Pink Noises

Pink Noises: Women on Electronic Music and Sound

Tara Rodgers

DUKE UNIVERSITY PRESS
Durham and London 2010

© 2010 Duke University Press
All rights reserved
Printed in the United States
of America on acid-free paper ∞
Designed by Amy Ruth Buchanan
Typeset in Chaparral Pro by
Achorn International
Library of Congress Cataloging-
in-Publication Data appear on
the last printed page of this book.
Frontispiece: Jessica Rylan
performing with the Personal Synth,
2006. Photo by Lawrence Braun.

FOR FRANCIS W. RODGERS

AND

SUE ANN HOOGKAMP RODGERS

Contents

Acknowledgments

I am most grateful to the artists I interviewed for this book and its web-based predecessor, Pinknoises.com. Their experiences and talents speak volumes, far beyond the scope of one book. I have been impressed by their work and moved by their willingness to communicate aspects of their creative lives toward this project. I hope that the book circulates their sounds and stories fairly and widely.

Karen Choy generously contributed her design skills toward the realization of Pinknoises.com from 2000 to 2005, and without her work the site would have been much less vibrant if not impossible to maintain. An extended network of people supported the site or my music during this period, which laid a foundation for this book: Adrienne Day, Chealsea Wierbonski, Lola Rephann of Deep See, and Brenda Kahn of *Womanrock* in New York City; Carla DeSantis of *Rockrgrl* in Seattle; the First Ladies DJ Collective in Washington, D.C.; Ladyfest in Chicago and Texas; Estrojam in Chicago; Brock Phillips at Motormouth Media in Los Angeles; Anne Hilde Neset at the *Wire*; Tomas Palermo and others at *XLR8R*, Emily Griffin of Electric W.O.M.B., the Sister SF collective, and Ninah & dAS of KPFA/No Other Radio Network in the Bay Area; DJ Cyan, CKUT, and Studio XX in Montreal.

Susan Smulyan at Brown University has remained over many years an outstanding mentor and friend; undergraduate music seminars with Carol Babiracki and Rose Subotnik also sparked interests that run through this project. I am grateful for many fruitful encounters in the MFA program in electronic music at Mills College, especially for Maggi Payne's attention to sonic detail; Fred Frith's open-mindedness and commitment to community; Pauline Oliveros's ideas about music and feminism; Chris Brown's enthusiasm for computer music; Alvin Curran's experimentalism; and David Kwan's gift for straightforward critique. In Montreal, Jonathan Sterne provided detailed feedback and superb advising. Darin Barney, Carrie Rentschler, Will Straw, and my colleagues in the graduate program in communication studies at McGill provided valuable input and encouragement. Andra McCartney at Concordia University generously lent her expertise.

Many other artists, journalists, and scholars offered information and support along the way. Whether in brief conversations or more sustained dialogues, my contact with them has meant a lot: Lisa Barg, Michael Bierylo, John Bischoff, Dan Cavicchi, Joel Chadabe, Owen Chapman, Tommy DeFrantz, Rebekah Farrugia, Anna Friz, Annie Gosfield, Donna Haraway, Elizabeth Hinkle-Turner, Dan Hirsch, Elise Kermani, Shoshana Magnet, Charity Marsh, Trevor Pinch, Ann Powers, Hildegard Westerkamp, and Richard Zvonar.

Lorne Falk at the School of the Museum of Fine Arts, Boston, gave me a wonderful teaching opportunity, and my students in the SMFA Sound courses in 2004 and 2005 lent critical ears and fresh ideas. Paul D. Miller (a.k.a. DJ Spooky that Subliminal Kid) has kindly promoted the *Pink Noises* endeavor from the start; William Clark of William Clark Associates in New York moved the project forward with patience and dedication. Financial support from the Canada–U.S. Fulbright Program, the Richard H. Tomlinson Doctoral Fellowship at McGill University, and the McGill Department of Art History and Communication Studies afforded me time to focus on this project's completion and push the work in new directions. I thank Ken Wissoker for having faith in this project and providing insightful and motivating direction, and Courtney Berger and others at Duke University Press for their tremendous assistance.

My family and friends, some of whom I mention here, contributed warm conversations, critical feedback, or equally helpful distractions: Jody Blackwell, Carrie Bodle, Jon Curley, Annie De Groot, Abe Doherty, Anne Feve, Westry Green, Sheila Hallisey, Andrew Jacobs, Ayako Kataoka, Antonia Kirkland, Chris Kubick and Anne Walsh, Rachel Levine, Praba Pilar, Goretti Ramirez, Monica Ruiz-Casares, Nancy Tobin, Vandana Tripathi, Natasha K. Warikoo, and Eve Zaritsky. I especially acknowledge Jane Chi Hyun Park for her insights on this book and countless other matters; Elise Baldwin, who read the entire manuscript and commented in sharp fashion; Kerry Rodgers, who keeps me on track; and Clover, whose formidable presence shadows every page.

Finally: my father shared with me his knowledge of audio equipment and enthusiasm for jazz, and my mother taught me as much or more about the value of careful listening. They were both educators, and each promotes social justice within their community and beyond. I have learned much by their example, and I dedicate this book to them.

Montreal
December 2008

Introduction

I first made electronic music in the mid-1980s when I was about twelve years old, using an Apple IIe computer that my father brought home from work. I was absorbed in it for months, coaxing melodies out of programs I wrote in the BASIC language. As a self-taught musician who had played piano for years without formal lessons, for me the computer was simply a new means of working with sounds. As I had with the piano, I would figure it out mostly by trial and error. Today, I still play the piano, and I also compose with MIDI instruments, digital audio, and the programming language SuperCollider (Rodgers 2006; MacDonald 2007). I often attribute my facility with electronic music to my father's interests and support. He is a self-described audiophile and early adopter of computer technologies, and he shared with me his record collection, enthusiasm for home recording, and knowledge about hi-fi audio systems and computers. It came as a surprise, then, when recently I unearthed in a closet an old 78 that my mother recorded as an amateur pianist in high school. *Mom cut a record?* I asked a few more questions and found out that in the early decades of the twentieth century, my great-aunt was a pianist for silent films in Albany, New York, and my grandmother used a stenotype machine in her work as a secretary. In a small town in western New York, my other grandmother was a Morse telegrapher and teletypist at her job with an agriculture company in the 1940s. So while my father's audiophility was an obvious lineage for me to identify and claim, it turned out there were clear precedents for music and computing experience in generations of women before me in my family.[1] Even after I had conducted dozens of interviews for this collection and its online predecessor Pinknoises.com, I still defaulted to stereotypical assumptions about gender, audio, and computer technologies in my personal history.

The terms *technology* and *music* are often marked as male domains, and the trenchancy of associated gendered stereotypes seems to gain force when these fields converge in electronic music (McCartney and Waterman 2006, 4).[2] This book attempts to disentangle these potent assumptions and open possibilities for imagining relationships of sound, gender, and technology differently. It endeavors a feminist intervention in historiography—suggesting what feminisms can do for electronic music cultures—and it proposes what sound, as a category of critical and aesthetic analysis, can offer to feminist concerns.[3]

Project Overview

This book is a collection of twenty-four interviews with women who are DJs, electronic musicians, and sound artists. The interviews investigate the artists' personal histories, their creative methods, and how issues of gender inform their work. This project emerged out of technical interests, social connections, and political affinities in my trajectory as a musician and scholar. During the past decade, I have moved from being an electronic dance music producer in New York, to a graduate student in an experimental electronic music program in Oakland, to a professor of sound at an arts college in Boston, to a doctoral student in Montreal, and—to quote a house classic by Crystal Waters—back to the middle and around again. In all these contexts I have encountered a curious lack of representation that profoundly underestimates the presence and diversity of expressions by women working with sound as a creative medium over the last century. Others have conjured this absence with wonderful, experiential analogies. DJ Mutamassik says: "When you look at how many cultures the women have been making the drums and beating them as well, you realize that we're living in a secretive Masonic society or something." Annea Lockwood called it "this great hole, a black hole of no info" about women composers (interview with author, September 25, 2004). Another artist remarked that her entrée into the world of electronic music felt as if she had landed on a planet where something had happened to make all the women disappear.

I first ventured into this so-called black hole or alien planet in the late 1990s when I set up a home studio for making electronic music. As I began to research production methods, I found that the spaces where knowledge circulated—primarily music stores and online discussion forums—were often populated by men who boasted about technical knowledge and were unhelpful to newcomers in the field. Many men were supportive, but electronic music cultures overall seemed to discourage or deny women's participation. This was made clear by the lack of substantive coverage of women in electronic music magazines and history books.[4]

My own impulses to learn electronic music production and start the website Pinknoises.com felt quite different. In addition to my established curiosity with music and computers I was inspired by the legacy of Riot Grrrl, the grassroots movement in the early 1990s that catalyzed feminist art making and political activism (see Kearney 1997). I also was motivated by the pervasive spirit in the United States in the late 1990s for creating online communities that could transcend geographic boundaries, and by feminist writing on rock, pop, and hip-hop. My interest in music's relationship to cultural politics gained fervor after I read the anthology *Rock She Wrote* (McDonnell and Powers 1995), Tricia Rose's *Black Noise* (1994), and an article by Ann Powers (1994) that encouraged more work by women as instrumentalists—which I took up as a call to arms. And, along with some other women of my generation who make electronic music, I have been inspired by traditions of women's music and political activism.[5]

In 2000, I established Pinknoises.com to promote the work of women making electronic music, to make resources on production methods more accessible to women and girls, and to provide an online space where issues of music and gender could be discussed. Curious to locate and talk with other women in the field, I sent e-mails to various online forums and soon heard from six artists. I interviewed them about their music backgrounds, creative methods, and ideas about gender and electronic music culture. Those interviews formed the primary content for Pinknoises.com's launch, along with essays and links about studio setup and production techniques. With the help of our web designer, Karen Choy, and occasional contributions from other artists and writers, we updated the site with new interviews and articles for about three years and, after that, much of the content remained archived online.[6]

The website and book have evolved using "friendship as method" (Tillmann-Healy 2003, 734), because with many of the artists my research methods have blended with mutual efforts to build friendships and cultivate professional support. I devote the majority of the pages

3

pinknoises.com

((launch party))

tuesday_january 16. 2001
tonic / 8pm-2am
107 norfolk st. / nyc

Pinknoises.com launch party flyer, 2001. DESIGN BY KAREN CHOY.

in this book to extended-form interviews in order to balance my perspectives with those of the artists. The selection of interviews, the
questions, and the organization reflect my decisions, but the artists
revised and approved edited transcriptions of their interviews. I rely
on the notoriously unstable terms *women* and *men* to frame the project
because these social categories significantly affect the organization of
electronic music histories and the distribution of resources in related
material realms (see Riley 1988; Scott 1988; Young 2005, 12–26). I hope
that this book will encourage further research in areas of sound, gender, and technology, including theorization of how electronic music
practices can destabilize binary categories of gender.[7]

The material in this book is emblematic of a "new audio culture"
that has emerged in the last half-century, in which musicians, artists,
scholars, and listeners are actively engaged with the creative possibilities of sound (Cox and Warner 2004, xiii). There is significant cross-
pollination among formerly more distinct academic, experimental,
and popular genres of electronic music. Artists cannot easily be cat-
egorized by their methods, as many of them move between roles as
DJs, electronic music producers, and/or sound artists.[8] Lines of influence run in all directions: Antye Greie (AGF), who crafts dense, digital soundscapes with vocal fragments, is partly inspired by hip-hop
MCs; Pamela Z, whose music combines bel canto and experimental

vocal techniques with digital sampling and effects, attended one of AGF's performances with interest (interview with author, October 31, 2004). The feminist electro-pop band Le Tigre draws inspiration from Yoko Ono and Laurie Anderson. Eliane Radigue, who for thirty years has developed a signature style of subtly changing analog synthesizer drones, collaborates with a younger generation, including AGF and the electronics improviser Kaffe Matthews. To take stock of this new audio culture, this book offers glimpses of contemporary electronic music practices through stories of several generations of women, all of whom are active cultural producers at the time of this manuscript's **5** assembly. It provides a genealogical investigation of a present moment, tracing lives and careers that intersect with each others' and with broader historical developments in the field.

The interviews are organized thematically because juxtapositions of genre and generation can reveal how sound and audio technologies connect otherwise divergent experiences.[9] Sounds are points of departure to realms of personal history, cultural memory, and political struggle. At stake, on one level, are questions of who has access to tools and opportunities for creative expression, and how women artists are represented in mainstream media. Moreover, the interviews show how women engage sound to work creatively with structures of time and space, or voice and language; to challenge distinctions of nature and culture using sound and audio technologies; to question norms of technological practice; and to balance their needs for productive solitude with collaboration and community. The section themes situate the artists' work (provisionally, since their work is multifaceted and changing) within categories such as time, space, nature, and embodiment. These topics are based on resonances among the interviews in each section and forge connections between electronic music practices and feminist philosophy, media, and cultural studies.[10] The themes also depart from familiar tropes like "noise" and "experimentalism" in existing electronic music histories, which, I will argue, have thus far conjured a canon of male composers and writers.

This collection will contribute the sounds and stories of some women to historical accounts which have thus far left them out. Yet its relationship to electronic music historiography is not to advocate an unattainable completeness in historical accounts but to be concerned with how histories are contained and contested in movements of sound in the present. It is thus necessary to lay out a broad critique of gender issues across multiple histories that electronic music inherits, including affiliations with militarism in the evolution of audio technologies, a logic of reproduction that operates in audio discourses and practices, and the politics of electronics manufacturing in a music culture that privileges planned obsolescence. Together these factors have informed electronic music histories by delimiting who and what counts in such matters as invention, production, and making noise.

Noise and Silencing in Electronic Music Histories

Much like technologies used in electronic music practice, electronic music histories have been imagined and structured according to tropes of noise and silence (see Kahn 1999; Cox and Warner 2004). Histories of electronic music often begin with a prominent origin story, the avant-garde noise of the Futurists in the early twentieth century. In the beginning, the story goes, there was Luigi Russolo's Futurist manifesto, *The Art of Noises* (1913), a bold celebration of the sounds of machines, modern industry, and war. Origin stories tend to normalize hegemonic cultural practices that follow, and in electronic music, "the beauty celebrated by aestheticians [is] often stained with such things as violence, misogyny, and racism" (McClary 1991, 4; see also Kahn 1999, 56–67). Indeed, themes in Futurist writings seem to flow naturally into the colonialist discourses articulated to electronic sounds in Cold War popular culture, the sexist imagery that has characterized many electronic music album covers and advertisements, and the militaristic language that inflects contemporary music-production terminology.

The tools for making electronic music are not innocent: true sound "mediums," they are an interface to ghosts of technoscientific projects past. In the United States, links between audio and military technologies were well established by the 1920s. Broadcast radio developed in conjunction with military investment around World War I, and subsequent amplification and recording technologies emerged directly from wartime expenditures or were funded for their potential military applications. Noises of new technologies in World War II were of such magnitude as to motivate extended research toward the development of new methods for controlling sound, to safeguard effective communication in combat. Postwar research in psychoacoustics and communications that addressed these issues shared with early electronic music many of the same historical actors, machines, and institutions (Chanan 1995, 8; Edwards 1996, 210–13, 220–21).

During the Cold War, electronic sounds became firmly lodged in the public imagination, especially in association with space age and atomic research. Space age pop music featured racially exoticized portrayals of women on album covers and used electronic sounds to signify the allure and anxieties of space exploration (Taylor 2001, 87–93). In 1962, the composer Herbert Brün recounted how stereotypes and fears of atomic warfare affected his audience's opinions of electronic music: "Throughout the population, in all social circles, people, when speaking of electronic music, use phrases like the following completely unabashedly: 'Electronic music is made of electrons. Electrons split atoms and a split atom is in some way part of the atom bomb, and one doesn't fool with such things. Above all, it shows complete lack of taste and tact, to want to make music with weapons of death'" (Brün 2004, 126). These associations persist today in the terminology of electronic music: DJs "battle"; a producer "triggers" a sample with a "controller," "executes" a programming "command," types "bang" to send a signal, and tries to prevent a "crash" (Katz 2004, 114–36; McCartney 1995; Peebles 1996, 12). The very act of making electronic music thus unfolds with reference to high-tech combat, shot through with symbols of violent confrontation and domination.

This persistent militaristic terminology and aesthetic priorities of rationalistic precision and control epitomize notions of male technical competence and "hard" mastery in electronic music production. These have produced and been constituted by their opposite: nontechnical or "soft" knowledges and practices that are coded as female (McCartney 2002; Bradby 1993, 156–57; see also Turkle 1984; Oldenziel 1999). In their interview in this collection, Le Tigre explains how standards of male-defined technological innovation do not apply equally to women:

Johanna Fateman: It really struck us that, when men make mistakes, it's fetishized as a glitch . . .

Kathleen Hanna: Something beautiful.

Johanna: And when women do it, it's like . . .

Kathleen: . . . a hideous mistake.

Johanna: Right, it's not considered an artistic innovation or a statement or an intentional thing.

Le Tigre maintains a goal of "technical innovation" for every project they do, but they define this standard on their own terms.

Much work by artists in this collection is likewise unfaithful to technoscientific priorities. Mira Calix, for example, is happy to use her new computer like a "big tape recorder" for compiling the eclectic mix of electronic, acoustic, and environmental sounds she incorporates into her compositions. She has little interest in the latest software developments and instead prefers to collect and record the sounds of unique wooden instruments. Annea Lockwood resists "fixing" recorded sounds with audio technologies, "'Cause I think they're essentially not fixable. Except that of course through media, we think, we feel we can fix them. But *sounds in their natural state* . . . are not fixable, are they?" Lockwood's recordings of rivers relay shifting movements of water and evoke transitory memories of place, defying the constraints of the recording medium on which the sounds are stored. Expressing a similar dissatisfaction with fixity, Laetitia Sonami strongly dislikes making recordings of her performances, in which she digitally transforms her voice through gestures of her hand: "The idea of commitment terrifies me—that you would have to commit a sound to a particular time . . . how do I know it should be there?" These artists cultivate technological sophistication in their work, but stake out philosophical positions that run counter to using dominant technoscientific priorities of precision and control as ends in themselves.

The question of what it means "to make music with weapons of death," while exaggerated in the Herbert Brün quote above, remains relevant given the pervasiveness of military origins and metaphors in electronic music technologies and practice. Indeed, electronic sounds might not be so compelling were it not for their associations with technologies of war—and, by extension, simulations of war in film and video games would not seem so realistic without their electronic soundtracks. Because the boundary between fiction and lived reality can be an *auditory* illusion that masks real struggles over life and death (see Haraway 1991, 149), work that challenges electronic music's technoscientific priorities is all the more crucial.

Clara Rockmore's performances on the theremin provide an alternative origin story for electronic music, one that may point toward better futures. Rockmore was the most widely recognized virtuoso of the theremin, a new electronic musical instrument in the 1920s. The theremin consists of two metal antennas that sense the position of the player's hands; by moving each hand in proximity to the antennas, the player controls an oscillator's frequency (pitch) and amplitude (volume). Rockmore's performances, including a showcase of the instrument at Town Hall in New York in 1934, helped to establish electronic and experimental music as a viable art form in the public imagination (Chadabe 1997, 8–11; Martin 2001). Her Town Hall recital "left the audience spellbound that such artistic music floated on air from a source seemingly uncontrolled by human effort" (Darter and Armbruster 1984, quoted in Montague 1991, 21). The *Washington Post* noted that the theremin "plays as if by magic . . . Toward it advances a young artist, Miss Clara Rockmore. Her right hand reaches toward, but stops short of the vertical rod. In so doing, she has penetrated the area of sound, and a beautiful tone results" ("Around the World" 1936). Rockmore was authoritative in performance; the *Post*'s commentary implies that she encroached on a phallic domain of virtuosity and technical mastery—reaching for the "vertical rod," "penetrating" the area—but that these transgressions were justifiable by the novel and transportive qualities of the sound. A *Times* critic wrote: "Stunning in a crimson dress, she stood over the instrument and evoked sounds . . . By moving her hands and fingers in the air she achieved tonal agility comparable to that of a singer, and a *living* tone-quality" ("Novelty Feature" 1947, emphasis added). The spellbound audiences were presented with a performance of electronic music as embodied, affective engagement with technology, characterized by nuance and care.

Rockmore opened an "elsewhere" within electronic music discourses (de Lauretis 1987, 25): a space for mutual encounters between humans and technologies, between familiarity and otherness, that motivates wonder and a sense of possibility instead of rhetorics of combat and domination. In her work on the cultural politics of emotion, Sara Ahmed writes: "The surprise of wonder is crucial to how it moves bodies . . . wonder involves the radicalisation of our relation to the past, which is transformed into that which lives and breathes in the present" (2004, 180). Electronic music can move bodies by way of technologically mediated or generated sounds that provoke a sense of wonder. Laetitia Sonami describes the first time she heard a Putney VCS3 synthesizer as a student in the 1970s: "I was like, Wow, what is that? I was hearing sounds that were very crude, but still there was this whole sense of magic, of electricity producing sounds in ways I could not fathom."[11] Sonami was motivated to develop an instrument that respects how technology is "a projection of our dreams, illusions, desires . . ." rather than one that reduces technology to an expression of "macho" control. So while the origin story of the Futurists infuses one's orientation toward electronic music with violent noise, Rockmore's mobilization of wonder—resonant in Sonami's and others' experiences decades later—suggests a different way to navigate the history. It calls for scrutiny of how electronic music can (or has failed to) express possibilities for more imaginative and ethical encounters with technology and difference now and in the future. It enacts a shift in emphasis from "weapons of death" to evocations of living.

Like noise, the function of silence as a privileged aesthetic category in electronic music discourses deserves critical attention. One of the most noteworthy works composed by John Cage, who is a central figure in electronic and experimental music histories, is 4'33", the "silent piece." This piece troubled notions of absolute silence and arguably helped to open Western music to wider range of sounds (Chadabe 1997, 24–26). Cage's body of work was innovative in the context of Eurological compositional traditions, but it has been taken up by some academics and journalists to define what constitutes "experimental" music in the broadest sense. This has worked to deny the influence of comparably innovative music practices by women and people of color (Lewis 1996; see also Oliveros 1984, 47–51). Thus, despite Cage's own efforts to disrupt hegemonic silences, the centrality of his work in subsequent electronic and experimental music histories has often had the effect of silencing others.

Moreover, the process-oriented compositional strategies advanced by Cage that seek to erase or reduce the influence of a composer's intent on the resulting music can be interpreted as a negation of identity; this may not be a universally desirable aesthetic for artists of historically marginalized groups who have suffered the effects of imposed forms of silencing and erasure. Indeed, feminists have often located empowerment within acts of breaking silences, by foregrounding aspects of identity. As Adrienne Rich said, "The impulse to create begins—often terribly and fearfully—in a tunnel of silence. Every real poem is the breaking of an existing silence, and the first question we might ask any poem is, *What kind of voice is breaking silence, and what kind of silence is being broken?*" (Rich 2001, 150; emphasis in original).

This is a useful question to put toward the politics of noise and silencing within electronic music histories.[12]

Just as recording engineers use the processing tool known as a *noise gate* to mute audible signals below a defined threshold of volume (like the hum of a guitar amp that would interfere with the relative purity of the guitar's sound in the mix), arbitrary thresholds have often silenced women's work in historical accounts. Some of the most important contributions to the study of electronic music and sound have positioned women as outside the scope of study (Kahn 1999, 13–14); defined DJ cultures as "distinctly masculine" with relative inattention to women's participation in these cultures (Reynolds 1998, 274–75); or used observational statistics, such as that fewer than one in ten DJs is female, to explain women's absence from the text (Fikentscher 2000, 124 n. 3). Another study that discusses women artists reached some unfortunately reductive conclusions—for example, that composer Suzanne Ciani was like "a woman in a man's world who wanted to have it all" (Pinch and Trocco 2002, 170). All the above studies are formidable works of scholarship for the accounts that they provide, but their cumulative effect gives the impression that women are rarely present in DJ, electronic music, and sound art cultures; that they have not made significant contributions to these fields to the extent that men have; or that gender categories ultimately pose restrictions on professional survival.[13]

There are other rhetorical approaches that have marginalized women's work in electronic music histories. The electroacoustic composer and scholar Andra McCartney has noted that Pauline Oliveros is often isolated as the only woman in textbooks that otherwise cover a variety of men's work in detail. Recognition of Oliveros is crucial and admirable, but her isolation has at times positioned her work as representative of an essentialized, "feminine" aesthetic (McCartney 2006, 31). Pamela Z, in her interview here, discusses a similar problem in the context of compilation CDs that feature only one woman composer. Such tokenistic representation often means that women's compositions are not analyzed in liner notes and album reviews with the level of rigor that men's work receives. In their interview, Z and Maria Chavez also comment on the politics of stylistic comparisons, noting that journalists tend to compare their work reductively to other women artists (simply because they are women) or trace their musical aesthetics to well-known men (whose influence they would not necessarily claim). This pattern enacts a double reinforcement of electronic music's male lineage, gendering important stylistic developments as male, and grouping women together as other to this master narrative. Le Tigre likewise discusses how they would like to fit in with what is considered to be "real" electronic music, but formal technical and stylistic regimes seem to exclude their aesthetic. Pamela Z concludes that gendered and racialized representations in music media tend to reduce otherness to a palatable symbol: "like the woman on the mud flaps of the truck that's the symbol of female form."[14]

Gender and Technology in Discourses of Sound Reproduction

Beneath the surface of these oversights and reductive representations, one obstacle to thinking women as *producers* of electronic music culture may be that they are always already entwined with a logic of *reproduction*—perpetuated in discourses of sound reproduction and materialized in related technologies—that ties women to age-old notions of passivity, receptivity, and maternality.[15] Feminists have demonstrated that women provide the material foundations upon which cultural worlds are built, and male modes of thought operate by denying the debt they owe to the maternal space from which all subjects emerge (Irigaray 1993, 10–12; Grosz 1995, 121; Young 2005, 128). In founding texts of Western philosophy, reproduction was established as a process in which a mother contributed formless matter, to be given shape by the father: a mother was considered to be "a mere housing, receptacle, or nurse of being rather than a coproducer" (Grosz 1994, 5; see also Ahmed 2006, 71; Irigaray 1985; Spivak 1981, 183).

In dominant discourses and practices of sound reproduction, technological forms and processes that are culturally coded as female or maternal have been systematically devalued and controlled. Histories of technology have routinely overlooked the active functions of "container technologies"—those technological forms associated with metaphors for female organs of storage and supply, and with types of labor traditionally done by women (Sofia 2000, 185). Magnetic tape is one such container technology, coded as a receptive matter to be given form and meaning by sound (Mumford 1966, 141; quoted in Sofia 2000). It is a kind of enabling background for electronic music, a passive (feminized) inscriptive surface employed to reproduce the workings of (male) culture.[16]

Control of this medium of reproduction—and faithfulness to an "original" sound—has informed technical and aesthetic priorities in discourses of sound fidelity. These values, elaborated on in popular magazines beginning in the 1950s and implemented in common practice, positioned women as threats to the self-contained spaces of hi-fi that men sought to define in middle-class homes. Women embodied the very potential for loss of sound quality by threatening men's requisite privacy to inhabit a controlled, domestic space in which they could cultivate an aesthetic appreciation of sound (Keightley 1996, 161). "Loss" was technically defined as the degradation in quality or clarity of recorded sound as it passes through the medium. In a similar way that women represented a threat to men's control of hi-fi settings in the home, the (feminized) medium of sound reproduction constituted an interference with the purity of the signal. Hi-fi discourses advocated maximizing sound fidelity by guarding the signal against loss and making the medium as transparent as possible (Morton 2000, 13–47; Sterne 2003, 215–86). A classic, masculinist technological fantasy is at work in this example: male attempts to appropriate the maternal function with technology typically exhibit a conflicting, nostalgic investment in the figure of the mother, and an antagonism and desire to overcome it (Doane 1999, 23, 29). While the medium of sound reproduction is necessary for male subjects to certify their relationship and fidelity to an imagined origin, male claims to creation are asserted through masterful control and/or erasure of this medium.

In other discourses of audio technologies, male claims to creation have been bolstered by stories of male birth and a concealed dependence on laboring women's bodies. In the mid-twentieth century, the distinctive, prized tone of Fender electric guitars relied on the laboring hands of Hispanic women workers, who meticulously wound pickups tighter than machines could (Smith 1995, 69; see also Rylan interview). Despite the crucial role of these workers, a biographer attributes the unique tone of the guitars to Leo Fender's innovations as "an American original" inventor (Smith 1995, 283). With rhetoric that does similar work, stories of male birth have functioned throughout histories of technology to confer value upon inventions by men. Thomas Edison, Samuel Morse, and Alexander Graham Bell proudly referred to their inventions as their children, a strategy by which they claimed a full role in the creation of an artifact (Sterne 2003, 180–81). In fact, at the turn of the twentieth century, women were central to how the

13

uses of phonographs and records were defined in social contexts, often redirecting their intended designs (Gitelman 2006, 60–62).

Electronic music historiography continues to follow this pattern.
Modulations: Cinema for the Ear, a feature-length documentary about
the evolution of electronic music in the twentieth century, was released in 1998 and screened internationally. The film presents a historical narrative of electronic music that begins with the Futurists
and John Cage and moves from Robert Moog, Kraftwerk, and the
"pioneers" of Detroit techno to contemporary sonic experimentalists

14   like Squarepusher and DJ Spooky. It celebrates "the nomadic drift of
the posthuman techno sound" and identifies the emergence of a "universal electronic sound."[17] The credits list nearly eighty informants, all
of whom are men. Patrilineality takes on an air of inevitability: a sub-
title hails Karlheinz Stockhausen as "the grandfather of electronica";
the Detroit techno producers are described as "the successors" to the
German pop-electronic group Kraftwerk; and in an interview about
the film, the director, Iara Lee, positions John Cage over Brian Eno as
"the father of ambient" (Lee 1998; Vaziri 1998).[18]

In one of the only scenes where women appear in the film, which is
framed before and after by men's testimonials about the significance of
the Roland TB-303 bass synthesizer in the history of electronic music,
there is a fleeting glimpse of a Roland factory in Japan where women
engage in repetitive labor assembling and testing keyboard synthesizers. The wide shot of many anonymous female laborers contrasts
sharply with the close-up angles and star treatment of the individual
male experts in the surrounding scenes. These scenes are accompanied
by upbeat electronic dance music, characterized by repetitive musical
structures and the seamless flow of a club DJ's mix. The audio connects
disparate economies of factory labor, studio production, and dance
floor pleasure along the same continuum of a global—and supposedly
universal—experience of electronic sound. Women are aligned with
the reproduction of mass-produced goods, while men are positioned
as cultural producers and arbiters of aesthetic innovation. Women laborers in the global economy are marshaled into a celebratory mon-
tage of cultural diversity; critical differences of gender, agency, and
cultural power are lost in the mix.[19] All the above examples suggest
how historical narratives and technical discourses of electronic music
have relied on metaphors of the feminine and maternal, as well as
on women's bodies more literally, to establish a male subjectivity in

sound and reproduce priorities of a male-defined culture. A patrilineal history of electronic music production is normative, and ideologies of sound reproduction circulate unmarked for a particular politics of gender.

To think against the grain of cultural ideologies that have aligned women with normative modes of heterosexual and capitalist reproduction, and to construct electronic music histories differently, we can consider how sounds themselves are reproductive. Reproductive sounds are variously *produced* by bodies, technologies, environments, and their accompanying histories; *reproduced* in multiple reflections off reverberant surfaces or in recording media; *reproducible* within spaces of memory and storage that hold sounds for future playbacks; and *productive*, by generating multiple meanings in various contexts. To account for reproductive sounds in all their temporal depth is to challenge the patrilineal lines of descent and the universalizing male claims to creation that have thus far characterized dominant discourses in electronic music.

Alongside such moves to expand the scope of existing histories, there is still some consistency among surveys that suggest that women DJs and composers number one in ten or fewer (Fikentscher 2000, 124 n. 3; Bosma 2003, 9; McCartney and Waterman 2006; Katz 2006, 580–81). The question of who is counted in electronic music historiography is inevitably informed by the politics of social and professional networks, and by limited definitions and standards of achievement.[20] What is important to take away is that the public face of electronic music—on CD releases, magazine covers, international festivals, scholarly publications—is typically male and does a certain kind of symbolic work. As Hanna Bosma points out, these forums "tell a tale of a world of creators and experts of electroacoustic music, and this probably influences the behaviour and thoughts of listeners, students, would-be composers and experts" (2003, 7–8). Another strategy is to emphasize the substance and diversity of work that *has* been accomplished by women, and this collection is a starting point for doing just that.

Throughout the history of electronic music, women have been influential as consumers and users of audio technologies; instrument builders and assemblers; directors, teachers, and students at academic electronic music studios; composers, instrumentalists, vocalists, and sound poets; producers, audio engineers, and software developers;

founders of record labels; events organizers and participants; and philosophers and critics.[21] Rather than linger on observations that women may comprise only one in ten DJs or composers, we can reframe the perspective by cueing Autumn Stanley's revised history of technology (1983): with their myriad technological innovations and sounding practices, "women hold up two-thirds of the sky."

Pink Noises and Feminist Waves

16 The interviews in this book demonstrate the relevance of feminist politics in "the cultural space of postfeminism" (McRobbie 2004, 6), which can be a formidable undertow to feminist movement. Portrayals of women in contemporary Western popular culture are postfeminist when "feminism is 'taken into account,' but only to be shown to be no longer necessary" (8). Women in objectifying or exploitative frameworks claim to act out of personal choice, for their own enjoyment and individualist advancement. Postfeminist representations are common in mainstream accounts of electronic music, as many of the artists I interviewed attest. Jessica Rylan comments that "things were better for women in the '80s or '90s. It was certainly a lot less exploitative than it is now." DJ Mutamassik critiques the images of "coquettes with drum machines" in hip-hop and music production magazines, whose skills as producers are overshadowed by attention to their voluptuous figures.[22] A recent *New York Times* article epitomizes postfeminist contradictions, showcasing several women DJs who are embracing their role as arbiters of urban fashion now that their musical skills have been taken into account. As one woman says, "Just to be able to blend records is not enough anymore. You have to have a look" (La Ferla 2007). After working hard to gain public recognition for their technical proficiency, women face renewed pressure to cultivate their appearance. Several interviews in this collection address women's negotiations of this atmosphere (see Passamonte and Maslen).[23]

The artists express a range of opinions about gender in electronic music cultures. There are contradictory opinions among different women and within individuals as well. Some feel that gender has not played a memorable role in their artistic and professional experiences; others argue that cultural ideas about gender significantly inform expectations about musical and technical competence, dynamics of group improvisation, and even the timbral qualities of sound. Some feel that women have been marginalized through biased media representations and employment discrimination; some acknowledge that women can redirect these sexist stereotypes in their favor, capitalizing on them for career advancement. Some claim that women make music and communicate about technologies in ways that are essentially different from men, and that these differences should be validated. Other artists' experiences point toward the myriad configurations of sexed bodies and gendered identities, indicating, for example, that masculine gender identifications should be integral to theories of women's musical practices.

The artists adopt a range of strategies for addressing perceived gender issues in electronic music cultures. Some enthusiastically organize women and girls through community-oriented educational projects. Many of them attest that music production offers women and girls a way to gain confidence in their conceptual and technical abilities—skills that are also applicable in other areas of life. Others say that it is unfortunate, although necessary, that women continue to organize in this way. Some prefer not to discuss or emphasize gender issues because they consider this to detract from their progress in gaining recognition as an "artist" rather than a marginalized "woman artist." Some claim not to think about gender issues at all unless others confront them with questions. Many artists harbor conflicting feelings within themselves and adopt various strategies in different contexts. For example, an artist's attention to and interest in gender issues may change over her lifetime and may also shift situationally from the relative privacy of the home studio to the more public contexts of performances and media appearances.

The interviews here also explore the intersectionality of gender with other aspects of identity, including race, ethnicity, class, and sexual orientation. Some artists delineate particular gender stereotypes that emerge in culturally specific music traditions. Some describe the joint operations of reductive and exoticizing racial, ethnic, and gendered stereotypes, which generate multiple axes of discrimination in media and professional contexts. For some artists, early experiences of racial and/or class discrimination motivated them toward creative expression; these motivations may have facilitated their capacity to challenge traditionally gendered relationships to music technologies and performance. Some artists have been leaders in organizing queer communities and/or communities of color around electronic dance music. In many cases, artists may be equally or more primarily invested in other aspects of identity than in a specific politics of gender; others aspire to a gender-neutral artistic identity. Many artists may not identify as feminist, because of personal or cultural reasons for feeling excluded from what they understand feminism to be. That said, the title *Pink Noises* encapsulates an energy of productive difference that has animated this project from its inception. There may well be important differences between how the artists situate their work and politics and how I frame the project here. It is my hope that the book will demonstrate how such differences—as well as various strategies and combinations of individual achievement and collective organization—can challenge and fortify feminist movement.

18

Perspectives of different generations of women are a crucial aspect of how this book documents and speaks to electronic music practice and contemporary culture. Typical "wave" models of feminism, which describe feminist movements as succeeding each other temporally in a linear historical progression, and tend to posit strictly defined generations of women as irrevocably at odds with each other's interests, are inadequate representations of women's complex identifications. Feminist waves might better be conceived as interacting sound waves. Sounds can be thought of as *pressure* and *movements*, doing cultural work.[24] In the propagation of sound waves, the most audible impression may occur near the beginning of a sound's generation, but the wave reverberates through space indefinitely, continuing to intersect with and influence the trajectories of other sound waves as physical matter in ongoing interactions. Likewise, feminisms and the reactions to them do not go away but continue to reverberate in shared discursive spaces. How debates *sound* within and across these spaces depends upon one's orientation toward an argument, how one listens selectively, and how some claims are masked or augmented by their relative power or position.

Feminist debates are sounding practices, to borrow the term that Andra McCartney uses to describe the work of the composer Hildegard Westerkamp. Sounding evokes "the mariner's slow and careful navigation through unfamiliar waters," a practice by which one finds a way forward by listening closely to gain understanding (McCartney 2000). Pauline Oliveros's philosophy of Deep Listening constitutes another valuable approach. Deep Listening is a life practice of cultivating awareness of all sounds across all of spacetime, formulated through Oliveros's own feminist consciousness and techniques of meditation. It suggests that attending carefully to all sounds enables more mindful and constructive intersubjective experience (Oliveros 2005; Oliveros and Maus 1994). Feminist movement, then, is a continual negotiation of sounding and deep listening.

In the title of this project, *pink* serves as a marker of female difference, and *noise* as a site of disturbance and productive potential. Pink is the most pervasive hue in Western consumer culture for socializing girls toward acceptable modes of femininity.[25] "Pink noise" is a term in physics and audio engineering referring to variations of white noise, or unstructured sound that contains every audible frequency. Pink noises have been filtered to emphasize low frequencies, resulting in equal distributions of energy per octave. Pink noise generators are commonly used in professional recording studios as test signals for sound systems; but while it plays a critical role in the operation of equipment, pink noise is typically kept out of the audible mix. Noise also has metaphoric connotations of discord and dissonance. In cybernetic theories, noise is a chaotic information source from which ordered patterns can be formed, as well as a disturbance that interferes with transmission of a signal. In this spirit, when I asked AGF whether she thinks the term "glitch" is appropriate for describing her music, she replied that "glitch" implies only a temporary disturbance, while: "i hope i am disturbing for a life time / ;)." Drawing on these definitions, I introduce the following interviews as *pink noises*: sonic interventions from multiple sources, which destabilize dominant gendered discourses and work toward equal power distributions in the cultural arenas where sounds reverberate.

Notes

1. On women's involvement with electronic information technologies in the United States during and after World War II, see Balsamo 1996, 152–53. For other relevant histories of women and computing, see Light 1999 and Plant 1997. On gender and technologies in office work, see Morton 2000, 74–107.

2. On the historical formation of "technology" as a seemingly neutral and universal term, through highly contested processes of gender, racial, and class differentiation, see Oldenziel 1999, 1–50. See also Wajcman 2004

for an overview of debates in feminist technology studies, and McClary 1991 on constructions of gender and sexuality in Western music.

3. Unless it is necessary to refer to a more specific creative practice, I will use the term "electronic music" to refer inclusively to electronically mediated sonic experimentation that takes many forms. It is worth noting, however, that some of the *Pink Noises* artists have turned away from the formal constraints or masculinism they associate with the terms "music" and "composition," in favor of the term "sound." I understand feminism to mean various strategies and movements to end sexist oppression, contest unequal power relations across multiple axes of social difference, and rethink the norms of gendered subjectivity.

4. A notable exception is Joel Chadabe's *Electronic Sound* (1997). See also McDonnell 1998 and Owen 1997 for an assessment of women's participation in electronic music cultures in the 1990s.

5. See Halberstam 2007; and Le Tigre's lyrics to "Hot Topic" (1999). Women's music in the 1970s tends to be associated with acoustic folk music, but events like the Michigan Womyn's Music Festival were the training ground for an early generation of women sound engineers as well (Sandstrom 2000; see also Matthews interview on music and the Greenham Common women's peace movement).

6. Pinknoises.com was reviewed in various music and general interest publications (see Neset 2001; "Separate and Equal" 2001; Warren 2003) and was nominated Best Music Web Site at the 2003 Webby Awards. See also Farrugia 2004 for discussion of how women have used online networks to make social and professional connections in electronic music cultures.

7. Other ethnographies would complement the perspectives in this volume. For example: women who use audio technologies nonprofessionally; women who work in industrial or commercial rather than artistic contexts; artists who are trans- or gender-queer–identified. On music in daily life, see Crafts et al. 1993. On gender in audio cultures, see Born 1995, 114–23; Gilbert and Pearson 1999, 83–109; Katz 2004, 131–36, and 2006; Keightley 1996; Perlman 2004; Schloss 2004, 57–58, 94; Straw 1997; Truax 2003. *Pink Noises* also addresses cultures of hearing. To theorize sound in ways that are inclusive of deaf cultures, feminists might build on themes of vibration and touch, as well as on relationships of signing and musicality (see Le Tigre interview).

8. Women may do this as a strategy of professional flexibility, and "this dialogic stance, rather than any one method or aesthetic position," can be read as a feminist aesthetics of sound (McCartney and Waterman 2006, 7).

9. Readers interested in a more chronological narrative of electronic and experimental music history, which includes information on some of the artists in *Pink Noises*, may consult Chadabe 1997.

10. The section themes are informed by passages in Grosz 2005, 1, 43–52; Halberstam 2005, 1–21; Massey 2005, 4, 10–11; Young 2005, 130; Har-

away 1991, 178, 195; Doyle 2005, 1–9; Sterne 2003, 287–92; Lee and LiPuma 2002, 192; Gilbert and Pearson 1999, 118; Grosz 1994, 5; Cusick 1994, 16–18; Hayles 1999, 1–4; Woolf 2005, 1–2; and McRobbie 2004, 11.

11. Many other women in the *Pink Noises* interviews verbalize their early encounters with electronic music as a kind of epiphanic moment: *"bang . . . this* is what I've been looking for" (Matthews); *"That's it!"* (Radigue); *"Whoa! . . .* This is it" (Chavez).

12. Feminist work on the uneven effects of silence and its disruptions, especially across differences of race and sexuality, has much to offer for thinking the politics of noise and silence in electronic and experimental music (see Cixous 1976, 880–81; hooks 1984, 12–15; Hammonds 1997; Hedges and Fishkin 1994).

13. In a relevant commentary on academic accounts of electronic dance music, Angela McRobbie summarizes how scholars have constructed it as "virtually a female-free zone": a domain in which recreational drug use, new technologies that dissolve human-machine boundaries, and a general sensibility of subcultural abandonment converge to offer "an escape from the whole bother of gender" (1999, 145–47). These accounts have tended to exhibit—and normalize—a lack of critical inquiry into how gender continues to inform the production and distribution of knowledge in these cultures.

14. Z's comment was allusive, but such iconic female figures appear throughout visual cultures of electronic music (Taylor 2001, 88–89; Sherburne 2002). An event featuring Canadian women artists at an experimental music festival in 2004 displayed the infamous mud-flap woman on its promotional materials (Anna Friz, e-mail to author, April 18, 2008).

15. To be clear, in this section I am taking issue with how electronic music discourses produce gendered subjects and technological forms. The perpetuation or contestation of hegemonic cultural practices can be enacted by individual people of any gender.

16. Another example of an audio technology coded as female form is an early version of the phonograph, which required singers to direct their voice down the horn—a "curious gaping orifice"—when recording. This was apparently an unsettling experience for some men. The folklorist John Avery Lomax, who traveled across America recording music in the years 1908–10, reported: "I lost many singers because the cowboys didn't like the looks of it" (Brady 1999, 40).

17. For a more thorough analysis of the relationship between posthumanism, music technology, and Afro-diasporic cultural politics, see Weheliye 2002.

18. Such examples abound in electronic music cultures, and these proliferating lines of descent rather comically begin to tie themselves into knots. Kim Cascone (2000, 14) identifies Luigi Russolo as "the 'grandfather' of contemporary 'post-digital' music"; the composer and engineer

Max Mathews (2008) has been called both "the father of computer music" and "the great-grandfather of techno"; DJ Frankie Knuckles, "the godfather of house" (Fikentscher 2000, 137).

19. For further discussion of how electronics manufacturing and toxic waste disproportionately affects the health and safety of women laborers and Third World communities, see the Rylan interview; Fuentes and Ehrenreich 1983; Grossman 1980; Pilar 2005.

20. For example, consumers of audio technologies typically are not considered to have invented the phonograph to the same extent as Thomas Edison; those on the dance floor are not recognized as producers of underground dance music culture to the extent that DJs are—and these roles are often gendered (Gitelman 2006, 63–64; Pini 2001).

21. On women's roles in defining the uses of phonographs, microphones, and electrification technologies in the early twentieth century, see Gitelman 2006; Goldstein 1997; Lockheart 2003. On women as modernist writers and avant-garde artists concerned with sound and aurality, see Cotter 2002; Cuddy-Keane 2000; Gammel 2003; Morris 1997; Scott 2000; Wilson 2004. See McCartney 2003 and Hinkle-Turner 2006 on women who were founders of academic electronic music studios beginning in the 1960s, developers of computer music software, and/or composers of electroacoustic music. For more information about women developing computer music and sound art software, see Chadabe 1997, 158–63, 334–36, 265–67; Gagne 1993, 297–332; Polli 2005, 2006; Rodgers 2006; Scaletti 2002; Spiegel 1998. On women who facilitated electronic music's popularization through science fiction soundtracks and music for advertising, see Chadabe 1997, 66; Epstein 1974; Hodgson 2001; Milano 1979a, 1979b; Pinch and Trocco 2002, 155–70; Sherman 1982; Wierzbicki 2005; Zvonar 2004. On women who are electronic and electroacoustic instrument builders, see Fullman 1994, 2003; Hutton 2003; Oliveros 1984, 36–46; Ptak 2008; Young 1982; Rylan and Sonami interviews in this volume. On women who are sound installation artists: Amacher 1994, 2004; Bodle 2006; D'Souza 2002; Gercke 2000; Grant 2004; Landi 2001; Licht 1999; Schaub 2005. For an overview of women's work in performance art, radio art, experimental vocal techniques and sound poetry, see Bosma 2003; Duckworth 1995; Hume 2006; Malloy 2003; Morris 2007; Sawchuk 1994; "Lily Greenham" 2008; Waterman 2007. For an account of women's uses of hi-fi audio components in the 1970s, see Pease 1978. On women in audio engineering professions, see Peterson 1987; Potts 1994; Sandstrom 2000. Resources about women who are vocalists, DJs, or producers of electronic dance music and hip-hop include Bradby 1993; Bridges 2005; Cooper 1995; Dove 2003; Guevara 1996; Halberstam 2007; Hebert 2008; Park 2004; Raimist 1999; Rodgers 2003; Rose 1994, 146–82; Siegler 2000a and 2000b; Snapper 2004; Walker and Pelle 2001. Female Pressure (2008), an online database of women DJs, electronic music producers, and visual artists, currently lists 970 members from fifty-one countries. Women who are philosophers and critics, as well as composers,

include Amacher (2004); Oram (1972); Oliveros (1984); Spiegel (2008); and Westerkamp (2000 and 2002).

22. These are variants of the machine-woman figure who has long served to market audio technologies; see Théberge 1997, 123–24, for a representative advertisement from 1989.

23. See Verini 2003 for another review of a DJ event that exemplifies postfeminist discourse. For views of other artists and journalists on postfeminism in electronic music cultures, see Romano 1998, Rabinovitch 2000, Maloney 2000, and Cepeda 2001.

24. I am echoing bell hooks's use of the phrase "feminist movement," where the emphasized term *movement* encodes an active, progressive force that resists the exclusionary connotations of "a" or "the" feminist movement (see hooks 1984, 17–41). I also follow McCartney's and Waterman's observation that the attribution of agency to sounds (claiming that sounds do cultural work) offers a way to examine how gender is "symbolically projected" (2006, 14–15; see also Diamond 2000, 107–8). For a pertinent analogy of feminist and radio waves, see Garrison 2005.

25. See Peril 2002. As Björk put it when discussing motivations behind the lyrics in her album *Volta* (Atlantic, 2007): "Part of it was having a little daughter and realizing what are we telling girls? [All] they want to do is be pretty and find their prince, and I'm like, what happened to feminism? . . . There are actually other things than pink jars and losing a glass slipper" (Stosuy 2007).

Part 1. Time and Memory

For the artists in part 1, electronic music
and sound art practices reveal time as a
flexible and manifold medium, a labyrin-
thine structure, an influential partner
in the creative process. Pauline Oliveros
uses delay effects as "a time machine"—
collapsing past, present, and future in
her storage, generation, and anticipation
of sounds in improvisation. Her choice of
tools joins together music technologies
that are out of time, so to speak, with
each other. The accordion, a nineteenth-
century instrument, and twenty-first-
century software gain new leases on
life in interaction. And her trajectory of
musical exploration, a time span of several decades, has included many turning
points as she adapted to new technologies, "going with the flow."

Kaffe Matthews narrates her musical history as a series of fortuitous events where "good old timing came along" and presented chance opportunities for her to change course and explore new creative realms. She builds her music from such "once-off moments," using electronics to transform the sounds of unique gatherings of people, place, and atmosphere. Matthews discusses the varying time-scales and memory capacities of humans and machines, and the interfacing of these in performance situations. When improvising with electronics, a performer must negotiate "this business about a delay"—the latency between gesture and machine response in real-time systems. In Matthews's account, composer and instrument find middle ground: computer technologies have evolved toward greater memory capacities, but Matthews limits her program's RAM to one minute, which is most compatible with her brain's capacity to remember information.

For Carla Scaletti, the relationship of electronic music to human experiences of time and memory is metaphoric. Object-oriented programming offers ways to transform sounds at multiple time-scales simultaneously, much like the biological and chemical processes that comprise human bodies. She also sees parallels between brain functions and programming: human memory, like an audio filtering technology, takes an inputted signal and transmits it back into the world with subjective coloration.

Eliane Radigue's slowly evolving compositions are shaped by the duration of individual sounds within them, and by the evoked temporalities of death and rebirth in Buddhist philosophies that inspire her work. The embodied time of her musical performance is constituted by spontaneous gestures to adjust the ARP's potentiometers, as well as the months she waits between initial recording and final mixdown. Her meticulous use of the same synthesizer for thirty years slows the march of progress in a music culture that valorizes brand-new technologies. Overall, Radigue's music promotes patience, and openness to disorientation, within experiences of time and memory: "This slow changing where we don't even know that it is changing, and when we hear that it has changed, in fact it has taken place long before."

Pauline Oliveros

Pauline Oliveros was born in 1932 in Houston, Texas. She became the first director of the Tape Music Center (now the Center for Contemporary Music) at Mills College in 1966 (see Bernstein 2008); was professor of music at the University of California, San Diego for fourteen years; and is now Distinguished Research Professor of Music at Rensselaer Polytechnic Institute and Darius Milhaud Composer-in-Residence at Mills. Her extensive body of work includes early recordings of tape delay systems (*I of IV*, 1966), some of which also incorporate synthesized sounds of the Buchla (*Beautiful Soop*, 1966; *Alien Bog*, 1967). She performs with an accordion tuned in two different systems of just intonation and often plays it in combination with the Expanded Instrument System, a processing scheme she designed with digital delays and reverb effects controlled by foot pedals (see Gamper 1998). She has also composed for soloists and ensembles in music, dance, theater, and multimedia.

Oliveros is a prolific writer and philosopher of music, feminist, and humanitarian issues. Some of her classic writings include the article "And Don't Call Them Lady Composers," originally published in the *New York Times* in 1970, in which she critiques cultural factors that work against the recognition of "great" women composers; and "The Contribution of Women as Composers," in which she compares analytical and intuitive modes of thought and argues against devaluation of the latter, which has been culturally coded as feminine (see Oliveros 1984, 47–51, 132–37; Taylor 1993; Mockus 2008). She also developed Deep Listening, a meditative practice that advocates mindfulness of sound to motivate personal and social consciousness, and founded the Deep Listening Institute, a nonprofit arts organization, in 1985. I interviewed Pauline in Oakland, California, in November 2003, when I was a student in her Deep Listening seminar at Mills.

: : :

Tara Rodgers: How did you become fascinated with sounds?

Pauline Oliveros: I was always. I remember it always being very fascinating for me, from childhood. As far back as I can remember I was always listening to what was happening around me. I lived in a rich environment of sound. In the Texas wetlands, there were lots of insects—it was like a really thick canopy that changed through the seasons: tree frogs, cicadas, crickets, all these wonderful sounding critters. It wasn't quite as droney as the sound of the freeway that we've got here. In those days, mechanical sounds were more exceptional. Over time, it's been a project for technology to conquer nature. Although nature fights back, like with the earthquake last night.

Over the years, you've worked with quite a range of tools for making and manipulating sounds. You've explored a lot.

Well, I'm just going with the flow, so to speak. The whole history of recording and reproduction of sound is something that has a huge trajectory, and I've experienced that for seventy-one years now. I remember having a phonograph, a Victrola that you'd wind up. The thing that was interesting to me was that it wound down. I used to like to listen to the sound winding down! [Laughs]

When did you develop an interest in working with electronics?

I was always fooling around with the radio listening in between stations, with the shortwave whistles and pops and clicks. So I guess I was always interested, it was about gaining access to the tools so that you could play with them. In the '40s, I had a wire recorder, where you'd record sounds on a wire, and by 1953 I had a tape recorder, which was new on the market for consumers. As soon as I had the tape recorder, I started recording and listening; and eventually I had a tape recorder that had two speeds and you could record variable speed by hand-winding the tape. There weren't any synthesizers or anything like that, so it was a slow process of gaining access to equipment that would allow you to do things.

The Tape Music Center, which later became the Center for Contemporary Music at Mills, got started in 1960 and had a collection of stuff. The Buchla synthesizer was invented and demonstrated in 1965 at the

Tape Music Center in San Francisco, but I didn't work on it until the next year, when I was first director here in 1966–67.

It's a long history of how things change from analog to digital. I still work with a hybrid kind of thing. I'm using Max, I'm using the computer as a programming and processing environment, but I'm still playing the accordion, which is a nineteenth-century instrument. All the sound is derived from acoustics rather than from electronics, but I use the computer system to process the sound. There's still plenty of places for me to go, even.

Tell me about your Expanded Instrument System.

Let me explain what that means. I think about using all these delays as a time machine. Because when I play something in the present, then it's delayed and comes back in the future. But when it comes back in the future, I'm dealing with the past, and also playing again in the present, anticipating the future. So that's expanding time. That's the idea there. It's not about just one delay, it's about a whole lot of them. I've got it up to the point now where I can actually use about twenty delays. If you're in a space, you're hearing delays all the time, different time-scales. What I got interested in, long ago, was the coloration of sound that happens in a space. This happens because of delays, so I wanted to work with that.

I started working on this in a piece called *The Bath* [1966], which was based on the distance between the record head and the playback head of an analog tape recorder. I was recording a dance piece, recording the sound of the dancers, and eventually opening up the delay to change the shape of the room, the feeling of the room. I would play back what I recorded, and play back much later what had been recorded into the whole piece, so that eventually it was a very complex texture but it was all made of sounds that they had already made and were making. So I've worked that idea over a long period of time into some fairly complex things [see Oliveros 1984, 36–46].

The most recent version of this system uses Max/MSP as the interface. I have a program running which can improvise with me so when I play, whatever I play gets taken up, but then it's treated algorithmically, and I don't know what's gonna come back. So not only am I doing what I said with the expansion of time, but also the expansion of the material. It's transformed, and I have to be open to that as it comes back. The algorithms are based on my own ideas of what could

Pauline Oliveros at the Buchla, Mills College, 1966. COURTESY OF THE
CENTER FOR CONTEMPORARY MUSIC ARCHIVE, MILLS COLLEGE.

happen to the material, but it's really unpredictable. I enjoy that situation of just listening and taking it in and responding. And the thing is, there's a half-second delay in the brain, so if you're going to do something, the brain knows before you know consciously, so there are evoked potentials already a half-second before you do things, but the brain remembers it as the present, which is a very interesting phenomenon. What it tells me is that the body knows what to do without the conscious mind intervening. Things get messed up when we think we have to control by our consciousness, or what we call consciousness.

That's what I think is going on in this work that I've been doing all this time, with Deep Listening. It has to do with understanding that, feeling that, trusting that you do know what to do. For example, I play with my feet. I have accelerator pedals that control the clock time of the delay so I can bend pitches and do transformations as I'm playing. And my feet know what to do, but if I tried to tell my feet what to do, it would be too late and I would lose the moment. It's almost as if there's somebody else there doing this. I know my feet are moving and I'm moving them, but they're moving—the feet are moving.

Over many years you've written about the status of women composers and the roles of gender in musical expression. What are some of your thoughts on this now?

Well, I've done a lot of work towards raising consciousness, and I have an article on my website called "Breaking the Silence" [Oliveros 1998]. I talk a lot about these issues and I give nine points of how to change things. And you're doing some of it by doing this project, but I feel that change has to go across the boards. Everyone has to be involved in changing it, or else it doesn't get changed. It means that music has to be taught differently; it has to be inclusive. If children learn to play music, they have to learn to play music written by women as well as by men, so there isn't a separation. And if a performer is playing a program, they need to play music by women as well as by men. And if an audience goes to a concert and there's no music by women, they have to confront the management about it. If that doesn't happen, the change is not going to take place. Especially in traditional, establishment music, people are educated to the music of the European masters, who are all men. As long as they're educated to that, that's what they're going to elevate. If there's no change at the root, at the very basic level, it's not going to change very quickly.

It's interesting that there's been an effort to make some of these changes, for instance, in literature departments, but I don't know that the same is true in most music departments.

I guarantee you it is not. I've had to bang my head against the wall to raise consciousness: You've got to start programming music by women, and you've got to fill the library with music by women. But it's hard to get that to happen, because the canon is so entrenched in all the educational institutions, and in music teachers, who don't give it a thought.

Recently I saw a photograph of you at the Tape Music Center in the 1960s with some of your colleagues, and you were the only woman in a group of men. I can't help but feel that not much has changed, since my graduate classes have had a similar ratio. I know you've been involved in an initiative to recruit more women here at Mills; tell me about this.

We did get more women, but we haven't gotten enough yet. It turns out that women are not so interested in composition; across a lot of different schools, I sent out a message to a lot of different schools that also said: that's the way it is here too. Annea Lockwood was teaching at Vassar, another women's college, and the women would sign up for harmony but they wouldn't sign up for composition. So why is this? One of the answers for me is that they don't see any future in it, for them, because what future do you see? You see all male programs, performances, you see all male faculties, music by men, you don't see any place for yourself. I was very determined that what I wanted to do was to compose music, so I just did it. Mills is different than it was when I was here in 1966, but it's not different enough.

I've done some workshops for women and girls different places around the country, teaching the basics of recording, and there never seems to be a shortage of interest, it's more that they haven't been encouraged to work with the tools.

They haven't been encouraged. They haven't been supported to do it. And that just continues, that boys are much more supported to do tech-y stuff than girls. And girls quickly learn to restrain themselves from being interested in things like that. So, it's a problem which I've grappled with, trying to raise consciousness and try to change things, but it's not easy. Because you run up against the canon of Bach, Beethoven, Mozart, Brahms. How can you not recognize this masterful music? [Laughs] Millions of people are educated to that. So there's a very strong force field. In the orchestra repertoire they play that stuff over and over again.

So being a composer in this time is not easy, no matter what the gender. Because there's not a place for composers, really, to be nurtured and developed and to have the excitement of creative music being as interesting as traditional music. The art market is a big market and a lot of money is put into that; some artists can make a lot of money that way. But profit being the driver in the culture, when you come up with some nice weird something—juicy, especially new—but it doesn't sell, then you're not part of the game. These are big issues, and they're there. The main hope is that people need to be nourished spiritually so that there's the understanding that creative work is of the spirit. If you don't nourish that creative part of the human being then you get what you've got in Iraq right now, and Israel and Palestine. You have death and destruction instead of creative energy. The energy's gone amok. All those things are embedded in what we've talked about. So you've got to just keep on keepin' on. Be subversive, very subversive.

: : :

Oliveros's recent projects include Adaptive Use Musical Instruments for the Physically Challenged, a collaborative initiative with researchers at RPI to develop interactive music software for children with limited motor skills. She is also continuing development of the Expanded Instrument System for improvisation and composition; composing *Urban Echo: Circle Told* for large chorus and the Leah Stein Dance Company, *Nile Nights: Remembered Texts from the Deep* with the author Ione, *Magnetic Fields* for violin and piano, and a *New Blues Peace* for piano and audience.

Kaffe Matthews

Kaffe Matthews has been making and performing new electroacoustic music since 1990. She is acknowledged as a leading practitioner in the field of electronic improvisation, using each performance site—with its unique acoustic, spatial, and social context—as her instrument. In 1997 she established the label Annette Works, releasing the best of these events on CD.

I was introduced to Matthews's work when I attended her performance at Tonic in New York City in 2001, the night she inaugurated the Lappetites collaborative project with Ikue Mori, Keiko Uenishi, and others. This group has played in various formations since, and released a CD, *Before the Libretto* (Quecksilber, 2005), featuring Matthews, Eliane Radigue, AGF, and Ryoko Kuwajima. I met Kaffe for this interview in March 2004 at her studio in London.

: : :

Tara Rodgers: Tell me about your early impressions of listening to or performing music.

Kaffe Matthews: I first got passionate about music when I was about six, when I started to play the violin from free lessons at school. I was brought up with this traditional, classical approach where music was stuff made by dead hairy old men that was written down, and my job was to stand and read and play their instructions. I loved it and my violin was my best pal. I got bored with it all, though, when I was about sixteen. I stopped playing and it wasn't until about five years later when I randomly picked up my violin one day and played it for the first time without any music, and—*wham! Jesus!*—realized that I had never, ever listened to anything I had ever done. All those years I was dealing with reading manuscript, I was always translating somebody else's visual instructions. And that was a really important moment. That was when I realized that I wanted to start to play music again, but without using any kind of written score, just to experiment with sound and get into listening.

I had been singing in a band at uni, and I was really bad, but I enjoyed that whole experience of playing music with people again. And then I was asked to play bass guitar in another band. That band, in fact—if we're going to talk about gender—that was with girls, and that band itself was kind of a product of Greenham Common, the English women's peace movement that was happening around nuclear issues. In the '80s in England there was a huge women's peace movement, and it was a really, really important time when we really thought that we could make a difference, make a change. It was a very inspiring time. It's funny, I'm probably sitting here sounding like some kind of ardent, extreme feminist, and I don't think I am, and I never thought that I was. Everything about the women's peace movement made sense. And playing in a girls' band was a lot of fun, and it made sense, but we were seen as radical and a bit extreme and all these kinds of things. We did have quite a few political songs and wicked haircuts. We were called the Fabulous Dirt Sisters and we worked together for about four years and made a few albums, and toured England and busked all over Europe. That was another important time: to learn about listening and playing with other people, and to experiment with writing music.

The Dirts was an acoustic band, but with the last couple of albums I got this feeling that mixing desks were kind of interesting, 'cause if you twiddled the knobs you could make stuff sound completely different. When the band split, at the end of the '80s, I got a job completely by chance in a recording studio in Nottingham as a kind of tape op/tea girl. I was saying, Look, I've got no experience, don't you have to be super brainy to handle this technology, isn't it really difficult? And the guys who ran the studio, they were pretty young, they said, You'll pick it up fine, no problem. But one of them did say, One thing you've got to realize, it's gonna be really hard being a girl doing this. I said, Oh, I can handle it. But I realized after awhile what he meant when, yeah, I was always the only woman around. When bands came in—rock bands were the way the studio made its bread and butter—it was all guys. When I was actually engineering, they were saying, So where's the engineer?, looking at me. And they'd sit behind me reading

Playboy, this kind of thing. The only girls that were around were gorgeous, sexy, superbabes who were singing somebody else's lyrics.

But anyway, I worked there for two years, and this studio's "thing," if you like, was acid house music, and it was in the early days. So there were samplers and Atari 1040 computers running Notator and two-inch tape machines all synched up together, and it was fantastic. But really scary, you know. I found the whole thing really confusing and frightening. Eventually I got to grips with it, and the sampler was very much the instrument that I got dead excited about, because during the last year of the band, I got very into drumming, West African drumming, and again by chance managed to get out to Senegal for three months where I ended up living with some drummers (my whole life is a series of glorious accidents!) on the beach who taught me traditional Senegalese rhythms, and that was, again, a really important moment in my musical life.

I came home, back to Nottingham, with this very simple, crystal-clear vision about music. About what the fundamentals of music were. Things like how the shape of your hand on a drum skin would completely alter a sound, and that sound therefore would have a different role in the pattern. It would also change the pattern, and the pattern would have a different rhythm, and the rhythm would have a different meaning. Really simple, basic things. So when I discovered the sampler, it was like, *crikey!* This is great, because all those hours of bloody practice I was having to do every day—although I loved those four-hour drumming mantras each morning which, looking back, were a really important time where I developed concentration and focus and listening, though I was splitting my fingers—but, wow, I don't have to do that with the sampler. I can't replace it, I can't replace that music, but I can do something different. Suddenly, I felt that I could *compose* music—that super-scary, ridiculous word that still seemed to assume some kind of God-given talent, and still seemed to assume men. *Composing*—you know? That word suddenly felt OK: Yes, sure I can do this, stick stuff together, when you've got a sequencer that you can use to shuffle sounds around.

There was this huge dance music scene that exploded in England, early '90s acid house, up in Manchester. I was the assistant to one of the top DJs there, Graeme Park. I was cutting samples, beats, and loops for him all the time. I'd spend days with all his vinyl, sampling it all. So I was learning a lot about beats and rhythms, and how to work

Kaffe Matthews with *Sonic Bed_London, music for bodies* in residence at
Rich Mix, 2006. PHOTO BY CHRIS GEORGE.

with the tools, but I myself was not really good at doing it. I decided
that this is what other people did, and even though I love rhythm and
patterns, I never attempted to really make rhythmic music myself. I
just got very much into the crazy things you could do with sounds,
and the accidents that would happen when samplers crashed. That
was always more exciting, that what the machine produced was more
interesting than my own ideas. These things would happen that were
not me. It was a product of what I did with this machine, and the machine would produce all this stuff, and I'd use that.

So the sampler was a great thing, but to play it, you either trigger it
from a sequencer or you play it from a keyboard. And I was not a keyboard player. So I thought, imagine if I played a sampler from a violin?
Again timing. I got invited to do a master's at York University in the
north of England, and I said to them, I'll come if you get a MIDI violin—and they did. But in reality, what a hideous thing it is. I basically
struggled with it for about five years. It sounds like a great idea, but it's
horrible to really play, because if you play it properly—violinistically—

it will resonate, so it sends out lots and lots of MIDI notes. I had to develop this very heavy-handed technique, which was not like being a violinist at all, so that different notes would trigger different samples, and bow pressure would affect filters, and change the pitch and the panning. I was working with an Ensoniq sampler (if you want to do live MIDI control, they're fantastic) but I kept finding myself in these performance situations where the material I had so studiously tweaked for hours in the studio, in the venue just didn't work. I kept finding myself wanting to work with the situation that the gig and the venue provided, and I needed to be able to improvise more.

Good old timing came along again and I got invited to STEIM [the Studio for Electro-Instrumental Music] in Amsterdam in January 1996. I was going to work with Big Eye, a video tracking system that in fact would demand even tighter control than my MIDI violin setup. But on arriving we talked, and on presenting my frustration at having to play with such control and restriction and that this didn't feel the best way to be going at all, they suggested instead that I should try this new software they were working on. My immediate response to that was, No, I'm not going onstage with a computer! But they pointed out that of course I already was—as a sampler is a computer—and that Apple was about to bring out a laptop that would be powerful enough to cope, so I said OK, let's go look.

We went straight down to the studio, plugged in my violin, and *bang*, I could play it and immediately hear stuff that wasn't violin, and I was like, yes, *this* is what I've been looking for. And that's LiSa, the software I still use. That simply has become my instrument, it really has. It's funny, in a way I'm pretty old-fashioned or traditional about music making. I mean, I need to move something physical to make a sound. I think that's why I stuck with the violin for so long, in fact. Essentially I make music by being in a place with an audience and playing with the sound and the atmosphere of the event, and I need physical gesture to be able to do that.

Do you think audiences respond differently when gesture is an overt aspect of electronic music performance, as opposed to when they see someone behind a computer?

Yes, and I think they do to me, now, because I insist on playing in the space rather than on the stage. So people can sit around me and get close and realize it's not a question of somebody triggering stuff from a sequencer on a laptop. I use a Peavey MIDI controller, and work with sixteen faders, so tiny gestures can cause quite big sonic events. I can have many different sounds coming and going within layers all at the same time.

I play nearly in the dark, the darkest I can, with a little light on the table, just so I can see enough of what I'm doing. I play in the dark because I don't want the audience to have to watch anything. This is another thing: music for me is about listening, and it's great not to have performing monkeys leaping around onstage, let's actually chow down and listen. People onstage doing stuff, yes, it's fantastic, and I'm not saying I've got anything against it at all. But the music that I do, I'm interested in actually being able to make music that is completely about listening and is not about watching. So hey, let's turn our eyes off and just listen. Most laptop electronic music has a negligible performance aspect anyway, it's not about watching. But humans still seem to want to do it, to watch a hand move and hear a sound. I don't know whether it will eventually go, that need, or whether it's just something that we're used to because music making has always been about performance. I don't see any reason why people shouldn't eventually be completely happy with listening, without having to watch. Although, of course, we'll have to stop presenting the seated-in-rows, proscenium arch situation for this to happen.

Tell me about what LiSa does.

It's a live sampling program. Imagine this: there's a box, or a buffer, which represents your RAM. It's an empty box into which you can put sound, and you can put sound anywhere in that box. When I first started working with LiSa, the laptop that I had, and the laptops that were available, were these heavy, chunky things. The max amount of sound you could work with was thirty seconds, and that was fine, that was enough. I eventually could get a memory upgrade and I had a minute, and then when I had a more powerful machine I could have had five minutes, ten minutes. But I've discovered, in fact, that my brain can't remember where a live sound is for more than a minute. So I still work with a RAM of a minute.

LiSa allows you to set up MIDI notes as triggers either to record a sound or to play it back, or even to play back a prerecorded sample. So I have assigned different switches on the MIDI controller so that some switches will record and some will play back. I've got five recording switches which will record into five different parts of the buffer, and the playback switches will play back different chunks of that buffer. I also have the playback switches set up on four different MIDI channels, so that I can process the sounds in four different layers via MIDI controllers with the same little bit of sound. I work with tiny bits of sound and I'm continuously changing what those sounds are. With such small chunks of sound, there's a moment that happens when your finger goes to press the switch, the switch is pressed, and there's a delay in the information getting through. You click record, grab the sound, it goes in the box, then playback.

One of the things I find is that a lot of people who play with electronics, they don't improvise. It can be very hard to improvise with electronics, because electronics are not nearly as much of an instrument as a traditional instrument can be. They're not as immediate. It's a different thing. In a way, I have an acoustic background to improvising, so I've come through all that, the way of improvising that acoustic instrumentalists have—which is about complete control of your instrument and being able to produce a particular sound from a particular gesture. So they don't understand being able to improvise with electronics at all. They don't understand this business about a delay, not being able to respond with a laptop in a way that you can with a string. But I think it's a really interesting area. And that's one of the reasons I work with LiSa, because I can improvise with that. I can be immediate with gesture and sound.

Often I'm playing back stuff as soon as I'm taking it, but I will play it back processed. I have an idea as to how it will turn out, because the more I've gone on with this, the greater my understanding has become as to what a particular sound is going to sound like when you grab it and play it back processed. But invariably, you gather something else, or if you're working with a loop, for example, the loop point is not where you think it's going to be. It's got to the point now where my work is really about riding that knife-edge between what works and doesn't work, absolute control and no control. Disaster and delight. Life, really!

Is operating along that border something you enjoy?

Completely. I think I love it. You don't know exactly what's going to happen. And it's still going back to this thing, the fact that the ideas get produced through my collaboration with this instrument. It's not me, on my own—my ego, my ideas—at all. It's very much about this process of what we do together. And that process is also a big part of being in a space, a certain kind of space, at a particular time of day or night, with a particular audience. You might be stuffed in a room this size in Germany with eighty people aged between seventeen and seventy-five, or you might be three floors underground in a completely dark cellar with it dripping and you can't see anybody because it's that dark, but you can kind of sense people's presence. And there's a nine-second reverb in the place. So all these things combine to make music. That's very much what I've been doing and what I am interested in, the fact that every performance situation is unique. The combination of people, this weather, this atmosphere, this feeling—it's never going to be repeated. This is a once-off moment, so OK, let's make music out of it, this now.

And that's true of your label too, right? You've released only live recordings.

Yes. It releases just live recordings because that's how I make music, although each CD has got progressively more edited. I've always been interested in being able to find ways of making music using electronics that are away from things being fixed and super-produced and predetermined and controlled. That's what digital instruments are so good at. They're perfect at reproducing the things that humans can't, i.e., producing something definite and perfect and repeated. That's not what humans do. So, yes it's fantastic to make digital music that does that, that really exploits that—the dance music industry, for example. But: there's also this other way with it, and I guess that's the field that I'm excited by. And I suppose that field is about sound. It's about different kinds of sounds that you can make and access through using digital instruments.

In your experience, how do you feel that gender has influenced the private aspects of composing, as well as the more public aspects of performing and being represented in the media?

I'm still quite perplexed or confused to understand why there are so few women involved; it's not an obvious question to answer. I don't have a definite answer for it. It used to not bother me that I would be the only girl around doing experimental stuff with a laptop, until about 2001. I was playing at a festival in Berlin, and it was running for five days. There were three shows a day, and I was the only girl for the whole five days. I suddenly thought, Hey, this is crazy. I went to one of the curators, who's a woman, and she said, Kaffe, tell me. Who else, who are the other girls that improvise with laptops in Europe? Tell me who they are, and they'll be here. And I was going, Mm, good point. Who are they? It was funny, it was the first time it ever bothered me. And it's not a feminist thing, it's more to do with the fact that, Jesus, it would just be more fun if there's more girls around. We'd have something other than shaved heads and gray everywhere, you know? Let's get a bit of glamour onboard! We do it differently; we make music differently. There'd be a greater variety of music here if there were girls here. So I got back home and sent e-mails around to everybody I knew: curators, players, whatever. Who are the girls who play experimental, improvised music? There were quite a few answers about women who work as DJs or who work with beats and their voice. But experimenting or doing more avant-garde or off-the-wall stuff, very few. The ones that there were, were all in the U.S.

About a month later, I got invited to curate a night at Tonic, and so I invited all those girls to play with me for the second set. We had such fun that night. That was the beginning of the Lappetites, which is this girls' group that I've had going ever since, in different formations.

You mention that you think men and women make music differently . . .

Yes, differently. Simply because we're different creatures, so of course we do it differently. And that's marvelous. So us playing together, or us listening—let's get all these different combinations happening.

: : :

Since our interview, Matthews has shifted the focus of her practice to sonic furniture building through "music for bodies," a collaborative research project she directs. This is a project for building specialized audio interfaces for enjoying music through the body rather than just through the ears. Recent works include *Sonic Bed_London*, which received an Award of Distinction for Digital Musics at Ars Electronica (2006), the Worldwide Bed Project, and the concrete *Sonic Bench_Mexico* (2007), permanently available for sitting in Mexico City.

Carla Scaletti

Carla Scaletti is a composer, harpist, and computer scientist based in Champaign, Illinois. She founded Symbolic Sound Corporation, a company that creates software and hardware for sound production, with Kurt Hebel in 1989. Since 1986, she has been designing and developing the Kyma environment, a graphical computer language for creating, modifying, and combining sounds. In combination with the sound computation engine, designed by Hebel, it is recognized as one of the most sophisticated sound design systems currently available. Kyma is used in a wide variety of contexts, including music composition, film, advertising, and speech and hearing research.

Inspired by science fiction, Scaletti is also developing a Mu-Psi Manifesto to provide a theoretical foundation for creative work with music technologies. She explains: "Just as a science fiction begins with the premise of some possible future universe and proceeds to fill in the details and consequences of that premise, a Mu-Psi sound work begins with a hypothesis, a 'what-if' premise, and proceeds to explore the ramifications of that premise."

I learned about Scaletti's work while studying computer music in graduate school, where colleagues who worked with Kyma praised the close relationship that Carla maintains with the community of users. We conducted this interview over e-mail in July 2006.

: : :

Tara Rodgers: Tell me about your early exposures to music and science.

Carla Scaletti: The earliest encounter with music that I can remember was learning lots of little songs in kindergarten and my teacher being surprised when I starting making up my own songs in the same style. My earliest exposure—not to science but to scientists—came when

I visited my dad's microbiology lab; he took one of my dirty fingers, rubbed it across a slide, and then let me look at it under the microscope. To me his lab was a mysterious place with giant automated centrifuges, acidic smells, mice, scary-looking biohazard signs on refrigerators, test tubes, and white lab coats.

In school I felt myself tugged in two directions. I was addicted to music but in high school, college, and even into graduate school I continued to take an interest in classes that most of my fellow music majors thought were crazy: mathematics, human genetics, astronomy, acoustics, light, electrical engineering, psychoacoustics.

This may sound odd, but I really identified with medieval composers—the ones who wrote isorhythmic motets. Or Dufay, who based his motet for the opening of the Duomo in Florence on the same proportions that Brunelleschi had used in the dome itself. In my music history classes, I found out that in medieval universities, the first thing the students had to master was the quadrivium—arithmetic, geometry, music, and astronomy—and I tried to arrange my own studies in the same way. The music history courses also introduced Iannis Xenakis, so there were intimations of others who were returning to the quadrivium.

In high school and college I used algorithms (worked out on paper) to generate parts of my compositions but had to keep it a secret from composition teachers and my peers, who would have considered it antimusical. The highest compliment was when the members of a student string quartet rehearsing one of my pieces intentionally added some subtle mistakes, just to test whether I really "heard" this music or whether I had just generated it mathematically. When I caught the mistakes, they said they could tell I had written the music "from the heart" and not algorithmically. But the truth is my goal was (and is) to make music with both. To me, the best music works at multiple levels in parallel: intellectual, sensual, spiritual.

When I was studying at the University of New Mexico, the composer Max Schubel did a residency there and produced several recordings for the Opus One label. He asked me to be his assistant, which basically meant that I was in charge of getting sandwiches. But it also meant that I got to sit and watch him editing, which at that time meant cutting tape with a razor blade. Seeing how he could piece together a new performance that had never actually occurred by splicing together bits and pieces from hundreds of takes made a deep impression on me; he was creating a new work, not simply documenting a live performance. As a reward for my work as a gofer and playing harp on several of his compositions, Max released one of my pieces on Opus One: *Motet* for bass clarinet, harp, male narrator, and mezzo-soprano.

I'm curious how your training or fluency on the harp may have influenced your approach to designing software.

To me, composing feels closer to programming than harp playing does; programming is more of an iterative, non–real-time activity with lots of rethinking and rewriting and sketching things out on paper as part of the process.

But now that you mention it, it's pretty clear that many of the things I wanted from Kyma came directly out of my experience as a performer. For example, I wanted to get my hands on the sound, to manipulate it, to hear the results in real time, to interact, to adapt. The mind/body/ear is a complex and subtle control system that we've been refining since birth, and which has been refined by evolution before that. Xenakis, whom I had so admired for applying mathematics to music composition, came to that conclusion with his UPIC system. He wrote that the hand was capable of capturing mathematics beyond what is possible with our current mathematical tools.

At some point you encountered an ARP 2600. When was this, and what impressed you about that instrument?

The ARP 2600 was (and still is) in the studio at Texas Tech University. When I discovered this instrument it was like everything came into focus for me; I suddenly saw a way to combine my (seemingly) competing interests. Electronic and computer music was the perfect melding of music and science. That may seem like an almost trivial observation at this point, but up until then I had been surrounded by peers and instructors who thought that music and math/science were polar opposites. Or mathematicians and scientists who thought of music as a recreation with no connections with their research.

Tell me about the time you spent at the University of Illinois in the early 1980s. How did you end up studying there?

My friends at Texas Tech knew I was insanely interested in computer music and one of them told me he had seen a book in the library called *Music by Computers* [von Foerster and Beauchamp 1969]. I checked out the book and noticed that most of the articles in it had been written by people at the University of Illinois at Urbana-Champaign. So I applied to graduate school there.

What was the focus of your work?

The focus was electronic and computer music. Though I also ended up doing a lot of new music harp performances my first year. But one afternoon I was down in the practice rooms trying to work out an exceptionally complex rhythmic combination in a piece written by a fellow composition student. In frustration I brought the score upstairs where I found him in his office quietly studying. I asked him to help me figure it out by tapping the rhythms on the desk and he just laughed and said, that's *your* job. At that point I decided that I would play only my own music, at least in public. To this day, I have a special admiration for composers who continue to perform live, who literally stay in touch with music making.

Were you influenced by certain mentors?

Yes, not only by instructors but also by peers. Those were lively and creative times at the University of Illinois; nearly every composer was developing software or building hardware. Sal Martirano had the SalMar Construction, a composing/synthesis machine built out of feedback shift registers that was, in retrospect, one of the earliest examples of a complex system capable of behaviors ranging from cycles, to quasi-cycles, and chaos. Herbert Brün had created the beautifully minimalist, almost algebraic sound/composition language called SAWDUST. John Melby introduced me to software synthesis; Scott Wyatt increased my appreciation for production values; Jim Beauchamp had built a hybrid digital/analog synthesizer controlled by [the University of Illinois computer] PLATO, and he was heavily into spectral analysis; Sever Tipei was doing computer-assisted composition. I lived in the graduate dorm, which meant that I could have dinner every night with students from all over the world who were doing research in everything from English literature to quantum tunneling.

I did my minor in psychoacoustics. Constantine Trahiotis had a reading seminar in Speech and Hearing Science where I learned how to read a journal article with skepticism, checking the units, critiquing the experiment design, making comparisons with other results, trying to replicate the results, and how to design experiments for the least amount of bias and clearly interpretable results.

Later, I was also influenced by Kurt Hebel and Lippold Haken, who were, at the time, electrical engineering students at the CERL [Construction Engineering Research Laboratory] Sound Group. They were the first people I had observed using computers in a fluent and relaxed way, in a way that solved problems rather than creating additional problems. At the School of Music, the computers were treated with a kind of reverence; the terminals were in special, locked, spotlessly clean studios. At CERL, there were cereal box stickers on the terminals, toys on top of the terminals. From Kurt and Lippold, I learned the problem-solving culture of engineers. I call it a culture because it was pervasive; it didn't just apply to engineering problems. For many people, if there is a problem, the tendency is to become outraged, to assign blame, to use it to cause trouble for someone else and to take over that person's resources. At CERL, if there was a problem, people tried to solve it; and if the first solution didn't work, they tried another, and another—they took a kind of pride in being so tenacious.

What inspired you to begin development of Kyma in 1986?

I needed Kyma for my work. There wasn't anything available that embodied the things I wanted to do with computer music. In Kyma, I tried to incorporate all the things I loved about electronic music: the direct shaping of sound, the concept of modulating the parameters of one signal by another (unheard) signal, the idea of controlling the sound with your hands, and the liberation of music from the "notes" of written music notation and movement towards a music based on "sound" objects. Computer music languages of that time used terminology like "instrument," "orchestra," and "score." Working with those languages felt like a step backward from the revolution begun by musique concrète and electronic sound synthesis.

As a programmer in the mid-1980s—which was well before the widespread availability of commercial music software that we're used to now—what future did you anticipate for the software you were developing?

Initially, it was a language I made for myself, for my own work. Then, when Kurt Hebel and I started the company in 1989–90 and sent

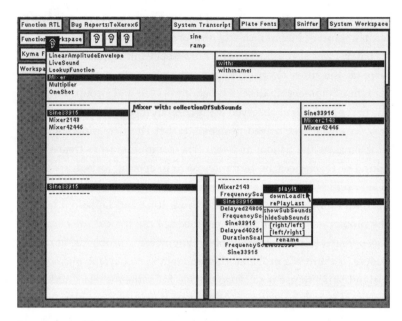

Screenshot of first version of Kyma, 1987. COURTESY OF CARLA SCALETTI.

out the first product announcement to the mailing list of *Computer Music Journal*, I had the completely naive idea that this was exactly what everyone had been waiting for and that we would be completely swamped with orders the very next day. In fact it took several years of explaining, of teaching, of spreading the word, and of proving ourselves before people trusted us enough to adopt Kyma as their working environment. Initially, I had imagined that the people using Kyma would be people very much like me. It's been a wonderful surprise and adventure to discover that Kyma could be useful to sound designers on films and computer games and that musicians could use it to make music in completely different styles. Kyma has definitely benefited from the input coming from all those different sources.

How did you happen to work in Smalltalk? Are there aspects of object-oriented programming that you've found particularly well suited to conceptualizing sound and music?

Smalltalk was a suggestion from Kurt Hebel. He knew I was working on a music language and during a winter break he had stumbled upon Adele Goldberg's book [Goldberg 1984]. The Smalltalk programming philosophy really appealed to him and he told me I should look into it. At the time there were some computer scientists looking at object-oriented programming as a way to model objects like instruments, an orchestra, a score, a conductor. I saw it somewhat differently: as a way to model a sound object at multiple time-scales and as a way of encapsulating and organizing complex networks so you could work at a high level for a while, plunge down to work out some low-level details, and teleport back up to the high level again while you were composing.

In your music compositions you often make reference to biological processes. From your experiences with music and programming, what connections do you see between genetics, human bodies, and future trends in music-making?

It's all signaling, networks, information flow, and patterns emerging at multiple time-scales.

Can you clarify what you mean by this notion of multiple time-scales—on a technical level?

To give an example from traditional music, a pitch-change curve at one rate might be heard as a motive; at a slower rate, it might be perceived as transpositions of the motive; at an even slower rate, it might be heard as modulation to a new key, and at an even slower rate it might be heard as different movements of the piece being in different keys or even different pieces in different keys. To give another example, in a Kyma improvisation, you might capture a gesture from the audio or tablet input and then play it back at different rates, using it as a control signal on different parameters of a synthesis algorithm. Or you might use the same algorithm to generate samples at the sample rate as you use to modulate the amplitude or frequency of those samples at a control rate.

In biology, different metabolic rates, the different rates of chemical reactions, and the different spatial concentrations of the chemicals can result in interesting pattern formation.

And on a more metaphoric level, what most interests or excites you about working with time in music, and within the realm of software?

Because it's a metaphor for our own interactions with the world. One time I had an idea to try to make a piece about memory—the way memories sometimes loop inside your brain, the way some memories degrade, the way some memories combine, the way some very old memories suddenly reappear. But the more I worked on it, the more I realized that *every* piece of music is, in some sense, a metaphor for the way memories replay inside our heads over time.

Memory is really interesting in that it adds coloration and, if you add feedback, allows for recursion (and infinity). Your brain has memory, delay, attenuation, and feedback—it's an IIR filter! By taking in ideas, (imperfectly) remembering them, letting them mix with other ideas inside your head, sending them out later to other people in their new forms and receiving feedback from those people, you are acting as a filter and adding color and structure to your corner of the universe.

In your opinion, what makes an interface (graphical or hardware) successful for working with sound? And what sort of expressive control do you envision for Kyma in the future?

The ideal interface would be one that disappears, one that could become so second-nature that you would no longer be conscious of the interface. Think of driving a car: the car may have foot pedals, joysticks, rotary controls, and read-outs, but an experienced driver is no longer aware of those individual controls. You drive almost as fluently as you walk. A more complex example is a musical instrument. It can take years before an instrument becomes your "voice," but an accomplished performer can imagine a sound and produce it on their instrument as easily as most people can think of a word and then speak it. The ideal computer/human interface should make it possible to achieve that same degree of fluency. It doesn't have to allow for *instant* fluency, it can require practice, but it should allow for the possibility of transparent fluency.

One of the things I have been exploring with Kyma is the use of an audio signal as a controller. Performers have developed a fine degree of control over their acoustic instruments; why not use the sound of the instrument itself to control the timing, processing, and synthesis? Instead of pressing a button or clicking the mouse, a performer can control the synthesis by changing the spectral, amplitude, and/or pitch envelopes on their acoustic instrument.

When we added support for controlling sound parameters with a Wacom tablet and pen, it had a bigger impact than we had expected— both with sound designers and musicians. Being able to control multiple parameters simultaneously using subtle tilts, movements, and changes of pen pressure taps into that mind/body/ear control system

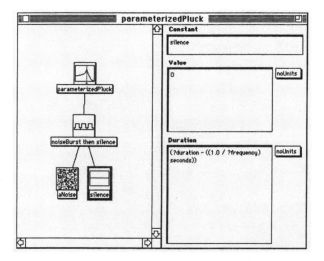

Kyma user interface, 1991. COURTESY OF CARLA SCALETTI.

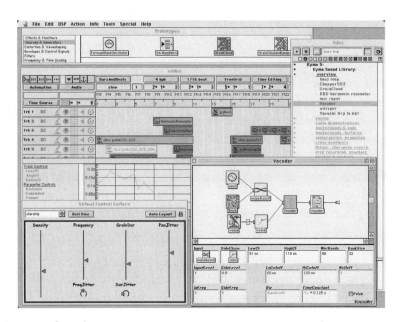

Screenshot of Kyma 5, 2000. COURTESY OF CARLA SCALETTI.

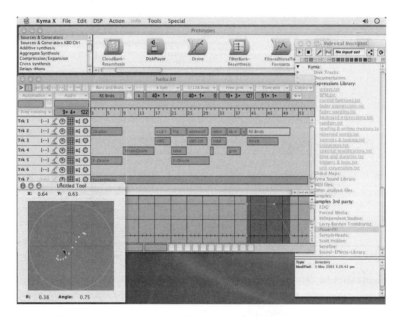

Screenshot of Kyma X, 2004. COURTESY OF CARLA SCALETTI.

and leads you to produce entirely different sounds than you would have produced using MIDI faders to control the parameter values. Another controller that works synergistically with Kyma is the Continuum fingerboard (designed by our old classmate Lippold Haken).

I'm convinced that the controller is as important a determinant of the sound as the synthesis algorithm itself. One of my goals for Kyma is to push it further along this mind/body/ear control system path, and to incorporate more physics into the interface.

In an article you wrote for **Computer Music Journal,** *you suggested that the development of any language, including programming languages, is a collective process [Scaletti 2002]. How has the community of Kyma users influenced your development of the software?*

Kyma has been one long continuous conversation. Someone will try to do something interesting with Kyma, maybe something that I hadn't anticipated, we make some adjustments, adaptations, or extensions to accommodate that new idea; these extensions lead us to another new idea which we implement in Kyma, which leads people using it to think of something else, and so on. This is not just a one-way conversation between the developers and individual Kyma users. Kyma acts as a nexus or a hub, incorporating new ideas from one field or style of music along one of its spokes and then spinning it out along all of the other spokes to people in different fields who are producing very different kinds of music and sound. It's like a virus acquiring new DNA and then spreading it among other minds (where it exchanges more DNA), etc.

In what ways has gender been an influential aspect in your work—in terms of your creative expressions, the philosophies behind your music and software, or your professional opportunities?

I suspect that might be one of those questions that is answerable only by an outside observer. I haven't set out to make a gender-specific statement in music or software but it must have had some influence (along with where I grew up, people I've met, where I went to school, etc). Life (biological and social) is a complex system with lots of entangled variables and one can never be certain which initial conditions have affected which of the results.

One way I've been lucky is that I'm genuinely interested in my work. Whenever I've run into a roadblock, my strategy has been to go around it. And the oblique path seems always to have led me to a much more interesting place than I had been trying to get to by the conventional path. There is some work that I feel driven to do and I have kind of stubbornly persisted in doing it.

: : :

Recent evolutions of Kyma include support for devices such as the Nintendo Wiimote, and new modules to support multichannel processing, recording, and diffusion.

Eliane Radigue

Eliane Radigue was born in 1932 in Paris, France. She studied electroacoustic music techniques in the late 1950s at the Studio d'Essai at Radiodiffusion-Télévision Française (RTF) in Paris, under the direction of the musique concrète composers Pierre Schaeffer and Pierre Henry. She married the artist Arman and devoted ten years to raising their three children. She assisted Henry again at the Studio Apsome in 1967–68, and began working on her own after that. Radigue departed from the principles of musique concrète to develop her signature style of slowly evolving sonic forms, which she builds from sustained tones of an ARP 2500 synthesizer recorded on tape, with barely discernible modulations of harmonics and filters. In the 1970s, she adopted Tibetan Buddhism as a personal philosophy and guiding principle for her compositions, evident on her recordings *Songs of Milarepa*, a tribute to the eleventh-century Tibetan saint and poet (Lovely Music, 2001); and *Trilogie de la Mort*, meditations on death and rebirth (XI, 1998).

I interviewed Eliane in January 2006 in the short time she had available between the sound check and concert premiere of *Naldjorlak* at Mills College, her first entirely acoustic work, for the cellist Charles Curtis. We met at Laetitia Sonami's house in Oakland, where Eliane was staying.

: : :

Tara Rodgers: How did you begin making music?

Eliane Radigue: I was fascinated during my early childhood by classical music. So I went, naturally, along this direction. At a point, I arrived to the twelve tones, which at that time were *the* story of music. But I was stuck with a feeling that it was very difficult to go further. I heard on the radio a program by Pierre Schaeffer, master of musique concrète, and thought, *That's it!* So I came to meet him. I went to the Studio d'Essai and worked privately with Pierre Henry, Pierre Schaeffer, and the people who were there, informally. It was in the early '50s.

I was married also and I had children. We were in the south of France, and it was difficult to get the necessary equipment, which at that time was very expensive and very rare. Pierre Schaeffer gave me a very nice letter to the broadcaster in Nice to introduce me, asking them to give me a few hours a week to work at their place. And the director was very nice with me, but made me understand that he had no time to waste with this! He sent a letter to Pierre Schaeffer that was very polite, but to me it was obvious that he had no interest at all in this kind of search. So then, it happened that I came to the United States in the late '50s and early '60s with my husband. We spent about one year in New York City, and I was in contact with several musicians. James Tenney was a mentor. I came to know several people like John Cage, David Tudor, Philip Corner. At that point it was very exciting. When I came back to France again, I was in the south of France. In '67, I separated from my husband and came back to Paris with my grown-up three children and started to work with Pierre Henry as his assistant. But I really started my work in 1968, after I left Pierre Henry. I had to leave him to do things on my own. Which means that I started rather late. I missed ten years in my life, ten years where it's very important, you know—like at your age—when there are a lot of things to do.

By that time, I was interested in feedback effects. Because, you know, synthesizers that did exist in the United States were quite rare: the Moog, the Buchla. In France, there were no analog synthesizers. So I worked with electronic sounds, these wild electronic sounds made out of feedback effects from a mic with a loudspeaker. It is very subtle to do that, because you have to find the right distance, just slowly moving it so the sound is slightly changing. You must be very dedicated and precise! The same when you make feedback with two tape recorders, by just a little whisper on the potentiometer, you may change a little.

In 1970, I decided that I'd like to come to New York, to have access to a real synthesizer. I came to New York University where Morton Subotnick had just installed a nice studio with a Buchla synthesizer. This was my first meeting with a real synthesizer, and it was a real fascination. Very naturally, I had been looking for these types of sounds I was already using, feedback sounds. A very simple vocabulary: pulse,

55

Eliane Radigue with ARP 2500 synthesizer, ca. 1970. PHOTO BY MOREAU.

beats, sustained tones. And then evolving from there inside, you
know? Some exercises I was doing, I was taking a beat—beating—and
by changing the inside of the sound, I would bring it into a sustained
tone, or conversely. Things were also sometimes more complicated.
But this was my immediate interest in this field of sound, which was
much easier to do with an analog synthesizer. So I spent one year here.
I had been looking at every kind of synthesizer. There was much less
to choose from than software now; there were the Buchla, Moog, ARP,
Electro-Comp, also a company in England. I really fell in love with the
ARP synthesizer. Immediately. Immediately! That was *him!* [Laughs]

What about it did you fall in love with?

I think he has a very special sonority. He has a quality, he has a voice.
A real voice. It's a very special quality of the sound. I like also the way
I could always figure out where I was on the patching system, with
the matrix. Not having to crawl into the wires of the system, like the
Moog or the Buchla, where if the sound is not here, you have to look
where by digging into it. So the ARP is much easier. Of course I didn't
use the keyboard, I left it in New York when I moved the synthesizer

to France. I didn't want to take the keyboard, because I was sure if at one point I got discouraged, I would have the temptation of going back to it! So by leaving it in New York, I was sure that I would just work with the potentiometers. So this is it, this was the beginning of everything. After that, I have been working with the synthesizer since 1970. Until recently, everything I have made has been made out of it.

Your pieces evolve so slowly. What is your process for making them?

It's a quite long process, because of course it is not made in just one move! [Laughs] Of course not, it would be impossible. This is why it has always been on tape, because it was impossible to do it live, it would have been impossible to perform. So this is my personal way of working. I am very bad at improvisation. I always have in mind what I want to do. Like with Charles Curtis, when he said he wanted to work with me, I started to work on the piece, and I suggested to him what I called the spirit of the piece. Whatsoever you name it, it's my leader. Let's say, I always know if the piece will be three parts, five parts; looking for the sounds which would fit every part, I'll know if this sound is good for the first part, the second part.

In analogical processes you have, of course, your oscillators. The basic frequency on the five oscillators is the same for the whole piece. When I decide that, I work the whole piece on that. And then come all the ring modulations, frequency modulations, amplitude modulations—and you have potentiometers where you can change the proportion, the ratio. And it is only on that, that I work. I don't work on the oscillators; when I have made my adjustment for one piece, it stays there. I work after that on all the partials. And of course, to end it up, the two beautiful filters on the ARP really make it. Everything is worked out with the potentiometers on the ARP. There are about thirty parameters that you can change easily, that you can change without having a complete disappearance—you know what I mean, with these sounds, if you go too far it just becomes anything else, just like lots of effects. Even with this instrument, if I change the frequency, it's another story!

It's a dramatic change.

Dramatic! So I always avoid dramatic change. This is what I've been involved with, and I am still involved in, is very slow changing, and also with a great insistence on the game of the partial, of the subharmonic and overtones. And for that, the ARP and its filters are a wonderful instrument. So this is how I make the sounds.

Then I have a pile of segments of sounds which are ready. At that point, I forget about it for at least one month, maybe two—to come back to listen to all this tape with fresh ears. It's quite interesting, because at least half of it goes to be thrown away. There are also some surprises, nice surprises—so I have to redo some of the parts.

Now I jump to the last process, which is very complex: mixing. I work with what were on these three reels of tapes, all these segments. But when I say segments, it's always at least ten minutes. Because the duration of a piece is definitely bound to the way the sounds change inside. This slow changing where we don't even know that it is changing, and when we hear that it has changed, in fact it has taken place long before. I know that, but even I don't hear it at the moment. And the sounds decide their own duration, somehow, because it's very obvious that you cannot go in one move from the beginning to the end or the sound will collapse.

When the sounds are made, with all this pile of tape, the organization of the mixing process is by far the most difficult part of it. By far. The idea's very simple: fading in, fading out, and crossfade. But it's another question to do it in the right time, at the right moment, in the right proportion. And when I was doing pieces which lasted for seventy or eighty minutes, if something wrong was happening at seventy-five minutes, *everything* had to be redone from the beginning. Everything. Now it's much more easy with ProTools. Except that I keep this organization with sounds on the three reels of tape, leaving some blank.

So you don't really edit on tape.

Oh, no. Very little. Just blank at the beginning to have the sharp beginning, and the sharp end. To know by sight where I was. And I always prefer working on slide pots for mixing, because you can play with at least four, or even six, at once. It makes that easier. But now, I couldn't do that anymore, it requires too much concentration and attention, even for fifty minutes. ProTools helps. I always have my analog tape, but after I transfer to the ProTools system it is much easier to organize. Except that for the crossfades, fading in and fading out, it doesn't sound exactly the same when it is drawn on the screen as when I was just carefully bringing it in with, you know, with the feeling. It's a little bit frustrating, because I love this feeling of crossfading very slowly, making even some stop here or there when it was working. With ProTools, no. You draw the line, you readjust it, and it does it by itself! But it's so much easier because if something goes wrong somewhere, you don't have to redo the whole thing from the beginning. And that's it. That's cooked. This is my cooking! [Laughs]

When you were learning about musique concrète in your work with Pierre Schaeffer and Pierre Henry, did that influence your way of working with tape?

That's a difficult question. Because I had already my interest, which was not exactly the interest of Pierre Schaeffer and Pierre Henry, as you know. This is why I had to quit at the time, because when I worked on my own, these two men were completely angry at me for what I was doing. I was the black duck of the family! [Laughs]

Because you worked with synthesizers, or in a different way with tape?

Because I was working the way I am working, which was absolutely an injury toward the basic principle of musique concrète, which has its own stylistic option, you know. I have been rejected by them, somehow, because of what I've been doing. This is why, at a point, I had to do my way alone. Just say, OK, thank you, men—I have tremendous respect for you and your work. I respect them; I think they did a wonderful, wonderful thing. But they didn't . . .

They weren't open to what you were doing?

No, absolutely not. I remember, Pierre Henry, the first time he listened to one of my things, he really got mad, he was almost insulting me. The only time nice that he said was, I considered you the best of my assistants, and look at what you are doing! Like he was expecting having me like a follower of his own way. That was rather difficult, in terms of affection. But, I've always been digging in the direction where I want to go, without paying any attention to how it was perceived. And by chance I had great encouragement from wonderful people, other musicians—Bob Ashley, David Behrman, Alvin Lucier, all these people—who immediately respected my work, which was very encouraging because it was a mutual admiration. And in fact, I've found this family over here in the United States. I used to say that my real family in terms of musicians is here. In France, I have been very much alone for a long time. Thirty years ago, I was a black duck in my own country! [Laughs] Now there are people who work in that direction also there. It's a big family now.

: : :

Since our interview, Radigue has continued composing for acoustic instruments, recording, and touring.

Part 2. Space and Perspective

Sound assumes many spatial qualities, among them site-specific acoustics, the treatment of recorded sounds with reverberation or spatialization techniques, and the imagined landscapes that inspire or are evoked by sonic forms. Maggi Payne cites the wide open spaces of her home state of Texas as an inspiration for her interest in textural details and spatial aspects of sound. She thinks of sound as a pliable structure that she compresses, stretches, and moves; she calls this "the architecture of the sound." Payne carries out a kind of architectural endeavor when she builds a coherent musical entity from juxtapositions of infinitesimally small sonic pieces. Ikue Mori also accumulates layers of rhythmic fragments and textures, which she describes as each having "their own space and control." She places these individual, sonic building blocks within contexts of improvisational performance, and they merge into a new, undulating, audible form.

Beth Coleman's stories from the early history of SoundLab document the politicized transformations of urban spaces in electronic music cultures. She recounts the artistic occupation of vacant buildings in Berlin in the mid-1990s, the efforts of promoters and artists in New York City to evade ordinances that prohibited dancing in bars, and the hasty conversions of spaces that are something else by day into party spaces by night.

Maria Chavez also describes the spaces of electronic music cultures as provisionally constituted and ever mutating. She notes that performance and installation environments are defined relationally among performers, sounds, and audience. As an improviser, she emphasizes accountability for one's place in that process: "being aware of my space, and taking it personally." Chavez's tools for improvisation include what she calls "ruins": vinyl records that have been warped or broken. The records themselves are decaying structures that bear the influence of the environments to which they have been exposed: a warm car, a worn bag, a stage floor. Overall, these artists illustrate how sound is a means for generating and inhabiting contingent spaces—spaces that take shape through dynamic interrelationships and are definable through the partial perspective of one's location.

Maggi Payne

Maggi Payne, born in 1945, is a composer, flutist, video artist, recording engineer, and historical remastering engineer. She is co-director of the Center for Contemporary Music (CCM) at Mills College, where she teaches recording engineering, electronic music, and composition. Her music exhibits meticulous attention to sonic detail, with subtle transformations of shifting layers of sounds over time. These techniques are exhibited well in *ReCycle*, a composition with recordings of a refrigerator, a freezer, a floor furnace, melting ice, boiling water, a Jacob's ladder, a faulty faucet, and noise during pauses in old 78 recordings (*Women Take Back the Noise*, Ubuibi, 2006); and *breaks/ motors*, which combines unwanted segments from her remastering projects with close-miced recordings of a tiny stepper motor (*Oasis*, Mills College, 2001).

At Mills, Maggi was my MFA thesis director and I was her teaching assistant for sound recording classes. We met for this interview in May 2004 in the CCM studios, flanked by the Moog IIIP and Buchla 100 synthesizers.

: : :

Tara Rodgers: How did you get interested in music and recording technology?

Maggi Payne: When I was really young, around five, my parents had me learn a little ballet, how to swim, a little bit of everything. One of those things was to play the piano. I really didn't like it, so I didn't do it for long, but at least I learned how to read music, which was good. But when I was around nine, I heard a flute, and I just said, That's it, that's what I want to play! I don't know where I heard it, I don't know how I heard it, because we didn't have much music around our house. So I picked up the flute and just went at it like crazy. I was self-taught, as most people are at that age. What I really loved was that when you're first trying to make a sound on the instrument, you make all these wonderful noises—whistle tones and air sounds. I started humming along and doing all of this stuff and I was thinking, Wow, this thing has a lot of capabilities. Then I started taking lessons, and I can still remember the teacher's name, it was Harold Gilbert. Here we were stuck in Amarillo, Texas, population 175,000, and here was this flute teacher who had to retrain me on the embouchure, but in the meantime, he was saying, You know, if you like those air sounds, it's fine. He was pretty wide open to anything, as long as I was also working on trying to get my embouchure correct, which was very difficult. So I thought that was really, really cool.

We lived on the outskirts of Amarillo, and there were very few houses around and very few people around. It was wide-open countryside, looking out across Route 66 and over to the cow pasture, forever! Incredible sunsets, but there was nobody there! [Laughs] So my dad, who always had an interest in technology—he was a doctor—he'd gotten one of the first 16-millimeter film cameras—he decided that he should buy me a tape recorder. I suspect his thought was that he would buy it for me, and I would either not figure out how to use it or get tired of it really quickly. But he was oh so wrong, because from the get-go, it was just amazing to me. Of course, it was not portable—it was a Webcor with a great blue "magic eye" meter. You were able to judge your amplitude by when it hit the center. The tube illuminated from both outer sides, and when these two blue streaks would join, you'd know that you were overmodulating and you'd have to back off. It was really cool.

And this was still when you were very young?

Maybe ten or eleven. It was when they first became available to the public. Since I was so isolated out there, I quickly figured out that I could record one part of a duet and play the other part along with it. So I was really hooked. A little later on, we replaced that machine with one that was much fancier. I guess that was closer on to junior high school or high school. At that time, I was so into the Bach B-minor flute sonata. The tape recorder had three or four different speeds, so I would start with the bass line and play it at quadruple time up a couple of octaves so it would bounce down to the correct octave, and then do sound-on-sound for each of the other parts, mix those onto the next track, until I'd get the entire accompaniment. After many, many passes, I'd get the whole thing. It was a quick lesson that you don't use vibrato, because when you slow it down two octaves, it's like *waaah-waaah, waaah-waaah.* [Laughs] So I got to practice sustained tones. But I was hooked. On both sides . . .

Playing as well as recording.

I loved playing. I was playing in all the orchestras that I could, and I went to Interlochen and Aspen. I went to Northwestern and was so busy with school I didn't record a lot during the first year, but I got a lot of session gigs at all the big studios in Chicago. And that was a wonderful education. I learned a lot about microphone technique as a player, in that you really play differently for a recording session than you do onstage. What I really liked about it was that, in all those many studios—CBS, RCA—the engineers were just so great. They didn't mind at all that I would come in after I finished playing and just pile on question after question after question. They were very generous about it all. So I picked up a lot of information that way.

65

I went to Yale for flute for graduate school and stayed there a semester, but I was kind of bored. They promised all this new music and there was new music on the undergraduate level, but not much on the graduate level. So I went to the University of Illinois at Urbana-Champaign instead, which was really happening. I got a first masters there and then here at Mills. At Urbana-Champaign, I averaged six concerts a week. It was really great. I worked with dancers, filmmakers, everyone possible. Gordon Mumma was there at the time, and I worked with him quite a bit. Also, this was the first time I met a classical electronic music studio, with the big oscillators, the big dials and everything. Jim Beauchamp taught a course in acoustics which I took, and I was truly hooked, and thought it was all amazing. He had one Moog module, I think it was some version of a harmonic tone generator, but I'm not absolutely sure. Gordon Mumma suggested that I come out here to Mills College, so I applied for the Electronic Music and Recording Media program and got in, and then was immersed in it. I remember Bill Maraldo and Bob Ashley opening the door to the Buchla studio and saying, You'll be teaching this next week. Showing me the way in and then closing the door! [Laughs] Like, no instruction whatsoever, a lot of learning on your own. It was kind of trial by fire, I guess. It was really good. It was a little while until we got the recording studio together here. I seem to remember it started as a four-track studio, and gradually grew to a 24-track studio.

And you've used the Buchla and Moog at Mills in some of your compositions . . .

Definitely in the early compositions. Actually, I used the Buchla on a few commercials that I did a long time ago and on some film work. The Buchla is so great because you can interlock all these sequencers. It's really a wonderful instrument. I love the filters on the Moog, so most of my compositions use the Moog because this early version of the Buchla didn't have filters. You know, that low-pass resonant filter is just amazing on the Moog. I think I've just always had an ear for filters—the filters in the Sonic Solutions system I use now are amazing. Thirty years later, that's where one of my interests still lies. I also filter white noise on the flute when I play it. As you blow into the tube, you change your fingerings and angle of the airstream. Timbre has always been so important to me.

Why is it, do you think, that you're so drawn to working with filters and timbre, more than other aspects of sound?

I relate this interest in the details of sound to the need in the huge expanses of the High Plains of Texas to find fascination in the details of the land. Every crack in the dry land, every snowflake in a blizzard, every cloud, every lightning bolt drew my attention. Since I often think of sound in visual terms, the connection is visceral for me. A complex sound with constant minute fluctuations can be quite fascinating, as the details become increasingly revealed over time.

Spatialization is also such an important and nuanced aspect of many of your works. Can you talk about perhaps one or two of your works where spatialization plays a significant part, and about your process for creating the spatial distribution and movement of sounds? Another way of asking this is: How do you conceive of space within a mix?

Spatialization has been a major concern of my works since the early '70s. I never do active panning during a mixdown. It's all engineered into the tracks or score. In my early works for Moog synthesizer I accomplished quadraphonic spatialization when I initially recorded each track. I would, for instance, have a slow attack time and release time on a signal that I was recording to track one. I would carefully calculate everything out so that when I overdubbed track two, I would start at the identical frequency (or sometimes a little above or below to produce beats), and start the envelope while track one was still sustaining, but would soon be decaying. Track one decayed as track two's attack took over, affecting a natural crossfade between these two tracks. I would do the same between tracks two and three, then three and four, and then perhaps cross over to track two from track four, etc. This is clearly heard especially in the quadraphonic versions of *Solar Wind* and *Crystal*, for instance. This is also the approach I used in a more recent work, *HUM 2*, for eight trombones, written for the wonderful trombonist Abbie Conant. The spatialization is built into the score.

In the many pieces of mine that use location recordings as the basis for the works I have some control over spatialization in the original recording that I make: the spatialization is inherent in the recording itself. When I record tiny stepper motors, for instance, I carefully place the mics so that as tiny as these motors are, the stereo field is enhanced. When these barely audible sources are played over speakers, the stereo field is greatly exaggerated.

I think of the sound architecturally, sculpturally. I'm sculpting the space or changing the architecture of the sound so that it becomes a tiny point source, a huge trapezoid, stretched diagonally, coming from the ceiling in the hall, coming from the top of your head, dead center in the hall, etc. Of course all of this is dependent on the acoustics of the hall, which are unpredictable, but it's always clear that the apparent space is being morphed in some way.

These days, you're doing a wide range of things—composing, historical remastering, and engineering.

A lot of historical remastering. Anything from as early as the '20s, going up typically around '65 into the '70s. I'm just trying to bring that music back to life. And it's really wonderful to be able to experience the performances from earlier times, many of which come to me so badly blemished and in need of repair. It's thrilling to be able to help breathe life back into them.

In terms of recording new works, it's so great to work on a project where you build tracks over time, and finally it just builds and builds and builds into this wonderful entity. Then in the process of mixing,

Maggi Payne at Bryce Canyon National Park, 1996.
PHOTO BY BRIAN REINBOLT.

everything gets revealed. It's just such an amazing thing to do, to put all these sounds together and work out their juxtapositions and layering.

It's really exciting to record contemporary music and classical music as well. It's a time-consuming process to do so many takes and then finally in the editing process, you're working in minuscule detail on every little bar or beat or thirty-second note—you're always backtracking a bit just to make sure the tempi match and the performance is solid—but when you finally start hearing it in larger sections, it's just like a miracle as it comes together.

And there's always that idea of always keeping your ears absolutely open for every sound wherever you are and wishing you had all your recording gear with you every second of your life, because as you run home to get your gear, often that sound has disappeared. It's just such a fascinating world of sound out there.

Do you have favorite sounds or sound memories, incredible things you've heard, outside or in a studio?

So many sounds. I did a piece a few years ago called *Sweet Dreams*, and it was about all the sounds that keep me awake at night because I don't sleep very well. I went out to gather sounds that interrupt my sleep, and I found that as I was trying to get those airplanes, the motorcycle, cars passing, all these sounds—I was really having trouble because the world is a wonderful mix of sounds, but when you're trying to get *one* sound it's kind of irritating. I was trying to get some sounds in isolation. Since I've been doing this for so very long, I'd go out to the same locations out in the country that I'd used before, and it was a bit terrifying to realize how much the extraneous noise level has increased. I would record as best I could, because of course the gear is much better, but many times I would go back and access the tapes that I made thirty years ago and end up using some of them because there was so much less background interference. It was just shocking. I was glad I used the best equipment I could ever find, always.

What's also really great, as I was listening and trying to find the spots on those tapes, I would just drop in and hear this sound, and I would go, *I remember that!* I recorded that in *this* location, at about *this* time in the afternoon, and it smelled like *that*, you know? And I'd fast-forward a bit, and I'd think, *I remember that!* Even if it's not perfectly logged in my records: Oh, yeah, I was in *that* tree! [Laughs] In *that* location. It's just amazing, all that sound brings to you. You'd think that because it's so abstract, that those memories wouldn't attach so strongly, but they do.

So, sounds that I love: I love sounds that I haven't heard before. When I'm doing my own work, I love sounds that I sense have a great potential for development. I'm already thinking of what I will convolve against this sound, what granular synthesis program might I use on this, because they each have different characteristics, you know? Or with a parametric EQ, if I cranked up this narrow band right up at the very top, there's just something that's very special there. So it can't just be a sound that's interesting on the surface, it's got to have that kind of potential to it. Like the piece *Distant Thunder* that I just completed, I recorded that great squeaky gas regulator over at Lisser Hall, and went to great pains sitting out there at midnight with my mics right on it. It was such a great sound, but try as I may, try as I might, I just couldn't use the squeaks. They just had too much character. But what I really loved was the sound of the flow of the gas through the pipe, as the pressure would keep changing. It was this very quiet world that was so wonderful. And then I tried and did that same thing with the bad washer in the sink in the men's washroom in the Music Building. I spent three hours in there one night when nobody was there—*klang-klang!*—just rattling the entire building. I was thinking that I finally have to tackle rhythm, because I don't typically use overt rhythm. I have microscopic rhythms, and then the large sense of rhythm and proportion. But I usually don't have what we typically think of as metrical rhythm. So I thought, well, here's my chance. And of course, that's not what I ended up using. I found a little fragment in between the strong rhythms that's just great. I think I tend toward the more sustained sounds that have a lot of fluctuating detail within, but not overtly rhythmic sounds.

Things that you have to discover.

That's right. And it's not even necessarily the complete sound, but a component within that sound that I can slice out and highlight and just go with.

I love gathering sounds. I think it's one of the more creative aspects of composing for me. I love that aspect. And then I go through all the logical trials of convolving them against whatever—so many times. For a ten-minute piece, I can get up to five, six, or seven gigs of trials on all these sources, before I go: Yes, yes, yes, no, this might work, this might not. So much material is not used; it's thrown away. It's a kind of sloppy way of working, and indulgent in a way.

In some ways, you can't avoid that.

I think not. Because I'm so efficient at my normal jobs of editing—efficiency's so important when you're working for clients—it's really nice to be able to take time in your own work, you know? When you build a piece, and really work with the materials over and over, juxtapositioning and layering the materials—that's when the logical side takes precedence, but then you're still making so many creative decisions. And when you start putting it together, it's such a beautiful combination of logic and creativity.

In my pieces too—the electroacoustic works anyway—for a long time, I've said that I like to think of them as inviting people on a journey with me. Attention is always difficult to maintain, so they're welcome to sort of take off on occasion, walk away and come back—in their minds—and come back and rejoin and go again, but it's like an invitation for a journey. And it's a music that hopefully is not such a controlling kind of music, where if you don't get this one part, then you miss the whole key to the entire piece. Or that you feel that you're so manipulated by any drama within the piece that you're controlled by the music—although there are certainly dramatic moments to my pieces—it's just that I try to make it more inviting. I really want people to join in the experience. I also talk about it as inviting people to experience the sound from the inside out, so that it's almost an internalized experience, a visceral experience, rather than an external experience that they're distanced from.

You've mentioned to me how you've been one of only a few women in certain professional contexts, at least in the audio engineering field.

When people ask me that, about how I got into all this: (a) a woman composer, (b) a woman engineer, and (c) a woman specializing in contemporary music, all I can say is, I never gave it a thought. It never really occurred to me to look around to see who else was there. When you're driven to do something, you just do it. I realize that we did study a lot of male composers, and very few women composers, and it's kind of a shame. And I'm glad that it's changing.

How do you feel that it is changing?

It clearly changed, for me, when I look back at it during my lifetime, particularly in the '70s. It's a major shift, particularly in composition. I wouldn't say that for recording engineering, but definitely for composition. We've got so many strong women. For the engineering aspect, there are a few more percentage-wise, but it's still very disappointing. When I go to the Audio Engineering Society meetings—and that's just a small facet of it—but still, I'm seeing one or two women in a room of fifty people, and there are very few people of color. But I am hearing of more and more and that's very heartening, and of course they're not all going to be joining engineering societies—they're out there working. I think since so many composers have also been getting into electronic music, recording has become part of that aspect of what they do. So they are definitely getting the skills in.

Do you feel any particular affinity with being at Mills College, in that it's a women's college? Did that have anything to do with your coming here?

I have to confess, in those days, we'd hear about an exciting place and we'd just go for it. It was on the strength of Gordon Mumma's recommendation, his saying that this was really the place for me, and I believed him and came here. But as I started looking out of academia and looking at the real world and realizing how few women composers there were, and how few women engineers there were, and how few women in electronic music there were, then it really did become a mission.

A mission in the sense of using your teaching to try to . . .

Change the world. Even if these women aren't going into these fields— and quite a few do, but not everybody—they have that confidence and that understanding of what they're listening to. And I hope they have a special understanding for what it takes to build a piece, to compose. Because in all my classes, that's what they're doing, even if they're not aware of that right away. But they catch on quickly.

: : :

In 2007, Payne premiered *Arctic Winds* at Mills College and had additional performances of her work in Los Angeles, New York, Paris, and Dublin. In April 2008, she completed *Liquid Amber*, a new video piece for which she also composed the music.

Ikue Mori

Ikue Mori, born in 1953, is a Japanese musician based in New York City. She played drums in the influential No Wave band DNA, with Arto Lindsay and Tim Wright, in the late 1970s. When the band broke up and she was looking for a new creative direction, she recalls, "Somebody gave me a really simple drum machine, and I just fell in love with it." Since the mid-1980s, Mori has remained a key figure on the downtown improvised music scene, establishing a unique vocabulary by using these "simple" drum machines—and now a laptop computer—as expressive, improvisational instruments. She is arguably the most prolific and accomplished artist to invert the primary function of the drum machine as a beat-keeping device.

I learned about Mori's work through Keiko Uenishi in 2000. I attended several of her performances at Tonic and continued to hear about the influence and reach of her work from many other artists. Ikue and I met for an initial interview at her Manhattan apartment in November 2002, and she answered additional questions by e-mail in January 2007, which are consolidated with the original transcript.

: : :

Tara Rodgers: When did you start playing music?

Ikue Mori: When I moved to New York in 1977. I started playing drums, acoustic drums.

Why did you decide to come to New York?

I always wanted to be out of Japan, since I was little, and then when I had enough money, me and my friend came just to see New York. It seemed like the most interesting things were happening in New York around that time, so we just came to see, like sightseeing. And we ended up meeting people and asked to be in a band, and it started so quickly. Within six months I went from never being a musician to playing CBGBs! It was really quick, yeah. It was an exciting time.

How did you end up playing the drums specifically?

I met Arto Lindsay and other people making No Wave music. A lot of young people who were not musicians just started picking up instruments, having a band, and playing. So I wasn't a musician, but I could fit in. My friend, he was a musician, and he was asked to be in a band because he was already playing instruments. So I was involved with people who were always jamming, playing instruments, and I was playing too. And then I met people starting a new band and looking for a drummer, and I started playing with them.

Many people still cite DNA as being hugely influential, despite the fact that the band existed only for a short time and produced few recordings. What do you think was different about what you were doing in music and performance, compared to other artists at the time, which created such a lasting impression?

Maybe because we were not trying to be something else but ourselves then. Songs were short and fast and the set was more like an intense small theater. In fact we had the same set for years. It became something else, beyond tightness. It was like a ritual ceremony every set.

What music were you listening to at that time?

Pretty much rock music from New York. It's always been rock music, even before I came to New York. Traditional Japanese music I was never interested in when I was in Japan. I kind of rediscovered it, and appreciated it, when I moved here.

When did you start playing drum machines, and how did you end up working with them?

From 1985 until the mid-'90s, I was pretty much playing only drum machines. For five years I was playing in one band, playing drums, and then the band broke up and I was looking for something new. Somebody gave me a small Roland TR-707 drum machine, a really simple drum machine, and I just fell in love with it. I found myself more enjoying programming than practicing. I can't really practice

Ikue Mori, 2004. PHOTO BY HEUNG HEUNG CHIN.

drums anyway, in an apartment. I've been living in this apartment twenty years. So it's convenient to use drum machines. And I was always more interested in making songs, composing things, rather than practicing things. Then I got more sophisticated drum machines that you can do a little more with, like making the different voices different pitches, making melodies. So instead of using a pattern and groove and repeating things, you can use the drum machine not just for keeping a beat but making more interesting broken beats and rhythms. And then I moved from using one drum machine to two drum machines.

Also around the same time I was involved in improvising music. Before, when I was playing drums with bands, we never improvised. Even though we were jamming, it was never improvising, it was really kind of set things. So about the same time I found the drum machine I was also involved in the improvisation scene, where you really have to react to other people's sound and music. So I began to program more and more in that way with the drum machine. I was still playing drums then; in the course of ten years, I kind of shifted to less drums and more drum machines, and then no drums and three drum machines, effects, and a mixer. I played with that setup for about ten years before going to the laptop.

People really don't see the drum machine as an improvisational instrument, since it's used more for preset beats. What inspired you to push its boundaries?

I was really never interested in using the drum machine as a beat-keeper. I use instruments to react, for improvising, to be more spontaneous. A lot of different fragments, thinking not just of beats but fragments of sound. So with a bank of sounds, you can preset sounds as numbers, or program the same sound at different pitches. Then the numbers trigger what I want to play or hear, more like an instrument.

How do you conceive of rhythmic structures in the music that you make?

I like layers of fragments—colors, broken beats, textures that have their own space and control—put together with depth, so that different grooves from each layer create new rhythm.

Do you have a favorite drum machine?

I've been using Alesis for a long time: the Alesis HR-16 A and B, and the SR-16—the small one. I have three different kinds because they all have different sounds, voices. The second one was more effective sounds, and the first one has more percussive sounds. Somebody tried to have Alesis endorse me, because in interviews I always say, "Alesis, Alesis . . ." but I think what I do is too broken!

Right, too unconventional. And more recently you've been working with a laptop. What software setup do you use?

I used the laptop starting in 2000, and it's really continuous from the setup with drum machines. People already playing with laptops showed me that I could do this setup in a laptop. And it was kind of a liberation from schlepping all the equipment. I realized, it's all sampling anyway, even if it's in the laptop. I'm using the same drum machine sounds, and using Max and MSP, which allow you to design a program sampling the same sounds that I was using. I have a key assigned for all the patches so then you can really play the laptop like a drum machine, pushing buttons. But with the laptop you can do even more processing and manipulation. So, for me, it's expanding the vocabulary to more sounds. But the sounds are still really percussive—it's an extension of using drum machines, you can tell.

What excites you most about the music you make? Are you always seeking new textures in sound?

Yeah! Mostly different sounds and rhythms. But I'm playing different projects with different people, and I have to be careful not really repeating too much of the same thing, because it's so recognizable. So I'm always kind of changing a sound, or seeking a new stretch, a new voice.

In your own work, or when you are listening to or improvising with others, what aspects of sound most attract you, or challenge you?

Nature sounds—stream, rain, wind, insects, birds—attract me most. Most challenging is to interact with jazz or rock licks.

I'm also inspired by a lot of visual things, like I really love film and old movies. I'm always watching them. Musically, I'm really influenced by film music. The movies that I really like are film noir, like '50s to '60s, dark, black-and-white movies.

In your albums that have been inspired by visual art (i.e., drawings and paintings by Madge Gill, films of Abigail Child, woodblocks of Tsukioka Yoshitoshi), how do you establish relationships between your sound compositions and the visual material? Would you consider it a process of translation from visual to aural?

That varies by project, and it is not always that the image itself inspires a certain idea of the song. Yoshitoshi's case is more like the stories and myths behind the images with moon that structured the album. Soundtrack for the film is more to do with each character and scenes. The pieces for Madge Gill are more direct inspiration from the images, although her life story is not forgettable, and the whole album *Myrninerest* (Tzadik, 2005) is about something very close to personal feelings and emotions.

Recently I started to play my own visuals in addition to my sounds, connecting via Max patch so that the images and sounds react to the same signals, and this opened up a whole lot of new possibilities.

Of your own recordings, do you have a favorite?

Well, I always like recent ones more than older ones. *Garden* (Tzadik, 1996), I like, because it's kind of the end of my drum machines era; by 1996, whatever I wanted to do with my drum machines was really established. *Labyrinth* (Tzadik, 2001), I like, too, because it's moving a little bit in a different direction from that, even though it's using the same sounds, a little more stretched.

It seems relatively rare to find women on the scene, and you're considered one of the pioneers. Do you see yourself that way, or did you when you were first involved with making this kind of music?

Yeah, and I still do; it's really only a few women. Electronic music is not even the worst ratio, you know—in improvising music, and jazz too, women are always kind of the minority. And sometimes I feel like I don't get taken as seriously as a man. But New York is great, though. New York has probably the most women musicians I can find, like at Tonic. So many women to work with. And they come here, too, because they find it's really comfortable for women working. Maybe in Tokyo it's like that too, but not everywhere.

Have you performed a lot around the world?

Mostly in Europe, but going to a lot of festivals I see a lot of women from New York! But women are really a minority.

Why do you think that is?

I don't know. What do you think?

Sometimes I think it relates to how women are not often encouraged to interact with certain kinds of technology the same way that men are.

Yeah, electronics especially. I mean, I'm still not a technical person at all. My interest in making songs is not in technical terms at all. Working with women, it's easier just to describe my emotional side. It's more easy to connect, in a way, because you don't have to really explain in technical terms. But I think men are more into using different expressions to communicate. I can be more personal with a woman. It's easier to express, and music can be more personal.

Do you think that comes across at all in the sound, in the musical expression itself, or just in terms of how women talk about how they use equipment?

How they react with machines, it's kind of different.

Having started out playing drums—the way you react to a machine in an improvisational setting compared to an acoustic instrument, it must be totally different.

Yeah, but see, I've been playing a drum machine for about ten years. And that's how I react, with pushing a button, and with the numbers. You know, how you find the sound by number; for me, that came from the drum machine. And processing is all numbers, with calculations.

In some ways, I guess it's like learning to play an instrument of any kind.

But it's not really a traditional instrument, you have to find a way. And now there's so many possibilities! Ten years ago, it wasn't possible to think just a laptop could do this. A lot has to do with the speed and calculations.

Do you plan to work with different kinds of drum machines in the future?

No, I think the drum machine is pretty done for me. Alesis is enough for me. Now, I'm using that but more developing a different sound out of it. Now it's not just a beat from a drum machine, now you can make a beat from scratch, and you can make granular sounds. Before, even though I was breaking the rhythms, I was using the factory sounds of the drum machines.

There are so many possibilities, it's sometimes hard to . . .

Focus! Because the machine can do so much, you really have to find your own sound, like your "identity" kind of sound.

Often with laptops, I find it's hard to distinguish one person's sound from the next.

That's one of my problems, too, listening. But sometimes a person will have their own sound and voice. There are exceptional people who have their own sound with guitar or drums also. You can recognize it.

Do you think that you have a particular "identity" that you've established in your sound? How would you describe it?

Most of the sounds I still use are from the previous drum machines. They are all very short patterns, and repetitions of different loop points and speeds. Layering them and putting them through the combination of filters make the unique sounds.

80

: : :

In 2007, Mori released *Bhima Swarga* (Tzadik), a film project that combines animations of traditional paintings from Bali with music that includes her renowned laptop electronics, and a Gamelan score by Matt Welch. She continues to perform at the Stone and elsewhere in New York City, and on tour internationally.

Beth Coleman
(M. Singe)

Beth Coleman (M. Singe) is the codirector of SoundLab Cultural Alchemy, founded in 1995. She has been active internationally as a DJ and sound and multimedia artist, exhibiting in such venues as the Whitney Museum, ARC/Musée d'Art Moderne de la Ville de Paris, and the New Museum of Contemporary Art. She has released recordings on various electronic music labels and produced multimedia works that combine electronic media, sculpture, and relationships of sound and space. The *Vernacular* software (2003), created with artist Howard Goldkrand, enabled users to mix multimedia objects in 3-D virtual space to explore the "interface ecology" that characterizes contemporary life. The installation *Waken* at the New Museum of Contemporary Art (2005) used generative code to create a "sonic prairie," a soundscape that emulated patterns in nature (Coleman and Goldkrand 2006).

Soon after I moved to New York City in 1995, Beth was becoming a fixture on the experimental electronic music scene. I was introduced to her work through coverage of SoundLab events in the *Village Voice* (Owen 1997). We met when she performed at the Pinknoises.com launch party in 2001, and sat down for this interview at a cafe in Manhattan in March 2002.

: : :

Tara Rodgers: Tell me about how SoundLab got started.

Beth Coleman: Howard Goldkrand and I started SoundLab in '95 after we'd been to Berlin for the summer with some friends from the UK. We basically invaded Berlin summer of '94, and it was a real transitional time where people were so off-balance with the Wall coming down, and there were a lot of empty spaces that got filled up by underground scenes, club nights, installations. And it was massive; the music was incredible, and there was a feeling of: We can do whatever we think of, as long as we can figure out the technical way to pull it off. Nobody had any money; you just scrambled to put things together. So we showed up in the middle of this and would do performances within people's things, like show up someplace with this really weird East German school record player, with the built-in speakers, and we'd attach a mic, and that was our basic setup. We did this kind of stuff where you just went and exploded all the time, and didn't worry about this, that, or the other thing; and it was a time and a place where it was really good to be able to flow and not worry about the consequences.

82

When we got back to New York, Giuliani had just become mayor and started the whole no-dancing-in-bars policy and all the rest [see Bumiller 1996], and we were really keen to have a speakeasy scene, under the cover of secretiveness, discretion, and basically those who hear about it come and hang out, listen to music, make music, make art, talk to each other. And, you know, Spooky would play there every week, and what was known as the "illbient" crew. People were working things out, doing their new music. SoundLab wasn't a club, so all those demands, like making people drink, it wasn't an issue. Anyone who showed up, they showed up because they wanted to see what the scene was—what people were listening to and what people were doing—not because they needed a certain stabilized, recognizable environment. And it was five bucks, so if you didn't like it, you could leave.

So it was in that context that I learned about making music and the equipment by setting up the equipment. It was me and Howard and Manny Oquendo, a central character in this whole scene. At three o'clock in the afternoon on Friday, we'd go to the Haus of Ouch on Walker Street and start literally laying the floor out, 'cause it was a dance studio and we needed to protect the floor. We'd build a whole installation from the ground up: set the sound system up, set the visual installation up. And different people would come in and debut their stuff, like Caspar Stracke, the filmmaker; Panoptic. One night we did an installation where we got fifty goldfish and strung them in bags of water and then had illumination on them, and we tried to figure out whether they liked the bass vibrations, whether they seemed happier, or do fish have ears, this kind of stuff. So some of SoundLab was analog, some of it was all teched out. But essentially it was—and is still—

very much a laboratory space where people are invited to work at their limits, debut new stuff, test out new stuff—that's what it's for.

I was listening to Spooky, and Wally, and Soulslinger, and drum 'n' bass was starting; by '96 people were really buzzing about that, and my first set was January '96. And Dr. Walker and Khan were there, and I knew they were going to play. So I remember their record was part of my set, and some dancehall; and that was my first official set at SoundLab, where I wasn't just playing at the jam at the end. And then I started playing basically weekly from there. I had the most ideal context to start working, 'cause I had really good teachers, really inspiring people to watch and to listen to; and it was my own event, I was the co-collaborator on making this happen, and booking. There was enough of an edge in terms of, heads are in the house, if you're bad, everyone will know! But I wasn't doing the bar at the Tribeca Grand, I was playing a set at SoundLab. And in some ways, the rule was: you had to do something interesting, which is not easy.

83

I was really nervous the first time I played, and I also was really elated, because it's cool—it's really exciting to DJ. And it's really exciting to produce music, and for me, the two are very closely related. Some people maybe wouldn't feel it the same way, but I was like: Wow, this is good, and I can hear this. I don't necessarily know how to make all the things I want to make, but I know, fundamentally, there's something I really hear, and it feels solid and important to find that, to work that out. So that's how I started.

So what's your main way of working these days?

Most of the production I'm doing is with Logic, and I'm starting to work with Max. I'm trying to do something that's minimal and grooving at the same time. I like using Logic as a platform because it still can do more things than I'm doing with it, and that's exciting for me. I'm working with an engineer to see, if I'm building Max patches and using those as plug-ins in Logic, what kind of manipulation can I get with that. One of the projects we're working on in the studio as a crew, which is primarily me and Howard, is a software piece where we're looking at finding not just audio data but multiple types of streams of information. Because, again, if a signal can be translated into digital format, which many things can be, then why can't that be part of a mix?

What I'm coming from with the whole history with SoundLab is, music in some ways is the most identifiable part of it, but it's been full environmental installations from the beginning, where we're working with new media and trying to see what can we make talk, what's the question of interface going on. That's in some ways the idea of architecture. So I'm working on music output, but for live performance, what I'm working off and testing out on different levels is that other idea of a whole electronic architecture interface. And I don't have to run everything. I like to be able to play solo, like have my own space where I get control of—whether it's a laptop or a laptop and decks— everything within that zone; but I like working with MCs, I like working with live musicians—well, I don't know if I like working with live musicians! I've worked a lot with live musicians, but I'm not really an improv kind of person.

You like to have your plan in place, more or less.

Well, I have a really different sense that very much comes from somebody who cut her teeth on electronic music, and not playing an instrument, not an acoustic instrument. Because a lot of what I've seen with improv, it's very interesting in terms of being live and spontaneous; but working with machines, working with these programs, you have a whole different question in terms of what's spontaneous and what's live. If you press playback, I mean, some of the live sets that go on with this stuff, people may as well just play the CD, because there's nothing interactive. Or the risk is, can I load all the programs at once, is it going to crash? I've done a couple of solo laptop sets, which is my preferred mode of working at the moment. I brought in my Logic mixes that I could then effectively dub out live.

Sort of like DJing but within the confines of the laptop.

That's right. So that works for me. As in with DJing, you have a certain amount of presets, in terms of: you brought these records. So there's that finite thing—that's not improv as such, but then within that, the way you make that combination, it's all improv. So in some ways, it's more conservative and also totally more blown out than what's going on with traditional acoustic or electroacoustic improv. I like to have some chance operations going on, but in DJing or electronic music you can make cacophony in two seconds. Like one of the easiest things you can do is make noise. And I've made a lot of noise over the last five years. I've definitely mashed and crashed and bashed stuff and really enjoyed it, and wanted to get groove and swing within the explosion. And people have been sort of hip to hearing that; so that's a very cool thing when people hear what you meant.

Like the sound system we work with, the Hill Foundation system, which is a classic Soundclash/West Indian sound system made by Scrambles, who's this Trinidadian cat, and his crew, Hill Foundation. Scrambles came from a more dancehall background, like big bass, and music with power, but not necessarily machine gun and broken beats and that kind of stuff. We really came up together. I started DJing a little before he started coming in doing sound systems with it, because SoundLab, between '95 when we started and '97, kept getting bigger and bigger and bigger, so we went to bigger locations and had bigger systems. I'd come in and basically play a set at all of the events, and I always wondered what Scrambles thinks when I break out the noise and whatnot. And one night, I think I was playing an electro/dance set, a more chilled-out set, and he said: So what happened? Where's the noise? And I said, You like that? You like that sound on your system? And he's like, It's your sound. That's what I hear when I hear you play, so I feel like you haven't played your set until I've heard your sound.

My feeling is you have to play with conviction, and you have to love what you're playing. And because the whole DJ scene and market is very hardcore in terms of, it's gotta be user-friendly, you've gotta give the client what they want. If somebody wants you to play a party, or a bar, the bar wants to know if drinks are increasing during your set; at the party they want to know if their clients were dancing. That's very, very heavily the culture. And I have respect for people who have their craft and can go kick it like that, but in that way, I'm much more a producer, where I hear a specific kind of sound, and that's what I reproduce pretty much whether I'm playing a DJ set or playing more and more my own material.

For my solo project, I've done all my own production, which is not always important to me, but I also didn't see any other way to do it. Because, in the same way that I don't know how interested I am in improv as I understand the history, I've worked with various producers and engineers a little bit, and I don't know how to work unless I'm actually making it. It makes me kind of frantic to sit next to someone and say, Can you make something like this?

Beth Coleman (M. Singe). COURTESY OF CHARLIE AHEARN.

Because what you're making is such an extension of yourself?

Yeah, or also, I don't necessarily know what the hell it is before I make it. Sometimes I go in with an idea of, I'm looking for this kind of sound, or this kind of rhythm, and often that's the clearest and fastest way to work, for me. Because once I get the rhythm matrix down, then I can stretch out a little bit in terms of: Here's how the bassline works, here's how the top end works. But I'm very beat-oriented. It's not surprising I get along very well with drummers. Like I played with the trio Harriet Tubman on some tours last summer with the drummer J. T. Lewis, who was part of Herbie Hancock's *Rockit* tour. And he and I were totally vibe, because even though it's a different touch, it's very much a touch issue with DJing and the way I play live electronics. That's the point of intersection where I feel I'm a percussionist, but I'm doing this totally vinyl, electronic thing.

And since you've been working, music technology has changed pretty significantly. It's become rapidly more software-oriented, and you've probably experienced that.

Yeah, in '95, people weren't playing laptop sets, the computers weren't able to do that; the software was in a more academic vein. Things were more hardware- and instrument-oriented, more MIDI-oriented in terms of how you connected the dots to make things play; and in the past five to seven years, it certainly has become more software-oriented. Which has suited me just fine, because I stepped into it just at the cusp of that change, so there are things I'm totally an idiot about in terms of some of the older craft using hardware and the connections there, and things that are pretty instinctual for me in terms of what it means to work with purely different softwares. I started on ProTools and then started to work with Logic.

What made you choose Logic?

It can do what I want. It can automate the things that I want, it can deal with MIDI. All the signs were there that this was a good step up, more flexible than what I could do with ProTools. I loved dealing with ProTools; that's where I started doing this kind of retarded hand-splicing and remixing and tiny recalibration of beats. And whether that becomes something where people hear my production, that's up to me. Because in some ways it's easy enough to just automate everything so it snaps to grid. I'm still working with combinations of interest, perversity, and how far can I go with this and what do I need to make the other parts sound like what I want. Which is part of the incentive to go in from time to time and work with other engineers or other producers, because I'm not opposed to hearing my music better or a little differently than it's in my head if I can translate it with somebody else. Because the bottom line is, I want to make the music so it sounds like whatever it should.

There's so much in production that's amazingly repetitive. I think when people are practicing scales on piano, there is this technical thing about what is correct, what is perfect—but there's a real physical aspect to that repetition. And one of the things that's really bugged out about doing it all in the computer is that it's absolutely repetitive in those same ways, but the gesture is not in sync. Which I think is too bad, and when I play the stuff back to do live shows, there is more relationship between the physical gestures and, like, stomping on my keyboard, in relationship to what's happening with the sound, which is really fun. That kind of studio thing, it suits me, because I like that repetitiveness; I think that's why I make this kind of music. It works for me, it helps organize what the zone is, even if it's annoying repetition. But, for me, electronic music is so much that really stupid slave-like repetitiveness mixed with a totally unbounded frame of what you can make there, and I like that.

I wonder if you can talk on the theoretical end, and of your own experiences, regarding gender and race in relation to digital technologies and electronic music.

My primary feeling about women and electronic music is that already we've seen a much larger ratio of women involved with electronic music, DJing, and production than you did in rock. You see already, if we're looking at a decade, let's say the '90s, you already have many more women who do this work in a recognized way professionally and also on the more underground tip; you go to a bar and chances are at least one DJ of the night is gonna be female.

I think with gear, whether it's guitars or computers, one of the primary ways people learn, especially with a DJ culture where it's primarily informal, is you're just around it. Like gangs of boys who skateboard together and then go home, do whatever they do, and play music. It's just your crew, it's part of what you do. Somebody must've had the initiative to get the turntables, 'cause that's money and organization, but you could have an eleven-year-old who learns how to DJ because his sixteen-year-old brother has got a whole group of boys who are doing that, and you just learn basically through osmosis. It's less likely that in this posse of boys you're gonna have an eleven-year-old girl who learns it as easily. So, you either get crews of girls who are learning it themselves, or you get mixed groups of both boys and girls. You don't get a total equal number because, in general, by the time you get to that junior high age, more often you get a diversion with girls dealing with dating, clothes, and that kind of stuff, and for the boys, the equivalent is skateboarding or tech or whatever. And it's still very much laid out in the culture that, whether it's your choice or not, that's often how people are directed.

But despite all that, we still see bigger numbers of women involved with electronic music right now, having seen that over the past ten years and in growing numbers. I've been involved in a few too many roundups of "who are the female DJs," and between '95 and '99 or something, I said: OK, I'll talk to you, I'll be involved with this article, because in some ways it is nice to know that other people are doing things, even if you just think: Oh, she's doing it, I could do it too! You know, it's not like sisters are always so charitable with each other! But, now that we are where we are, I'm like, all well and good, now fuck it. People can either say, I'm interested in Singe, she's a good producer, or I'm not interested in her, I don't think she's a good producer; I feel like we're along this road enough.

89

In the background, I do have a vested interest in doing media awareness and teaching media with groups of girls, different ages; some are adult women and some younger. I did a birthday present for a friend's daughter who was turning nine; I did a DJ workshop with her and her little homegirls. She'd come to see me play, especially at the park gigs during the day, and she was like: Wow, that's really cool that she does that, and it meant something to her that I was a girl, and a brown girl, doing it, because that's what she was—just a littler version. Howard and I have taught at art schools in Europe, and David Goldberg, who's part of [online music provider] Beta Lounge, was teaching at public schools in San Francisco, so he invited us to do something where we brought the turntables in and did sessions with people. We talked about DJing, but also talked about using other technology as well. Because you don't just have to use turntables—the basic message is, hack whatever gear you need. If you're designing websites, then look to see what's in the field, look to see what people are doing. The basic intimidation, being afraid to touch something or to find information, get over that and just see where you are. If all these people wanted to become professional DJs, that'd be a little grim—I doubt they do. But that fundamental skill of being able to identify something and convert from in your head to on paper, on the screen, or on CD, that's an important skill to stimulate with people. I mean, I wasn't trained to be a DJ, I just happened to really like it!

In terms of coming into places and playing, a couple of times, people have said, Where's the DJ? and I said, I am the DJ, but they get over it. Usually, it's more an issue of, What the fuck did you play? And, happily, it's more often good shock than bad shock, because I think it's worthwhile to play something that deals with the present moment. Unless you're in a really foul mood and just want to blow a place out and fuck them up, I don't really want to go in and play a set that nobody wants to deal with. I mean, that's a really weird calculation; you're dealing with the devil on that one, 'cause you don't know what your audience wants to hear, you only know what you want to hear. So what that imagination is about, in terms of what's enjoyable, what's interesting, what can I invite people to listen to—that's interesting to me.

I've had some really irritating moments dealing with some local New York crews, and some of them my own crew, where I just figured this was initiation—any new DJ gets this—where more senior dogs in the pack come over and start woofing at you while you're on the decks. Whether it's, Hey, how ya doing? or, Don't play that!—well, people don't quite say that, but a couple times people reached over and changed my EQ, and I'm just like, you can't fuck with that. If my stuff is making their ears bleed in the back of the room, and I'm too dumb to know it, then that's my bad, and people are free to not invite me back, but you cannot step to my mixing desk and touch it, because it's just ill, you know? So I feel like I've gone through a certain degree of the big dogs woofing at me when I'm trying to play sets, and one strategy is, and this is totally ill, but it's like driving a plane during war. Like the bombs are flying but you've still gotta drive the plane. You still have to be able to do it even when something just broke, your needle just glitched, the record you want to play just fell to the floor and is scratched—you still have to play. And that's part of, hopefully, the excitement. Like NASCAR racing, any moment you could wreck up on the side of the walls, but the people listening don't know unless you crash!

You need nerves of steel to do this stuff, and it doesn't mean that you're a hardass, it just means that you're dedicated to what you're doing, whether it's in your studio or live, because that's the sweet part of it and that's also the rugged part of it, to be able to follow it through. Whatever, maybe I'll get sued for this, but I don't think that women are very often encouraged to be dedicated to their projects. I think they are well encouraged to be dedicated to their company, their man, their partner, whatever; and the women we know—I mean, we both have met incredible producers—like people who are crucial to making projects happen, but more often than not they are not the directors of the project, they are not the artistic directors, they are not the vision people. They are the totally capable second-in-commands. I see this over and over again, in the same way that in grade school the girls are smarter, but by the time you get to college, girls are no longer participating in math and science courses. And in general—there have to be a million and one signals to girls and women to be good at what you do, but don't be too good at what you do, because are you ready to take the fire for it? So, we can still count on solo female artists who are really huge and really inspiring, but it's still disproportionate in the same way that if ten of the people are DJs, one or two of them are women, and that's better than maybe twenty years ago.

We both, and especially you, have been involved with initiatives where it's just women making music. And I think we'd probably agree on some of it, in terms of it's a little forced to ask people to unite under the sign of gender, but like some old-school feminist initiatives, it's still necessary. I think it's worth doing, and if there's an idea of there's something in common 'cause we're all women, we could deal with each other more, work with each other more, and support each other more. I think that women could be chilling with each other on purpose. Making a point, and also make it not personal. You don't have to like everyone; there are people we all work with who might not be your personal preference, but there's a bottom line of respect.

In terms of the race thing, it's like the difference between arty music in galleries and museums, and club music for clubs and bars. The zones are largely separate. I mean, you tell me if the experimental music scene in New York is not predominantly white. Obviously, there are exceptions: myself, some other people. In the same way that, are we gonna say that underground hip-hop in New York is all black? No, we're not, but there certainly is a certain kind of vibe and aesthetic going on. Like Def Jux, that's an incredible crew. And everything about them is, if hip-hop's black, then they're black, because that's the way they're doing it. And the producer for that label, he's a white cat, doing most of the production. Anyway, the point I'm trying to get to is, one of the things Howard and I had in mind in setting up SoundLab was "cultural alchemy"—that despite this city being so incredible a mix, and so sophisticated in how it does its mixes, he and I would go to different events in different places and it'd be totally segregated. I mean, it's not strictly segregated along race lines, it just often falls that it matches that way. But in some ways, the first point of segregation is aesthetic—what you think your crew is. If you think your crew is part of the tradition of the whole John Cage thing, then you get a more academic, more white scene. And if it's more club-oriented, if it's hip-hop, electro, certain brands of Detroit electro, you get a lot more brothers. I mean, like the drum 'n' bass scene here is a largely white scene, and largely post-rave, and in the UK that shit was not like that. In the UK, it was very underground, garage, black. And the splits where production went into different ways, got more techno, and got more and more white by degrees. You can see the fractures in terms of the differences in production and also the differences in the crews.

I think it's absolutely fucking boring that people have to make an extra effort to make sure that there are women or cultural diversity on a program. In general, dealing with clubs and dealing with bar scenes, there's always some kind of a mix. It's rare, even if you're in Germany, to find a totally white scene. I went into Electro, this huge, classic temple of techno in the middle of Berlin that was in this old electric power plant. And I come in, there's chains on the walls, the room is shaking, people are dancing, and looks like a primarily white, gay boy scene on the dance floor. So I go up to the decks, and there's this sister from Detroit flexing it! Now, that was not about affirmative action, that was not about, We're looking for a black woman to fill this slot, this was about, We give respect to Detroit techno. It was Kandi who was playing, and she ruled, so that was what it was. The same way with K. Hand. These are women working in the tradition, and that's just the way it is. So there's a way in which the mercenary logic of commerce and clubs and bars, for whatever reason, more often, if they're good and interesting, they will have a bill with different kinds of people playing. What I'm dealing with on the bar and club scene is, if I'm doing divergent beats—beats that are not all within the same pattern in a set, which, believe it or not, is a very radical thing for a DJ to do, to play divergent beats—and that's part of what I do—it's more of an issue on that.

On the more esoteric arty scene, I'm always surprised that people are so corny about what kind of mix can happen. I've had pretty good luck on both sides of the track, and because I've had that, I also am down with, if I can be helpful for some other people, I'll do the event. But there's also some shit I'll say no to, because I'm like, Don't call me four weeks late, with no money, and need a woman of color on your fucking panel, because I don't care. You figure it out.

"Race in Digital Space" [a conference at MIT in 2001] was really cool, because it was nice to have a gathering of the tribes. A lot of different people were involved; I was happy that we were able to talk about things. In the same way that it's too bad, but necessary, that we still need to organize things under the title of "women in music," it is too bad, but necessary, to have a big, bold placard that says Race in Digital Space. This world still works that people need the placard. They need the subtitles, they need an explicit reference—even though I don't remember *Wired* ever being called "white digital culture." You know, it goes without saying that things are white, if it's mainstream culture.

Even the more underground electronic music magazines, I felt like they started out with the initiative that this is about cultural mix. All these places understand that sampling something about hip-hop culture, and hip-hop style, is a mandate. It doesn't even have to be a black face anymore, there's just something about graphic design, Triple Five Soul and all these things, that this is part of cool youth culture. The advertisement of what this last decade was going to be, some of it got swept away with the media/tech revolution, and while people were trying to assimilate so much information about the new and the rich and the software and the tech, some of the identity issues and cultural politics of who's there as part of it fell into default mode.

But it's a good time to be working. And I say that even when things are crappy, and maybe it's just because I'm interested in doing this!

: : :

Coleman is now a professor at the Massachusetts Institute of Technology. She has been working on a networked film project titled *Boba Fett's Day Off.*

Maria Chavez

Born in Lima, Peru, in 1980, Maria Chavez grew up in Texas and moved to New York City in 2005. Since her introduction to improvised music through her mentor David Dove in Houston, she has quickly established a distinctive voice as an abstract turntablist and improviser. She pulls a wide range of textural sounds from a limited palette of vinyl records and styluses, ranging in condition from "immaculate to ruined." This is showcased on her debut CD, *Those Eyes of Hers* (Pitchphase, 2004). She has toured extensively and performed with artists including Kaffe Matthews, Thurston Moore, and Christina Carter. In 2006, she completed an artist residency at the Issue Project Room in Brooklyn and was selected to be a resident musician at Dia:Beacon with the Merce Cunningham Dance Company.

I became familiar Maria's work when she sent a review copy of her CD to Pinknoises.com; we met for this interview in Brooklyn in July 2006.

: : :

Tara Rodgers: When did you start playing music?

Maria Chavez: I played the piano and the guitar when I was a kid. I think there was a time when I wanted to be a big rock star, when I was thirteen! [Laughs] I started DJing when I was sixteen years old. My boyfriend at the time, he got turntables and I wanted to learn, and I caught on really quickly. We became a duo, and then we formed a DJ crew in Houston and played around in raves and clubs. In college, at the University of Houston, I was doing art history. I got onto the Rice University radio station as just a general DJ, but my real goal was to get the electronic show. It was the coveted spot, because the radio station spanned about 150 miles. Something happened where the station manager took the show off the air, and when I got to the station, I wanted to bring it back. That station manager was gone, and everybody liked me and knew who I was, so I started the show up again with a Rice University student. There were two other DJs, and we would switch, but I was the one doing mainly the house music and dance music. I would also do music history, talking about Vangelis in the '70s, early Japanese MIDI composers, and a show focused on the Roland TR-808 drum machine. I would have new talent on the show, like drum 'n' bass DJs. It was whatever was happening.

I also listened to the jazz and improvised show on Sundays, and once they said that Joe McPhee was coming to town with his trio, Trio X. For some reason, I'd never been involved in the avant-garde, improvised scene at all. I wanted to see what it was about, so I decided to go. I sat down and watched the show, and I was *totally* blown away with the whole idea of improvised music. I knew it was there, and I'd listened to it, but I always felt like there was some kind of inside story going on that I wasn't understanding. But when I went to that show, I understood that there wasn't—it was just what it was. And I really appreciated it for that. David Dove, who's the director of the Pauline Oliveros Foundation, was there and I asked to be part of his organization as an intern.

During this time, I dropped out of University of Houston when I was a junior, because I didn't have enough energy to do art history anymore. I went to the Houston Community College and did their audio engineering program. I needed an internship, so I used the Pauline Oliveros Foundation as my internship for two semesters. Dave had an improvised class at MECA, the Multicultural Educational Counseling through the Arts, an organization for inner-city kids in Houston. I had to go as part of my internship. I said, I don't play an instrument! And Dave said, Well, bring your turntable. So I brought one. I didn't know what I was doing. I really didn't play throughout the class, 'cause I was really self-conscious, I didn't understand what was going on. It was a class of ten people. He put everybody into groups, and had me play with him as a duo. We played, and I had this insane out-of-body experience that I'd never had before! [Laughs] I was watching my hands do all this stuff—you know, as a DJ, you don't scratch your needles and your records, you don't drag it across—you're ruining your shit, you know? I never would've wanted to intentionally do it. But the needle had popped off in the perfect way where it was gliding across the record, and I was able to do all this stuff that I had never

Maria Chavez at the Issue Project Room, Brooklyn, 2006.
PHOTO BY WESTRY GREEN.

done before. And once the piece was over—the piece was great, I really wish we would've recorded it, but it's in my heart for sure—I came to, and I looked at Dave, and he looked at me, and everybody was like, *Whoa!* And I realized, This is it. Ever since then, I stopped DJing and just went full, head-on into improvised music.

When you're performing your solo work especially, and in your recordings, what are your ideas about form and structure?

It's very open. It's mainly being aware of my space, and taking it personally. I don't have a start, a chorus, and a finish. It's really a matter of what feels right at that time. When people ask me, How do you know what records to play, and what needles to pick, I can't answer it. You could give me a ruined record and I could tell you what it would sound like, with certain needles, just by looking at it. So that vocabulary's already built. It's just like when you want to write something down. You have your piece of paper, you have different pens. You don't have a reason why, you just decide. And then it kind of creates itself. I'm very sensitive to finding the end. I hate turning it down really slowly, fading it out. I really like abrupt endings that just feel like, that was it.

97

So when you say you're really aware of the space, it sounds like it's both a space within the music itself, as well as the performance space.

The environment, of course. Yesterday, before we played, the bassist and drummer were like, So how loud can we get? And I said, Don't think that there's any limitations to your noise level, just take it personally. If you were in this space, how loud would you want it to be? Don't listen to me, just listen to yourself. If you really want it to be loud, then by all means. But take it personally, because it's so important to put yourself not just with your instrument, but with the audience. And understand that it's a relationship, rather than a self-indulgent process. That's what I mean by environment.

That's a generous view. Lately, I've heard so much loud music, like noise shows that really blow you away. Sometimes I wonder if people have lost respect for dynamic range, like for the ability to play quiet as well as loud and have it be just as powerful. If loudness is important, and that's your thing, then I understand it. But otherwise . . .

It's very restrictive. I think people have a view of being loud, being abrupt, as being very aggressive. But silence is really aggressive too.

And people that don't want to see that, they've already set their own limitations. But to each his own.

True. Tell me more about all the tools that go into what you do—your needles, your records—how you choose them and incorporate them into your work.

That's been an ongoing process. It's a very organic process. That's one rule that I laid down from the beginning, was that this needs to be an organic process. Records can be ruined intentionally; I've had some people ruin records for me, but I really don't use those very often. I have a couple that I ruined myself that I use maybe once every few months. But the records that I actually use the most are the ones that have been naturally ruined on their own. Because I keep them all in my backpack without their sleeves, so they're in and out, they move around, they touch each other. So there's always new scratches. Sometimes I'll leave them outside, or leave them in the car, just so they can kind of mold into each other. Some will stay put, some will warp around it. And I prefer it that way, because it's organic. Because my needles break during the performances, they break in their own ways. I would hate to have my records *have* to be manipulated in order for me to play them. I would much rather it be something that happened naturally, so that when I play them, I have a better understanding of what sound is gonna happen when this broken needle touches this record that's warped this way.

I like the way things work when they're stuck together. The wax kind of just melts it into itself, but it's very soft. It's not like if you put a lighter under it and it just fell into itself. It's just a really soft, gradual process. And it's always changing. There's always something new. I prefer it that way, 'cause it kind of goes along with how I play. It's very natural, I have to feel it. If I don't think this record belongs at this time—it's either 'cause I don't think the sounds will work, or I just don't like the way it's messed up right now.

How about the content of the records? Do you have a vocabulary that you're working with?

I do. I have a set group of records, eight to ten of them. I have a tone frequency record, for testing record players; *Jesus and Friends* filmstrip record; *Children and Their Music*, for children learning how to make music; a reading record, for kids learning how to read; *The Be-In*, from

'68, one of those environment records used for background noise. I have Kaffe Matthews's *Weightless Animals* album. She gave it to me when we recorded together, and I ruined it. [Laughs] These records, I only use little portions. There's a part of the record or a side of the record that I use.

And you have a stack of broken records you work with as well, right?

There's a method. My records are normally spread out around me, so if I need something I know exactly where to look to just grab it. I don't want to just sit there while the piece is going; I would hate to do that to the audience, have them wait for me to figure it out. My main records stay on my left, and everything else is around me. It starts by size, moves by sound, by content, and then by how ruined it is. So 45s and novelty, small ones are all normally on my left. And as it goes on, it's my 78s; and then my larger records that are more environmental sounds and noise records that people have given me; into things with more content, people talking; into ruined records that have been manipulated by hand. And then it breaks down to all my records that have been broken. I have little pieces of vinyl, 'cause I like to put the piece of vinyl while another record's going, and have the needle try to keep hold of it. If you have the record going backwards, you just hang onto it and the needle moves around trying to grab onto whatever it can.

But the eight to ten that are your main records—why those?

Those records get my point across. They have the sounds that I'm searching for on a regular basis. I can't use a Vivaldi. It's really hard, 'cause when you put the needle on the record even for a second, it already has its own space, you know? Like there are notes there already, you can't really manipulate it 'cause it's all melded together. And then when I play it, people will recognize it, even if it's a split second.

Which is not what you're going for, because then it becomes more like sampling, which is something else. It's fine for what it is, but not . . .

Not for what I do. I don't want people to get confused, you know? There's enough people sampling! I don't need to be one of them.

My vocabulary is pretty much set now. When I first started to perform, I was doing two turntables and picking and choosing. But I felt like my pieces were really long, and I really wasn't paying attention. It

Maria Chavez's records, 2006. PHOTO BY WESTRY GREEN.

was very scatterbrained. I finally decided, after a year and a half of it, that one turntable is enough, for now. And that was about three years ago. So now I've only been using one turntable and my mixer, and just now getting comfortable to maybe think about, maybe in a couple years, using another one. But it won't happen for a while. You want to zone in on just one thing.

I guess I'm an involuntary purist. I don't mean to be, and I'm not being pushy, but I really don't need anything else, because there's already so much going on. Some people ask me if I sample, or what outside equipment I use besides the turntable. I'm like, This is it. And my mixer—I use my lows, mids, and highs, but that's as far as it goes.

But within that, you can express so much.

Of course. Less is more.

How many needles are you working with on a continual basis?

Eight. That's a whole other organic process in itself. 'Cause everything keeps breaking, or it gets worn all the way down to a nub where you can barely hear anything, so then you've got to throw it out and start all over again. And then the good needle will break, so you need to get a new needle. The Ortofon DJ needles are very sturdy needles, it's very hard to break them. I almost feel like I should be a spokesperson for them: "I can ruin them in twelve shows!" They really put up a fight. I like the way they break, too, 'cause sometimes they'll curl into themselves, when it gets too hot. I love it when it does that. Then it can glide across the record, but still read everything as it's gliding, so it sounds like radio, when you're switching through.

So you've talked to me before about being the only girl in certain situations. I wonder if you have anything more to say about that, how issues of gender have factored into your professional experiences, or your creative practice.

It's been a very superficial presence. I don't consider myself a female musician. I don't think anyone would want to. And I don't think my sounds are feminine. If someone heard what I did, they would assume I was a guy.

Why do you think that is?

Some people say my music sounds like dark noise. And I resent that, because I don't think it's dark at all. A lot of guys, whenever I play, they'll say, It's so funny to watch you play, because it's this really dark and heavy music and you're so light and bubbly and nice. And to me, my music isn't that way at all. I just think it's very textural, and a very natural sound.

Which isn't gendered masculine or feminine?

Yeah. But people tend to gender dark, low-end, textural, skipping . . . I mean, records and turntables are a very masculine thing.

The whole female thing, it's just a superficial thing, but it helps. I'm not gonna lie. I dress nicely. And from a PR standpoint, if you want to get superficial about it, then let's do it. I have to just accept who I am and use it to the best of my ability. But actions speak louder than words. I would much rather just keep playing, and people can say all they want. One of my reviews for *Those Eyes of Hers*, this guy was like, She's so exotic, she's Peruvian, she's a turntablist, so the "exotica mounts up"! ("Maria Chavez" 2005) So the female aspect opens some doors, but in the end, the music speaks for itself.

People also tend to compare me to Otomo Yoshihide and Christian Marclay—following in the footsteps of Christian Marclay! It's always "following," even though I don't sound anything like those guys. I didn't even know who they were for the first two years that I was playing. I thought I was doing something totally brand new! When people started coming up to me saying, Have you heard of this guy? Then I'd listen. That's what I like about being a turntablist is that everyone is so different, but we're all using the same thing.

It's all very superficial: if you're a girl with a turntable, you're just a novelty. Besides the fact that you're with a turntable, you're just a girl—that's a novelty in itself, to be a woman in the world. My mom told me all the time, You always have to be five hundred times better than any man—that's for any woman—but for you, you have to be a thousand times better, because you're Hispanic and you're a woman. And you're playing on a turntable! [Laughs] My mom's so great—she calls it "music of the future."

: : :

Since our interview, Chavez won a Jerome Foundation Emerging Artist Grant, which supported her performance of a live visual and sound piece called *The Recorded Motion of Fiasco Transmutation*. She has also performed at venues and festivals including STEIM (Amsterdam), El Cervatino (Merida, Yucatan), the Kitchen (New York City), and the Wien Modern festival (Vienna) with Otomo Yoshihide. She collaborated with Kaffe Matthews on a project in 2008.

Part 3. Nature and Synthetics

Audio technologies and sonic aesthetics
are inflected with cultural understand-
ings of life, death, and decay. The artists
in this section use sound to complicate
boundaries between the natural and synthetic and suggest how the dynamism
of nature inspires audio-technological
variation. Annea Lockwood describes her
experiences working with synthesized
sound in an electronic music studio in
Cologne in the 1960s: "The sounds which
were assembled with all that care, all that
mathematical interrelationship . . . struck
me as not really being alive . . . So then of
course I had to ask myself what, for me,
constitutes life in a sound?" She left this
question unanswered but, in subsequent
decades, some of her most prominent
works feature recordings of rivers

interspersed with interviews of people whose lives the river intersects. Lockwood implies that synthesized sound—sound that is generated electronically through analysis and recombination of a sound wave's parts—lacks the kind of "life energy" that permeates flowing water and the cadences of human voices.

By contrast, the composer Mira Calix is drawn equally to working with analog synthesizers and wooden instruments because they *share* certain lifelike qualities: technologies made of analog circuits or wood seem to fluctuate and breathe like "little creatures." She uses recordings of her voice just as she would the sounds of any other instrument, because her voice, like a quirky analog synthesizer, has its own "unique imprint."

Jessica Rylan, who designs and builds synthesizers, prefers to use analog circuits because they follow "very simple, natural laws, just like breaking a tree branch, or like water, or even like birds flying in a V— they push and are pushed into that pattern because it's the path of least resistance." For her, nature and artificiality align with a distinction between the analog (which she describes as a natural process) and the digital (in which a computer makes the same binary decision, on or off, over and over again).

Like Rylan, the installation artist Christina Kubisch situates electricity and the technologies that channel it as thoroughly grounded in nature. She maintains that sounds associated with natural environments, like recordings of rainforests and birds, can seem "less genuine" than the electrical hums in contemporary industrialized areas. For each of the artists here, sound and audio technologies are media and metaphors for engaging what it means for living and nonliving things to encounter, interact, and transform.

Christina Kubisch

Christina Kubisch was born in 1948 in Bremen, Germany. She studied painting, flute and music composition, and electronics. In the 1970s, she participated in video performances and concerts, and since 1980 she has created an internationally recognized body of work with sound sculptures and installations. She added ultraviolet light as a significant stylistic element beginning in 1986. Many of her sound works are realized with techniques of electromagnetic induction: magnetic fields arise from interactions between specialized headphones and electric wires distributed in a space, and listeners wearing these headphones can access individualized combinations of sounds from the wires as they move through the space.

Kubisch creates synesthetic experiences in which embodied navigations of space become indistinguishable from musical form. Visually, her painterly treatment of wires references winding tree branches and other organic forms; sonically, boundaries between what is "natural" and "artificial" are deliberately confused. In *Oasis 2000—Music for a Concrete Jungle*, for one example, Kubisch transformed a concrete patio in London with wires and electromagnetic headphones so that listeners navigating the space experienced an unpredictable playback of sounds of rainforests, birdsongs, and flowing water recorded around the world. She posed the question, "What is true and what is false?," suggesting that sounds with natural origins can seem "less genuine" than the synthetic sounds that permeate urban environments (Gercke 2000, 47–48). Her recent cycle of works, the *Electrical Walks*, change the perception of everyday realities by amplifying the electrical fields in an environment (Kubisch 2006).

Kubisch has been a professor of sculpture and media art at the Academy of Fine Arts in Saarbrücken since 1994 and a member of the Akademie der Künste, Berlin, since 1997. She answered these questions via e-mail in August 2006.

: : :

Tara Rodgers: I've read that you have very specific memories of sounds of your childhood. Can you tell me more about this?

Christina Kubisch: I grew up in a very flat part of Germany. People say that you can see today who will visit you tomorrow—which means it's so flat that you can look far into the distance. I remember the absence of loud, dramatic sounds/noises. Not much was happening besides wind, rain, little everyday sounds embedded in those from nature.

Your work is now recognized as having a strong synthesis of sonic and visual elements, but for many years you studied these disciplines separately and from different approaches (painting, flute, piano, improvisation, composition, etc.). How does your current work draw upon this formal training, or turn away from it?

When I studied there were no possibilities of studying something like new media, sound art, or other forms of synthesis of different art forms. Music was music, no images aloud. Painting was painting, and sounds were seen as disturbing the purity of the image. When I started to mix up things, many critics said I did it because I was neither a good musician nor painter.

Formal training is still very much present in my work. I have difficulties to let things happen in a chaotic way. The apparent beauty or clean structure of my installations hides the more chaotic things behind. So sometimes at the first glance things seem very aesthetic, but then become disturbing after a while.

During the early period in your career—roughly the 1970s into the early '80s—which of your many performances and exhibits stay in your memory as the most interesting to you, and why?

No choice. The process is the work, the risk is part of it, and nothing ever is really finished.

When did you start working with electronics as part of your creative process?

Early in the '70s. My composition for piano and five players, *Identikit*, from 1974, uses headphones and prerecorded rhythmic impulses. When I moved to Milan the same year I started to experiment with

Christina Kubisch. PHOTO BY MIGUEL ÁLVAREZ-FERNÁNDEZ.

all kinds of electronic stuff, serious or not. Many of them were modified analog electronic instruments, but I used custom-made objects as well. I always have collaborated with technicians and engineers, because you only can invent new stuff if you know something about what is already existing. The research on electromagnetic induction started in 1979, and the first installation with this technique using self-built receivers was in 1980.

110

Your technique of working with electromagnetic induction is unique and so characteristic of your aesthetic. Conceptually, what motivated you to create this system?

The wish to be independent from classical musicians and the world of classical music; the wish to create works where people could come and go whenever they wanted; the wish to create permanent longtime pieces and sound spaces.

It started when I studied at the Technical University of Milan in the end of the '70s. I had bought a telephone amplifier out of curiosity and tested its qualities in the laboratory of the school—strange sounds were coming out. After this, I investigated immediately about electromagnetic waves and induction principles.

On a technical level, what was your process like when you were first developing it? How has the system evolved over the years?

I tried to change what was used technically for amplifying the voice (in such systems as simultaneous translation) to better sound quality, by using different sizes of coils, putting them as well in various positions. Then, together with my engineer, I developed portable wireless headphones, which, from the original headphone, had only the speaker left. As well I built a system of induction loops, which were sound carriers and were used as visual and acoustic material for many sound installations. In recent years, focusing more and more on the origins of induction, the electromagnetic waves, I built a new series of headphones which are particularly sensitive to these waves.

Especially for your works that are inspired by architecture, what aspects of a space are you most drawn to? Are there certain spaces you've worked in which have been most inspiring?

Hard to say. Mostly places which have lost their original functions, which were used in many different ways, but have been destroyed, al-

Christina Kubisch, *The Bird Tree*, Taipei, Taiwan, 2005.
COURTESY OF TAIPEI FINE ARTS MUSEUM.

tered, forgotten. Places of power that have become storage rooms, for example; a mansion that has turned into a hospital; a palace that has turned into a manufacturing space, etc.

In your works with light or solar panels, the interplay of light and sound is very integrated, becoming more like a sense of atmosphere. Is this something you strive for?

Atmosphere and sensual experience are very important to me. Much more than systems or programs. Though often there is a lot of precise work behind the work, like compositional structures or formal aspects, which you cannot see or hear. This is a remaining part of my strict classical education, I guess.

Many of your works are clearly tied to a certain space. But within that, there seems to be a very layered relationship with time—since you often draw on history, memory, and the real-time unfolding of sound and light. How would you describe how you approach time or temporalities in your work?

What a nice question. Time means flowing, changing, fragile structures. It means as well personal experience (you need time to have your individual discoveries of sensations and memories). Therefore I try to avoid making clear, symbolic, or pedagogic statements. Things cannot be identified immediately, so you need time to decide what it is all about. You have to put to yourself questions about your very own memories.

Silence and stillness figure strongly in some of your works. I wonder how you conceptualize or define "silence." Has John Cage been influential to you in this regard?

The history of art is not a chain of logical events. When I met Cage he impressed me because of his openness, his use of noise (and of course silence), and his ways of integrating chance operations and risk in his work.

I usually prefer silence to intense sounds, the quietness to strong noise.

But lately, since I started again with live mixes, I use the recordings of electromagnetic sounds, which can be very intense and even loud. I continue the work on silence for a new installation series as well.

Mostly silence and sound are connected to each other. Before the time of industrialization, very few poets used the word *silence*, because it was not something which was rare or in danger (this is my personal idea, of course).

Another theme in many of your works is a questioning of what is natural and artificial, or "true or false." Tell me about your interest in exploring this realm.

Please ask yourself how many things you know by real experience and how many by digital information. When did you smell a humid forest ground the last time, or when did you observe a sunset or a real bird in the sky for a long time? I use these very commonplace examples because they are not common originally as an experience, but instead by their transmitted image or sound, by advertisements, and so on.

Tell me about your Electrical Walks *series.*

I always heard the basic sounds of electricity when using the induction headphones. But since the middle of the '90s there were more and more places which had other sounds like small rhythms, pulsations, and strange signals. I remember this particularly for an installation in San Sebastian in 1999, where I heard some mysterious signals coming into my own sound transmission. I found out that behind the walls where my work was installed was a computer office. I decided to include these sounds and tried to know more and more about magnetic fields created by digital technologies. With the help of my engineer, Manfred Fox, we developed very sensitive headphones for hearing them better. The variety of what we got was really surprising. But the walks are as well a work of personal discovery of cities which, though familiar to you, change completely when walking around with electromagnetic headphones. This links again to "the true and the false," and what is behind the surface.

And of course, the sounds are beautifully frightening.

∶ ∶ ∶

Kubisch's recent projects include an *Electrical Walk* in the city of Haarlem (2006); *Licht Himmel*, a permanent light and sound installation in a former gas tank in Oberhausen, Germany (2006); and *Night Flights* and *Five Electrical Walks*, two CD releases on Important Records (2007).

Annea Lockwood

Annea Lockwood was born in Christchurch, New Zealand, in 1939, and completed her bachelor's degree in music at Canterbury University there. Beginning in 1961, she studied at the Royal College of Music in London, at the Darmstadt Ferienkurse für Neue Musik, and with Gottfried Michael Koenig at the Musikhochschule in Cologne and Holland. She moved to the United States in 1973 and taught for several years at Hunter College and then at Vassar College from 1982 until her retirement in 2001. She has been a rigorous experimenter, amassing a diverse body of work that includes collaborations with choreographers, sound poets, and visual artists; electroacoustic performances, recordings, and installations; and compositions for acoustic instruments and voices. Her many works include *The Glass Concert* (1967–69), a performance with shards of industrial glass; the *Piano Transplants* (1969–72), in which she drowned, burned, or planted old pianos at locations in the United Kingdom and United States; *Conversations with the Ancestors* (1979) and *Delta Run* (1982), built respectively from interviews with four women over eighty and a dying sculptor; *A Sound Map of the Hudson River* (1982), an installation based on field recordings; *Three Short Stories and an Apotheosis* (1985), a performance piece with the Sound Ball, a mobile receiver and six speakers designed for her by Robert Bielecki, placed in the hands of the performers and audience; and *Ear Walking Woman* (1995), a prepared piano composition for pianist Lois Svard. *Jitterbug* (2006), commissioned by the Merce Cunningham Dance Company for the dance *eyeSpace*, incorporates her recordings of aquatic insects and photographs of rock surfaces that are read as scores by two improvising musicians.

I first heard about Annea's work when Maggi Payne mentioned that Annea was borrowing her hydrophone to make recordings of the Danube River. I met her in September 2004 at her house in upstate New York, where she lives with her partner, the composer Ruth Anderson.

: : :

Tara Rodgers: What led you into making experimental music? You've mentioned training at the Royal College of Music in London, and studying electronic music with Koenig in Germany. But then you began recording rivers . . .

Annea Lockwood: And burning pianos and things! [Laughs]

Exactly! How did that happen?

Oh, a nice convergence. Like you, I also grew up as a pianist, and I really wasn't interested in playing other people's music too much. I enjoyed it, but it wasn't a passionate interest. And I didn't see the point in replicating other people's music, at all. Why do that? So I wanted to strike out in a different direction, not necessarily new—one hopes for new, but that may or may not happen—but a different direction, a fresh direction.

Growing up in New Zealand, I lived in parts of the country that were rich in environmental sound, so had grown up really listening and loving what I listened to. Obviously I wasn't thinking about how to work with it when I was a kid, but those sounds were beloved sounds. They were rich and plentiful. And I was lucky again that my training happened during the '60s. We were really convinced that we could do anything, and that it was really fun to do anything. I developed as a personal guideline that when I had an idea which I thought was unreasonable, that was *exactly* what I should try to realize. So I followed that for a very long time. It was really a useful guideline that took me in all sorts of directions. But the zeitgeist was this wonderful, sort of bubbling, imaginatively energized sense that categories were permeable, categories were crumbling, and any of us could move into any medium that we needed to move into for purposes of realizing a particular project—it was great!

What other artists were you around at that time?

Lots of people. A very good friend was Hugh Davies, an English composer and chronicler, in a sense, of the history of electronic music and its machines, who made his own devices and his own instruments.

We were very good friends all the time I was in England. He was an excellent improviser with live electronics. At a little more remove, as soon as I found John Cage, he became a very liberating influence. Cage's writings on sound and what sound resources we have, and the breadth of those resources, were completely aligned with my own personal experience of sound in New Zealand. It merged perfectly—gave me a great rationale for what I was inclined to do anyway! [Laughs] And then Pauline Oliveros, we made contact towards the end of the '60s. We started writing letters to each other; I think we recognized kindred spirits. She got me involved in the *Sonic Meditations* when she wanted to organize them at a distance. And I was sending her stuff that I was doing, and so on, responding to each other. That was an invaluable friendship. And then little by little I began to reach more Americans. The Sonic Arts Union people [Robert Ashley, David Behrman, Alvin Lucier, and Gordon Mumma], in particular, were great to me. And so on. After awhile I felt like my natural community was the American new music scene. There were people over here I really loved, and whose work was really exciting to me, and I very much wanted to get here.

Ruth Anderson, my composer partner, had started the Electronic Music Studio at Hunter College in 1968. It was the first CUNY studio. She founded it, and was directing it, and finally got a sabbatical, and called Pauline [Oliveros] and asked her if she would like to direct the studio that year. Pauline suggested that Ruth call me, so she did! It was something falling into my lap that I'd been wanting for ages. So that was how I got here, and how Ruth and I met. I substituted for Ruth that year, which was fun and sort of a challenge. In England, I had a little experience with voltage control [VC]. This was '73, and voltage control was more advanced here than it was in England. Ruth's studio had a lot of Moog stuff in it, so I remember spending a hectic summer in England working through Allen Strange's book [1972], trying to learn everything I could about VC-operated signal processing before I came over and started teaching it. It was good for me!

You started your River Archive as early as the '60s. How did that come about?

In hindsight, it was because I loved and was interested in rivers in New Zealand, which are quite wild, many of them. It was inevitable, I guess. But at the time, like Pauline and many other people, I was looking at how sounds and our bodies interact. I was trying to probe that as much as I could; the physiology of how sound affects our bodies. 'Cause it seemed to me if we were putting all this sound out there, we should at least know what it was doing for people, and to people. I came across a reference in a book by John Michell, *The View over Atlantis*, to a very old Peruvian tradition of taking people who were mentally off balance and emotionally disturbed to riverbanks for periods of time because they were found to be calming. And I got curious about that. It's clear to me how the visual element is very calming. You have this not quite monochrome surface, but compared with the surface of the land around bodies of water—which is full of information and tends to be very busy with trees and bushes and God knows what all else—an expanse of water is much less information dense. It's really relaxing; the brain isn't taking all that information in. But I was curious about how the sounds of moving water affect us. And so I decided to do this absurd thing of recording all the rivers of the world, making an archive of all the rivers of the world—obviously impossible. And getting my friends involved—Pauline amongst others—in recording rivers when they traveled, and sending them back to the archive. Then I started doing installations based on the archive. And the more I worked on those sounds, the more I became really very strongly drawn to the sounds themselves, and the textures of the moving water sounds. And still am. Anywhere I can hear some moving water, I listen for a little bit. They're very intricate textures, all sorts of rhythmic patterns and unpredictabilities and seemingly random sounds emerging and disappearing, and layers of pitches—very complex.

Part of it was because when I was studying electronic music with Koenig in the early '60s, the process was very much like those early Stockhausen pieces—*Studie I*, *Studie II*—assembling blocks of sounds from multiple oscillators and filters and ring modulators. And the sounds which were assembled with all that care, all that mathematical interrelationship—you know, struck me as not really being alive. I just didn't much like them. I loved the idea of being able to make sound from scratch, right?

It's a thrill.

It's a great thrill! That's amazing. But the sounds we were making from scratch seemed to me to lack life. So then of course I had to ask myself what, for me, constitutes life in a sound? The next step was, well, I won't know that until I focus on sounds which satisfy me and then figure out what satisfies me about them. And I started working with water and fire and glass, and all sorts of nontraditional sound sources. Which pulled me away from instrumental writing right away. I was looking for nontraditional things. But water was one of the most interesting to plumb because I never yet feel that I can hear every last component of any one stretch of water sound and hold it all together in my mind.

Right, of course you never can, because it changes . . .

It changes constantly.

And erosion happens, and it's a totally different thing.

That's right, which is delightful!

When you've recorded rivers, what is your process for selecting locations and sounds?

Well, I'll talk about it in the context of the new piece, *A Sound Map of the Danube* [2005]. Structure is very easy with a river—at least for me, it seems self-evident—I start at the source and work my way down to the river mouth. So the river gives me its structure. I'm just back from the last of the field recording trips. This trip was a long one, it was six working weeks. Ruth went with me, and we covered 850 kilometers of river, which is a bit less than the actual road distance we would have traveled. So let me give you some concrete examples of sites and what I'm listening for. One of the early decisions that I needed to make in relation to the Danube was, Does a site's historical significance trump its sound? The Danube is a river with a tremendous history, and its history is really important to how people have worked with the river, and how people have sought to control it and modify it; the Danube's configuration and location has determined a lot of human histories. Well, there's this one spot in southern Hungary where the Turks comprehensively defeated the Hungarians in 1527—Mohacs—it's right on the river. So that was an enormously important battle, and there's a very beautiful commemorative site there, with poignant abstract sculptures. I very much wanted to record there, and did. The river didn't make particularly interesting sounds, so I went to the commemorative site, which wasn't too far away, and spent some time re-

cording there, and got back and listened, but it really wasn't interesting. My decision all along has been sound over site. The sound has to
be compelling, to me. That's how people are going to experience it.

Another time, we started at Orşova in Romania. Orşova is beside
what used to be the wildest stretch of the river. There's a series of
gorges there through the Transylvanian Alps, the Kazan Gorges. There
were rapids and whirlpools and reefs, and there was passage for ships
only at certain times of the year, and they had to be guided by spe-
cially certified guides. In the 1960s, a huge dam was put in by Romania
and Serbia jointly, and the gorges became a lake and all that wildness
disappeared from the river. At Orşova, there was a particularly dan-
gerous stretch of granite reefs running across the river bed called the
Iron Gates. There were rocks jutting up out of the river every which
way; it was like a labyrinth. I wanted to record at the Iron Gates, but
knew it would be really tricky because of the dam and the reservoir
and the stillness of the water. I went down to the riverbank and found
some small wave action, and a most amazing chorus of frogs! [Laughs]
Really marvelous. There were some fishermen sitting on a wall behind
me when I recorded. I went down to the shoreline and sat in the mud
and the silt, basically, and was able to put my microphone on a stand
which I've been immersing in water for ages—this little stand has
tolerated everything! I stuck the stand out about six or seven inches
underwater and set the mic on it, then waited until the frogs got used
to this presence and started up again. So in Orşova I got this great
chorus of frogs where I didn't expect to find frogs, which satisfied me
a lot.

I choose sites according to how much their sounds grab me, really.
As I got down to the lower reaches of the river, towards the end of
the river, I began to notice a number of sites which I'd heard before—
heard in the middle stretch of the river, maybe, heard somewhere
else. I'd go down to the river and hear some wave action, and it was
nice—perhaps a passing barge kicked up some more wave action—but
the details of the sounds were fairly similar that I'd already recorded
somewhere else. So I didn't take it.

At another site, Tutrakan, which is an old fishing town in Bulgaria,
we often stayed overnight so I could record very early in the morning
or in the evening when everything quieted down; you know, people
went home to dinner, everything got tired. In the evening in Tutrakan,
for the longest time I couldn't find anything. The Bulgarians had built

Annea Lockwood recording the Danube at Gederlak, Hungary, 2003. PHOTO BY RUTH ANDERSON.

a sort of rampart of cement against flooding—a levee with this great, long cement slope, sloping away from it down to the river, right into the river, which gave very little sound indeed. But then I found a little floating dock, floating on about four oil drums down in the river, and the planks of the dock were separated just far enough apart for me to be able to rest my mic between two of them. The water flowing through the oil drums and through the underlying metal structure of the dock was making lovely gong-like sounds. But what was even nicer was that you could hear how fast it was flowing quite clearly. Your ears could get that information just from the sound. So I spent quite a long time down there recording. A little boy came running onto the dock so I put my finger to my lips and he quieted down immediately! Didn't say a word, he was great. And then he very quietly tiptoed over beside me, and sat down beside me—made not a sound! He got it right away. And I put the headphones on him and he sat there sort of entranced for quite a long time, not having ever heard the river quite like that, right? And tiptoed away.

Do you process the sounds when you are composing or mixing?

No, maybe a little filtering sometimes if necessary. And sometimes I work a bit with EQ because there's a component of the sound that particularly drew me to it, maybe a particular frequency in the mid-range that's very beautiful and I'd like to bring out a little bit more. I recorded in Vukovar, for example, in Croatia. Vukovar is a tragic place. It was besieged by the Serbian army and militias for three months, and many people died and the town was very much destroyed, and is being rebuilt. So it has a really tragic atmosphere. I found a little tributary flowing into the Danube there [the Vuka Rijeka], which at one point sounded particularly fierce—really. So with that, I was recording under a pedestrian bridge. The bridge was an old bridge, and there was a little weir under it, quite an old one, rocks and cement, which had been broken so that the water was flowing through a tunnel which produced really nice, interesting resonances. And the spectrum of the water shifted from one side to the other, because of the broken structure of the weir. Low-frequency sounds were particularly potent there. So when I put that onto my computer, I brought up the low-frequency EQ a bit to really bring that out. Other than that sort of thing, I'm doing very little processing. And I'm doing very little editing. I'm looking for stretches where I don't have to clean the sound up at all.

121

I'm also interviewing river people: people who work on the river, a pilot who's been going up and down the river all his life, a woman who owns a restaurant on a bank of the river in Austria who was flooded out in 2002 and had mud in her restaurant halfway up her walls and how she got rid of it, how the Austrian army pitched in to help her get it out of her yard. If you don't live near a river, you tend to assume that it's almost a static entity. We believe that we have rivers under our control, and I'm very interested in the fact that rivers are actually not totally under our control at all. They do take over from time to time; floods are the obvious mechanism for that happening. So I'm talking to people whose lives are impacted by the river, in their own languages, asking them, What does the river mean to you? Could you live without it? And little fragments of those interviews will be woven in with the river's sounds so that the river's people are inside the river, as it were. These won't be translated, they'll be in the original languages—those are wonderful sounds, those languages! [Laughs] Ten different countries, seven different languages. Mostly I could either talk with people in German or in English and have them respond in Romanian, Bulgarian, or whatever their language was. Somehow it was always possible to find enough language in common.

You've used such conversations before in your work, like Conversations with the Ancestors *[1980], and* Delta Run *[1982].*

And interviews are part of the Hudson River sound map [1982], too. I started recording people talking about their lives at a point at which I was interested in what I call the rhythm of memory—how people's speech, inflections, and tempo change when they're remembering something. Between that little transitional period when the memory is not quite solid, you're groping for it, and when it comes in strong, and then when it tails off again. I like these rhythms. I'm just interested in the experience of feeling people's *being* energy, life energy. I find it touching, when people are willing to relax enough to let that come through.

Tell me about your earlier works with pianos: the burnings, transplants, and drownings.

I was burning a piano in '68 because I wanted to record fire. I knew there were many defunct pianos around London, because I had been working with one. So when I wanted to record fire, I decided to record a piano and overstring it, you know—thinking that the strings would pop and make great sounds. But I had to pay for the piano to be moved, and I was pretty poor at the time. When a small festival wanted me to do something on the Thames embankment, I talked them into moving the piano and we burned the piano there. And I recorded it with some old mics I didn't need anymore. I wrapped the cords in asbestos—at that point in time asbestos didn't worry any of us! So we could burn the mic, put a mic right inside the piano—I always believe in getting as close as possible!—and let the mic last as long as it did, and record as long as possible. The audience gathered 'round really close, and talked its head off for quite awhile until the piano got too hot, so the recording was useless! But the thing became a beautiful visual spectacle. Then I wrote a score for it after I'd done it. The instructions were to put a little lighter fluid down in one corner of the piano, and set it alight, and let it go.

Sometime later I was living in Essex out in the countryside in England. The cottage I was living in had this attached garden area with laurel trees and bay trees. It was a really old-fashioned, Victorian place. It was running a little wild, so I decided to put pianos out in the garden. A little grand, and a couple of uprights. This is for fun, you know? And dug a trench, and put one in it like the Titanic going down. But what I was curious about in the garden was to see the moment at which young saplings would start to force their way up between different parts of the structure of the instrument. That paradox, that beautiful thing, that young plants look so fragile and are in fact so strong. So this *Piano Garden* was designed for that to happen.

When did you return to writing instrumental music?

I had done something absurd and not untypical in one's mid-twenties; I said to myself: Instruments, instrumental sounds are the common currency, still. They induce their own constrictions for all the obvious reasons. I won't use them anymore! I would move in all sorts of other directions, but not in that direction. By the mid-1980s, I'd been doing quite a lot of performance pieces, working with people's memories, the Sound Ball piece [*Three Short Stories and an Apotheosis* (1985)]. So I began to look at my work and wonder if I wasn't on the verge of repeating myself, which I didn't want to do. And also, I noticed that I was thinking of instrumental and acoustic writing as taboo, and that seemed in itself a limitation. Why would one put a whole major area of sound work aside? That seemed absurd. So, much to my pleasure, I've been doing both electroacoustic and instrumental music ever since the late '80s. It's a nice balance.

But I ran into various dilemmas. Down in the basement, I have various instruments from all over the place. Small instruments, percussion instruments, sound-makers that I've collected over the years that I really love the sound of. And rocks and stones, all sorts of things! When I started writing acoustic music again, instrumental music, what I was drawn to were alternative techniques, of course. But also, I started incorporating these objects that I'd been collecting all these years into my pieces. Some of them are hard to lay your hands on. And each one

Annea Lockwood with the final Piano Transplant, an installation
titled *Southern Exposure*, at Bathers' Beach, Western Australia,
in the Seventh Totally Huge New Music Festival at Perth, 2005.
PHOTO BY HEUCHAN HOBBS.

has a very specific sound, so that if you find its replica in some store
someplace, it's not going to make quite the same sound. So I started
lending all this stuff to my musician friends. You know, I'd write pieces
for them, lend all this stuff out, and then not be sure whether to get
it back or leave it in their hands. When scores start to circulate, what
am I going to do? Call up Lois Svard and say, Can you send those two
rocks I gave you? [Laughs] So it has its own problems.

Specificity of sound is really important to me. So even with the extended techniques that I come up with or use, the exact nature of the
sound is really important. And you can't depend on its replicability.
You run a superball mallet up a piano string, and you have to leave a
lot of loose areas around the qualities that sound's going to have. So I
learned acceptance.

Which of course parallels your philosophy with the rivers.

And with glass, too. The glass is unpredictable. Which is one of its
beauties. Replicability, forget it! [Laughs] In *The Glass Concert* [1966],

from one time of working with two particular pieces of glass, to the next, the details of the sound would shift.

There are these very different trajectories in the history of working with sound—on one hand, there's the spirit of musique concrète, with composers like Pierre Schaeffer who would catalogue and classify sounds and their properties so extensively. And then there is this other way of working, which you describe, which involves discovering as many sounds as you can, but mostly accepting them and leaving them as they are.

125

Or not needing to *fix* them. 'Cause I think they're essentially not fixable. Except that of course through media, we think, we feel we can fix them. But in their natural state, *sounds in their natural state*—that's a concept I sort of like—are not fixable, are they?

Right, fixing is something we tend to impose. Tell me about your source material for The Glass Concert *[subsequently issued on the recording* The Glass World, What Next? Recordings, 1997].

I went to the glass monopoly in England, Pilkingtons, and asked to go to their factories and see what they were producing. They were producing all sorts of glass—industrial glass, laboratory glass, glass that one doesn't see normally, commercially or domestically. And they gave me the run of the factories, bless their hearts. Like research scientists, they're very interested in very different applications of what they work with. I collected all sorts of types of glass, much of which I no longer own. There was one byproduct of some process that produced something like glass cotton candy. When I took a couple of chunks and slowly rubbed them against each other, the most ferocious sounds would come out! [Laughs] All of this being very close-miced, which is how I got into close-micing in the first place. Or, for electron microscopy, a very thin form of glass is produced, and before it's cut into slides it's sized in six-inch by four-inch sheets. I discovered if I held one of them gently at one end and just shook it a little bit in front of the microphone, the frequency range was very, very low. It produced these thunderous, wonderful rumbling sounds which bore no relation in magnitude to the actual size of the piece of glass! Just this wonderful discrepancy in proportion.

From something so fragile, too . . .

Right, producing something so enormous. So it was a wonderful medium to work with. And I started looking at glass precisely because so little had been done with it in the way of sound. I thought, here's a medium whose sounds cannot be associated with traditional music in any way. An audience is not going to make that association; they're going to have to really listen to the sound. I wanted people to really hear the sound itself rather than snapping into a sort of traditional context right away. Or to hear each sound, instead of hearing pitches in their melodic or harmonic relationship.

Returning to that topic of specificity, and how particular sounds can be *just right* with exactly the right fortuitously found tool, and you can't replicate it: Ruth and I were in Greece at one point, and we found an amazing beach which was loaded with these egg-shaped, pure white rocks, or sometimes with a black streak through them. They're all egg-shaped! How could any one beach be so consistent? [Laughs] I happen to love that shape, and I love rocks. So to her disbelief I came home with a whole lot of them and started distributing them to musician friends to work with, for example, to Lois Svard, for *Ear-Walking Woman*, which she commissioned in 1995. The rocks that I found for that piece are slightly uneven on the surface, so these are not perfect ovals by any means, there's a very slight irregularity on each one. When I get Lois to set one rocking on the piano strings, and it does an accel, the rock is interactive with the energy of the string. They feed each other. So the rock starts vibrating the strings, and then as the rock's energy diminishes, the strings take over and start the rock going again. So there's this fluctuating accel-decel at all sorts of speeds, and it goes on for ages. The perfect marble eggs you can find in any gift shop anywhere don't do it, 'cause they don't have that little irregularity! But I've just about run out of rocks from that beach . . .

It's funny, the lengths we go to for things like that. I have a collection of broken toy organs from the 1960s, which I bought cheaply but have invested dearly in shipping them from place to place every time I move. Once you find those sounds . . .

You can't relinquish them, no. How one gets caught in transitoriness: you can relinquish them, everything is ultimately transitory, but one certainly doesn't want it to be before it *has* to be! We work in a thoroughly transitory medium.

Rivers really bring that out. They're never the same, day to day, in any one spot. I had a month's residency in Krems, Austria, in May, beside the river. One of the things I had planned to do was to go to the same spot by the river every day and just record a little bit each day, to show how the river is *never* the same from one day to the next. It's in an area called the Wachau, quite a narrow, long valley that goes through some very old hard-rock hills where the river marvelously just decided to cut through the mountains, rather than go around the base of them. But of course, everything's jammed together: the railroad, the roads, the river, the river traffic. And I could never get down to that site early enough in the morning to outrun the traffic. At five o'clock in the morning, it was already noisy. Couldn't do it. And I couldn't get up at four—well, I couldn't see my gear at four in the morning! But I really wanted to touch on the transitoriness of water. Didn't work. But that's nice, too, the way one's plans get overturned.

::: ::

Lockwood's surround-sound installation, *A Sound Map of the Danube* (2005), traces the river's course from the Black Forest to the Black Sea, interleaved with the memories of its people, in thirteen interviews and location recordings made at fifty-nine sites. In 2008, she released a CD of the complete installation on Lovely Music.

Chantal Passamonte
(Mira Calix)

Chantal Passamonte was born in South Africa and moved to London in 1991. Pursuing her interest in music, she landed a job at a record shop and began organizing parties and DJing; she soon found work at the labels 4AD and Warp Records, where she was a publicist from 1994 to 1997. Through DJing she began to experiment with music equipment and compose, and since 1998 she has released numerous EPs and albums on Warp under the name Mira Calix. Her music has a textural organicism and coherent eclecticism: on *Skimskitta* (2003), sounds of stones, vintage synthesizers, and elusive vocals intermingle; unpredictable imperfections construct a fragile and percolating soundscape.

Calix has DJ'd extensively and toured with colleagues on the Warp label, but her compositions have increasingly found an audience outside traditional contexts of electronic music. She has received commissions from the Natural History Museum in Geneva to create a composition using sounds of insects; from London's Royal Festival Hall for development of the insect piece in collaboration with the London Sinfonietta; and from the Barbican Art Gallery for a site-specific installation.

We first did an interview by e-mail for Pinknoises.com in January 2003 and met for this interview in March 2004 at a cafe near where she lives in the east of England.

: : :

Tara Rodgers: Why did you decide to come to England from South Africa?

Chantal Passamonte: Well, I grew up under sanctions, and we had a cultural boycott, so a lot of things I was interested in I couldn't get when I was there. My parents are Italian with lots of family in Italy, so we'd actually come to Europe every year. We'd go to France and then to Italy and England. So I was lucky, I traveled throughout my childhood. And I had some friends here. Where I come from in South Africa is Natal, which is the last English outpost, so there's a lot of British connections. A lot of my friends' older brothers and sisters would come to London. Language is the main thing, but systemwise also, it's not that dissimilar to England. So I came over here and stayed with some friends, and I really liked it. I came like someone who's thirsty, 'cause I used to buy the *Melody Maker*, which doesn't exist anymore, but we'd get it shipped, so we'd get it six weeks late, so everything I'd read about had already happened. Being able to go to gigs or even buy certain books or see certain films, it wasn't really accessible to me, and that's really what I came for. I wanted to be able to do all those things that I used to read about that I could never do. People didn't come to perform in South Africa; it was far away enough, let alone all the political situations.

When did you first become interested in music?

I think I was always very interested in music. My dad actually plays, and my grand-dad used to compose, but I never learned to play any instrument. Tried to play the clarinet, that's what my father played, but miserably—wind instruments don't work for me! And so I never actually learned to play anything, but it was always very important to me. I think my father in particular had a big effect on that. He used to travel to China a lot, so whenever you got in my dad's car he'd always have Chinese cassettes. It was always things that were quite unconventional: jazz and lots of Motown, when I was really little. It was a big part of growing up.

How did you get interested in electronic music specifically?

It was a very natural progression, 'cause I was very into what I call indie bands, like Stereolab, My Bloody Valentine, and Spaceman 3. They were always using synths and sometimes drum machines, so it didn't seem particularly weird when I started doing electronic stuff because I was already used to all of that. Also from Orchestral Manoeuvres in the Dark when I was really small; I remember having *Dazzle Ships* and just being absolutely fascinated by these weird sounds and samples. Obviously I didn't understand how it worked, but later, it was just very normal because I was already listening to stuff that had

Mira Calix, 2006. PHOTO BY GEORGE KTISTAKIS.

those kind of sounds in it. It happened very slowly, definitely wasn't an epiphany.

I think the one thing about that kind of music, and probably the thing with my dad's music, it was all music with unconventional structures. So I got used to that at quite an early age. Although I like a lot of pop music, I liked a lot of music that wasn't structured in that way. It never seemed that weird to me; I just thought it was good.

At what point did you start making music yourself? Did you approach it through DJing?

Yeah, completely. My flatmate used to have some effects pedals and three decks, and I just started messing around. And then really just went from there to working with a Roland TR-606 [drum machine] and analog gear. Just a very slow process of trying to make things that sounded good. So again, it wasn't particularly a plan, it just sort of happened really slowly. And then I bought my own drum machine, and then bought something else, and really slowly bought a kit. At first all I had was a computer and a drum machine and a little mixing desk, you know, and that entertained me for quite a long time!

[Laughs] Probably not anyone else, but I was entertained! And so it was a very, very slow, natural evolution of curiosity, and just doing something and having fun, so you carry on doing it.

You said you didn't take to the clarinet really well, but you were fascinated with drum machines. Why do you think that is?

I think I'm probably inherently lazy because I tried to learn guitar and had the same problem! I really have so much respect for people who play instruments well, because it requires so much dedication. I'm quite impatient, you know. When I first started writing tracks, I wanted to write a track—like a *whole* track—*today!* And the thing about using electronic equipment is, you can do that. And you can teach yourself how to use it. It's just tools. They don't make any music themselves; you just have to learn the rules of those particular items. But you could be very impulsive, and you could do it really quickly. So it's a lack of patience in the sense that I wanted to create something, and I wanted to create it *now*. I think if you want to create a really nice song on the guitar, you are going to have to practice how to play that guitar for quite some time, and even if you're very naturally gifted, it doesn't happen in a day. You do have to practice.

The one thing I was always fascinated with, and I still am, is the piano. Even as a child, I loved the sound of wooden instruments and strings. So anything that falls into that camp, those are all my favorite sounds. They do something for me; it moves me in some way that I can't explain. Something about wooden instruments breathes—they constantly change, the wood breathes in itself. It's the same with old, analog synths. The fact that something is inconsistent, I find really attractive. Even though also you can tune a guitar to imperfection, or a cello, when it goes off on its own accord I find it quite interesting. They're like little creatures, you know, they breathe.

In the process of learning to make your own tracks, were you spending a lot of time by yourself?

I did, but I grew up as an only child and I've always been someone who actually needs a lot of time on their own, to quite an extreme, actually. Although I'm quite sociable, I need to counteract that with being alone a lot. So actually for me it feels quite comfortable, 'cause I enjoy solitude. I don't ever feel particularly lonely. I'm sure I have in my life,

I'm not saying never, but it's not something that I mind particularly. So that thing of working on my own for hours in the studio, I'm quite content.

Do you have a routine for making music?

I don't really have a routine, but I do like to write during the day. I don't really write much at night at all. I tend to get up in the morning, I go for a walk almost every day, even if it's just to go buy milk or something. And then I go into the studio, sort of run off 'til lunchtime, and work mostly through that period until it gets dark. So in summer I work much longer than in winter, 'cause in summer it gets dark around ten, and winter it's about four or five. It fluctuates a lot; I'm very seasonal! [Laughs] All my studios have had big windows. I like to be able to have a lot of light. I'm not someone who works 'til four in the morning, at all. I will stop and get up the next day. I'd rather start at eight in the morning. My circadian rhythm is very defined. I want to work in daylight hours.

Literally, I live on a farm, so if you don't put the TV or the radio on, you have no idea what's going on in the world. There's no time thing, there's no rush hour, you wouldn't know the time of day. You can tell by the birds and you can tell the seasons, but humanity doesn't run at a clock around you, and that's actually quite nice, it's quite liberating. When I was in Sheffield, I lived in the center of town, and you knew it was a Sunday because traffic had reduced to such a level. And I quite like not knowing if it's a Sunday. Because those things are not relevant to me, 'cause I'm lucky enough to work for myself, effectively.

Is there a typical process of how you put your music together? Like do you tend to focus on gathering found sounds, or is it more about melodies?

It really depends. I haven't developed a particular system; it depends on what I'm trying to write, if I've got an idea, some image, or something that's carrying me. But a lot of times I actually just sit there and play in melodies, and I can literally do that all afternoon. I just record and record and record, and then start working from there. So all my melodies, they're all played in. As simple as they are, I really love just sitting there, just playing stuff in. It works really well for me. And you do land up with loads of things where you think, Oh, that's great! But it's so not right for what I'm doing. And then you save it and venture off into some other track and then come back. It does lead you into other places and I think that's what I like about it, 'cause it makes you drift off. It's not necessarily the most focused way of working, but it's the most fun. I tend to work around that.

Right, as opposed to saying, I'm going to work on this eight bars until it's perfect.

Yeah, I never work like that, I can't. It's just not in my nature. I can pull it out when I really need to, but for me, the thing about being in the studio and having a studio at home, I'm not paying anyone for my time, so it's just about going in and exploring and having some fun and playing something. If something good comes out of it that day, great. And sometimes it doesn't, but at least you've actually had a nice afternoon even if it doesn't quite take you where you want to go. 'Cause you've learned something, or you've done something.

What sort of instrumentation are you using?

I really like a lot of folk instruments and because I travel a lot for gigs, I tend to buy local, little instruments and things. So I've got a lot of very strange, mostly wooden instruments. Lots of bells and things like that. I tend to work with them a lot. I really enjoy that. And honestly, I don't play them in the structured way that someone's learned to play it. You know, little funny harps and string instruments and stuff. But you can get such amazing sounds out of these things. I definitely like to collect. But not to collect to own them, simply to collect to use them. Especially Eastern Europe is amazing for a lot of those kind of things, and Africa.

It's interesting that on one hand, you're working in the realm of cutting-edge computer technology, but at the same time you prefer the sounds of wooden folk instruments.

Sitting there with a wooden shaker, yeah! I think that having an amazing computer and all that technology, like I said before, it's really just a tool. The computer itself doesn't do anything, if you know what I mean. Unless you make it do something, it doesn't do anything. So it's really allowing you to manipulate those other instruments or sounds, whether it's some pebbles or another instrument. First of all you can record it, you can multiply that recording, you can dissect that recording, you can do all those things and that's really exciting.

But to me, the important thing about making tracks is that the sounds are sounds I find really attractive. And also that have something *about* them, some quality. It's attractiveness in that there's some quality that resonates. When you're using something external like a wooden instrument, it has its own timbre and they're all different. There's a physical resonance that's unique, 'cause even if you buy two calabashes they're different; or if you buy two guitars, essentially they are different even though maybe they shouldn't be. I'm really into error. Things don't have to be perfect for me. The imperfection is interesting. Some people would call those things imperfection and I see them more as what makes—it's a cliché—but it gives it character. And the old analog synths have that. You know, you can have ten Roland SH-101s and they're all different.

And you use analog gear a fair amount too.

I do. They can drive you mad, 'cause they're temperamental and you just think, God, I really need this to work right now, and it doesn't. But then it does something, and it can be so annoying but it can actually be really illuminating. Something good comes out of it. But yeah, there are moments of sheer frustration, when you press record and then the thing's gone insane! And why? There's no rhyme or reason. I like all those things, they kind of keep me on my toes. They make things interesting.

What are you using—well, I'm less interested in what software you use, but in how you use it. Is it mostly an arranging tool for you?

I use it as an arranging tool, but obviously for processing sounds as well. I'm using loads of little programs for that. But I don't use virtual synths or that kind of thing much. You can see why they don't appeal to me greatly. Although some, I have to say, I've come across, and gone, Wow, that's really great. I'm not snobby about it, it's not like I will never use a virtual synth, but it's not generally the way I work. I do use things on occasion. But I like the physicality more. I'd rather have a knob I can turn. So yeah, it's basically just a sequencing tool and a processing tool. And that ability to record loads of audio. I wrote my first album on a really old Mac with very little audio capability. Having more and more audio capability, for me, is really attractive. With hard drives, I've seen it go from 64 megabytes, to now, we're sitting there with 80 gigabytes or 120 (and by the time this book comes out, that will seem small), so it's just massive, so much more you can store and use and manipulate. For me, that's been the thing that's facilitated so much. The other side, the software developments, they're great, and some of them I really do use and appreciate, but actually having so much space and being able to manipulate it and deal with that much audio recording, that's really been a big plus for me. I know a lot of people who say, You're just using it as a big tape recorder, but, you know, I'm quite happy with that!

Do you feel that gender issues have affected your practice of making music, or how you're perceived as a performer?

I think the only place it makes a real difference, and it's quite weird saying this back to you, is in interviews. 'Cause I can't think of an interview I've done where it hasn't come up, and I must've done hundreds. And that's quite amazing, because I've been out on tour with Plaid, or everybody pretty much on the Warp label, and they're never asked about being a man. Even working publicity, sitting there with Squarepusher, it's not like anyone's ever said, Oh, so you're a man . . . how do you feel about that? So I think that's the only place it makes a difference, is that it's something that I constantly have to consider or discuss, or just give an answer to. On a day-to-day level it doesn't really make any difference. In the studio it doesn't make any difference, but if you go out and do interviews, it will be asked. And then it's weird, because you have to consider it and you have to give and answer, but there isn't an answer and that is the truth.

In that you've worked on both sides of it, as an artist and a publicist for Warp, I wonder if you find the media depictions of women making electronic music to be fair.

Well, I'm not conventionally pretty, so I don't fit into that sort of thing, and I think the only difference is that there is a weird, silent pressure. You do feel that you need to turn up looking relatively respectable and so even if you're not pretty and you're not gonna be sexy, 'cause I don't enter into that game, you still gotta have clean hair and look relatively kempt, which I've seen with the boys really doesn't count for much. There are different acceptable rules. A guy can turn up like he hasn't bathed for a week, and when a girl does that it's accepted a lot less. Even though you've been on the same tour bus and it's the same situation, there's no reason why you should look any better. But that's society in general, people expect that. For the most part it comes naturally, it's not a chore, 'cause you do want to have a bath, you know what I mean? [Laughs]

But the media will choose the prettiest picture, you know that. I know, 'cause I've worked as a journalist and I've worked as a photographer and I've worked in PR. It's not something that bothers me particularly 'cause I've seen it from both ends and I do understand why. It is a little bit sad that in this point in history we're still playing that game. But what bothers me more isn't that somebody wants you to look pretty in pictures, but when I look at magazines and so many of the people being interviewed are male, and all the people in the adverts—in very little clothing—are female, what that sends out is a message that women are just there to look nice, and men are the ones who can look like anything but they can be intellectual and therefore interesting and we can accept them on their intellectual capacity. But that has nothing to do with me being a musician, that's something where I think, if I had a little girl, I wouldn't really like her to see the world like that. I would like her to think that, irrelevant to what she looked like, if you are a capable, interesting person you will be interviewed if your field covers it—whether it's science or art or whatever you are. So I find that sort of disappointing. But it's not something I spend much time being bothered about, though I can see it happening all the time.

You've performed and toured extensively. What do you like best about performing? And do you enjoy performing, or do you prefer time alone in the studio?

I like both. They're very different. I probably like being in the studio more. Gigs are strange, because some of them can be amazing. I think because I do so many, even when they're shit, they don't really devastate me because I know I've got another one soon. And also you know there's always gonna be a percentage which is a disaster! But when it's really good, it's good because the crowd makes you feel welcome. You know they actually want to hear you. I've played great gigs to very few people and shit gigs to loads of people. It's not necessarily having a crowded room, but if you have a crowded room and they're on your side, there's nothing better, really, that's such a nice feeling. 'Cause you can feel they're on your side. And you just know. I'm not really a person who looks up and interacts with the audience much; I'm quite like the classically shy, retiring electronic musician. But if you can feel that they're on your side, it's really lovely, 'cause you know you can go anywhere with them. So there's that element.

And the second element, which is even more important in a way, is that it *sounds* amazing. It sounds so good that you get carried away with actually hearing it. And on a much vaster system than what you have in your studio, or just different, so you notice things that you didn't notice, or you hear almost an extra melody. It makes you think differently, or it gives you an idea for something new.

It's such a politically charged time in the world, I wonder how you feel that electronic music culture in general, or your work specifically, addresses that.

I haven't noticed it in any music at all. Doesn't mean it doesn't exist, but I'm not aware of it. In fact, it's almost the opposite, it's almost as if we're all hiding from what's going on. So everything's nice and sweet and sugary. And that's quite interesting, that so much is happening in the world over the last few years and it doesn't seem to be reflected in music. In other times of great strife, usually art is the place where you see it. As far as personally, how I work, I think all those things do influence me as a person. I'm quite news-obsessed; I watch the news, same thing with the radio, at least three times a day but usually more. So those things have an effect on me, but not in a direct sense. I don't think I would sing about something like that; it is there, but I'm not shouting about it. But that's just because I never would've been in the past and I don't particularly feel the urge to now. I am quite a political person, I express it now, but not in my music. Maybe if I was a singer-songwriter I would maybe express those opinions more. I'm happier to do it in an interview than in my music. It's not that I don't want to make that point, it's just that I don't really see a way of making it within what I do.

Talking about your voice, you use it a lot in your recordings, but it's often almost inaudible.

Yeah, I always have. I think it's really 'cause I actually like the sound of my own voice, which most people don't, but I do. And so I like to use it. It's a tool. I work with it like the SH-101 or the guitar. It's just something else to make a noise with, and I like the sound it makes. I like what comes out of it. And when I don't, I sort of screw it around enough so that I do like it.

Is it less about communicating words than communicating sound?

Yeah, it's more about the sound, it really is. And also 'cause voices are a unique imprint, and so again, my voice is my sound, your voice is yours. So I don't see any reason why I wouldn't use it, 'cause it's mine and I can. Just seems very natural to want to use it in samples, even if it's to make a kick drum or a bass tone. It's there and I can use it; it's free! [Laughs] Don't have to pay anything for it. But yeah, it's weird about politics, 'cause it's just not there in the music.

What's interesting to me about electronic music is that there's perhaps more independence, compared to other genres that are released on major labels, in terms of what you can do and get released. But then again, maybe because we make music that doesn't have words as primary content, political content is more abstracted.

Yeah, you can give something a title that's politically provocative, or shove loads of CNN samples in there, which I'm never going to do, 'cause it's not the way I work. It doesn't feel natural to me to work in that way of sampling George Bush or something and cutting it up, you know what I mean? But you can be political in your personal life. It's something that's important to me, but not necessarily linked. Although it is, 'cause it's life, and life is obviously music. Your life makes you who you are, and therefore that's the music you make.

: : :

In 2007, Calix performed a site-specific work at Pollinaria, a new project in Italy's Abruzzo countryside dedicated to promoting interactions between resident artists and scientists and local organic farmers. She continues to receive commissions for music that combines acoustic and electronic instruments.

Jessica Rylan

Jessica Rylan, born in 1974, is a sound artist and electronic musician who designs and builds modular synthesizers with analog circuits, which she also uses in live performance. Based in Boston, where she grew up, she has toured extensively in North America and Europe under her own name and as the noise band Can't, and she has also created sound installations for venues including the Boston Center for the Arts and the Massachusetts College of Art [Mass Art]. She holds an MFA in electronic music from Bard College and is a research affiliate at MIT's Center for Advanced Visual Studies.

In performance and on her limited-edition recordings, she can be both high-energy and disarmingly intimate, expressing a range of emotion that is uncommon in noise music. Her synthesizer designs combine conceptual and stylistic elements from 1980s guitar effects pedals, 1960s and 1970s modular synthesizers like the Serge and Buchla, feedback methods of avant-gardists like David Tudor, and contemporary techniques of circuit bending. Her instruments include the Personal Synth, with two oscillators, noise, and a mic preamp; and the Natural Synth, which she describes as "good for doing fluttery and swishy sounds, like water and leaves." She builds synthesizers that are small-scale and battery-operated, designed to be comfortable and inviting to play, with a wide range of sonic possibilities and a certain immediacy of access. In 2006, she launched Flower Electronics, a small company dedicated to producing editions of her instruments, which until then had been one-of-a-kind.

I became familiar with Jessica's work through mutual acquaintances when I was teaching in Boston in 2004–05. We conducted this interview at her home outside Boston in July 2006.

: : :

Tara Rodgers: What is your background in music?

Jessica Rylan: I've played music my whole life. I was classically trained, I sang in a children's choir, I learned to read music, and then I played instruments. I used to play bass in a rock band.

How did you become interested in building things?

My grandfather was an electrical engineer, and he and my father did ham radio when my dad was a boy, where they'd communicate with people all over the world and get postcards in the mail. My grandfather was the first person who talked to me about electronics. We made a radio one time, a crystal radio, just the diode, no battery. He hooked this wire to a water pipe in the ground, and then you'd listen with the earphone and it was really quiet.

How old were you when you were doing that?

That was when I was five or six. Then when my parents bought this house and we moved in, the guy who lived here before was a tinkerer and left this big collection of *Popular Electronics* magazines in the attic. So I used to read those, and I was really interested in the ones about electronic music. I would read about it and think, God, I bet that sounds really cool. I was actually also listening to electronic music but I didn't connect the two things, as weird as that is. One time I had a babysitter who was listening to the stereo and sitting right next to the speaker, and she had the radio all the way on the left end on FM. It was really heavy, probably punk. So then I just copied her and put the radio all the way down on the left. I would listen to WZBC, a different station than what she listened to, and I remember hearing stuff like Alvin Lucier's *I Am Sitting in a Room*. They would never announce what the records were, so I never connected the two things. But somehow I was interested in it. I didn't start building my own stuff until a lot later than that, about eight years ago.

What tradition, if any, do you see yourself working within?

I'm not always sure what my focus is; I have a multiple focus. I like building things, and I like *designing* circuits now more than building. I did a few installations and would like to do some more, and I like being a performer, which is a totally different thing. At one point in my life I was really interested in experimental music—that there was a real value in experimentalism, whether or not people wanted to listen to the results. A lot of people like simple melodies or pretty apparent rhythms. So when you are doing music that doesn't have those things, or that is specifically against the harmonic series, intensely dissonant, or with close intervals, people don't like that. Or with noise, where you don't even deal with pitches and melodies and it's more textural, some people are attuned to that and other people aren't. For me, it's those tensions between, I am interested in super-abstract music, but I'm also interested in really recognizable music and pop music. I like writing songs and lyrics. I've been trying to do that within the genre of noise, but I think I hit my limit with that.

As far as traditions, the history of electronics is so poorly documented. The history of electronic *music* is pretty documented, but every book that you read just mentions the exact same people, and you wonder, is it really that there was only five people doing things, or was there other people that didn't get talked about? If you read the history of live electronic music, you read about David Behrman, Richard Teitelbaum, David Tudor, Pauline Oliveros, and Gordon Mumma. I'm interested to read about these performances, but as someone who's interested in electronic instruments, how was that documented? I've read lots more detailed technical descriptions of early computer music, like Max Mathews, Laurie Spiegel, and the GROOVE project. Whereas Louis and Bebe Barron, I've never seen their schematics; I've barely seen any of David Tudor's schematics.

I've started to think more about the aesthetics of electronics. I've been dancing around the edge of that for so long appreciating it, but I never systematically tried to analyze it. Like, what's the point of trying to do anything in hardware anymore? You can do it all in software—it's cheaper, it's easier, you can replicate it for free—it's the ideal business model. But people spend thousands of hours on a piece of software, and ten years later it's obsolete, because that computer system doesn't work anymore.

Or even one year later, with an OS update.

Totally! And does that invalidate everything they did? It's a very important question, probably most important to artists that use technology, because does that mean that your art is obsolete? If you do a piece now using a dual Beta deck, does that have any aesthetic value, or is it just retro? I remember when I first went to Mass Art, in their equipment room they had tons of reel-to-reel video recorders. I wanted to do pieces on those, and everybody was like, Why? What's the point? Woody and Steina Vasulka already did that fifteen years ago! Well, OK, but does that have any value in itself? Why did they use it?

It's an interesting question, because the speed at which things are changing now is so quick. Like if you think about the violin . . .

It's been the same for a thousand years.

Right, with only minor changes. But people can still find new ways to express.

Or they find old ways that make sense to people again, or that fit into the consciousness right now. But then, I'm attracted to the physicality of objects.

I think there are a couple of issues: one is, as a performer and creator, what interface you find pleasurable or expressive. Two, if there's something about the hardware that makes the sound aesthetically different or compelling.

I just like things that are simple. I like things that I can kind of understand. My big problem with the computer is that it does things in a time you don't have access to. It does it in these discrete intervals. I'm really interested in things in the world: trees, plants, rocks, water falling from the sky, a stream, a waterfall, the wind going through grass or somebody's hair. I love those sounds! We listen to sounds that have those simple relationships, and it's been in our DNA to hear those kinds of sounds for hundreds of thousands of years. There was a radical changing of the soundscape over the twentieth century, and I guess we like our lives better now 'cause we keep going further into this machine-noise environment. People are happy to trade being cool for having an air conditioner. Which, if you really like the sound of the real world, that's the last thing you want to hear! But we don't care about noise pollution. It's just not important to people, for whatever reason.

The thing with analog circuits is they follow very simple, natural laws, just like breaking a tree branch, or like water, or even like birds flying in a V—they push and are pushed into that pattern because it's the path of least resistance. With analog circuits, I like that you just put the stuff together, and whatever starts it, like you turn on the power, it's just following whatever the vibration would do. Whereas with the computer it is only making that one decision so many times over and over again. *Yes, no.* You end up with a more complicated result with the computer, but the analog circuit is real-time, it's really happening! And the sound it produces is the exact same as the electricity producing it. To me, that's so interesting. In the computer, whatever goes in and out is so abstracted, so many times. If you write a computer program, it's probably going to get reinterpreted as C, and C is going to get recompiled into assembly language, and *that* gets redone inside the processor itself. You get down to the level of, What is a digital computer? NAND gates. That's all it is!

And speaking of the aesthetics of electronics, one of the things with the changing of technology in modern capitalism, when there's so many layoffs and downsizing, is that no one expects that they'll be with a company for forty years or even five years anymore. The mid-twentieth-century model of capitalism where you work at a job for your whole life with wonderful benefits and get a great pension, that was totally a fantasy and can't happen. There are a lot of people that had skilled jobs, then those jobs disappeared because of technological changes. Like the Sprague capacitor factory, which Mass MOCA [Massachusetts Museum of Contemporary Art] bought and now there's an art museum there, that was a pretty great place to work in Western Mass for a long time. They probably dumped a lot of stuff into that river and didn't clean it up, but all that stuff became automated and now it's all offshore. I think there's one capacitor factory in the U.S. now. And a lot of engineering jobs don't exist anymore, like engineering drawing. Now all engineering design is done on a computer, whereas it used to be that all different people had those jobs drawing by hand. What happened to drafting? It's such a cool art form that had a firm hand in the history of drawing, but also was a focused skill. Well, anyone who had that specialty is definitely out of business at this point, or in early retirement. And that's really kind of sad, because the aesthetic of a hand-drawn diagram is a lot nicer than the computerized ones you get now, which are only about the information and not about the way they look. They look terrible. I've been thinking about it a lot with schematics especially.

In terms of building electronics, I enjoy drawing schematics by hand. I don't enjoy building the instruments one by one, though. Now I'm laying out circuit boards on my computer, because it's easier to

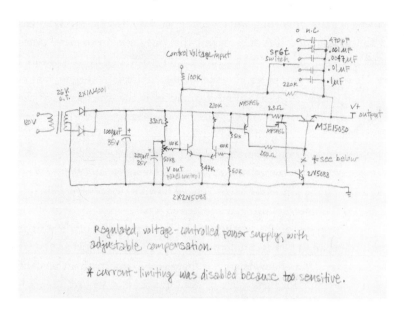

Schematic designed by Jessica Rylan, 2006: "Regulated, voltage-controlled power supply, with adjustable compensation."
COURTESY OF JESSICA RYLAN.

build things that way. That was something I was completely against before. It was like multitrack recording, it's cheating! [Laughs] With recording, it's easy to fake a super-human proficiency 'cause you can do endless takes. In a way, it seems unfair to the average person playing music. With laying out circuits, I felt like you should do everything with paper and pencil, 'cause the computer is like an unfair advantage over the past. But then I heard Vito Acconci speak at MIT, and he was saying if we can do things now using these new tools that were never possible to envision before, as artists it's our duty to do that. And that kind of blew my mind. I wrote a note about it that day, that I have to start using my computer to lay out my circuits. But I like doing schematics by hand. I just feel really connected with those instruments. I have a lot harder time getting used to the idea of digital music production. I know there's a lot of intellectual property that's produced, and that's very important. But there's something so ephemeral about it. Like programming: whenever people say, I *built* this on a computer, to me it's a really jarring statement, semantically. I have a hard time relating to it. In a way, it's like I'm in the nineteenth century, physically building something.

I recently built a little console as an experiment. I did everything totally different than I usually do, using this inverted circuit topology which is really interesting to me. The way they built power amplifiers in the 1990s, especially the really high-powered ones for PA systems, they would do this inversion where instead of the output coming from the output, it comes from the power supply. It's this weird kind of black-magic strategy that's counterintuitive, so I tried to use that. I had a job at a place that makes guitar amplifiers and pickups, fixing amplifiers for them. I worked with the engineers, so I was always looking at schematics and talking about designs even though it wasn't part of my job. I was talking with one of the engineers about my design, and he said, Why are you doing it like that? Who cares what the schematic looks like on paper, you just want to make a design that will work well. But I was like, Isn't it cool? Everything's arranged; it was bilaterally symmetrical. He was like, Who cares? Only the person who sees that schematic will know that; that doesn't affect the way it works. I was like, Can't there be a poetry to circuit design? They totally couldn't understand that. It's a valid way to work, but talk about a niche! [Laughs] That's like being a mathematician who's into writing poem equations that five people in the world will understand!

Well, that's been part of my interest with SuperCollider, is using the language so it can read like a poem as well as function as a sound generator. I like that poetry can happen on multiple levels, in the sound that comes out as well as in the technology that's making it happen.

It seems important, somehow. It's important to me.

For me, what's missing in a lot of computer music is that people can build really complex software and that's enough for them. To not care on a different level about what it means or where it's coming from, I don't really understand that! [Laughs]

I like seeing the context of it all. When I was at Bard, I quit doing electronics for three or four months. I got really concerned about the environment and upset about the labor of electronics and the way that work gets done. As I did more research about it I learned the electronics industry is really fucked up, and especially the computer industry. Where does your computer come from? If your computer is such a great tool for all these wonderful political things—which is totally a load of crap anyway, and I'm glad that there's a little more recognition of that now—but certainly ten years ago, everyone was so into hyping the technology, and hyping computer music. I got really offended by it. Like, your music comes from sweatshop production. You think it's so great, you carry around this thing that only weighs five pounds and that's all you have to do. But where did that come from?

I read a book about Malaysia and the semiconductor industry, and all these women staring through microscopes hand-soldering and basically going blind from looking at this small stuff all the time. At the time I was also really into knitting. I found a book in the trash about knitting; it was all these traditional patterns from an island off of Ireland. It was a very specific and advanced folk tradition. The book mentioned that in the seventeenth century in those far-flung places, there wasn't a lot of ways to make money. So a lot of women would sit around in the winter knitting stockings, and then they'd sell them all. It was a major source of cash income because they'd be sold all over the world. I thought it was so interesting that at one point in time there were all these women that made their living and also probably supported the family that way. So I knit this hat, and I brought it to school as my winter work project. Everybody was really mad about it. They were like, Well, this has been done *before!* And I was like, You know what? This is news to me. I didn't know the conditions of electronics manufacturing. Everyone's been keeping that a secret! You guys that are into computer music, you *never* want to talk about that stuff. I have to find out about it through the back door. Why is that so hidden?

Maybe on the surface it seemed like a knee-jerk, ill-thought-out feminist piece, but the other side of it for me, too, was feeling self-conscious being a woman who built circuits. Because, actually, *all* that stuff was built by women. If you look at consumer electronics manufacturers, they only hire women to do assembly, 'cause men can't focus! It's just biological. If you think about guitar amplifiers—Leo Fender—his employees were Hispanic women. Hartley Peavey hired all women in the circuit board department. He had men doing test and sales, and building the cabinets, but all the circuit boards were assembled by women [see Achard 2005; Smith 1995]. Within the arts community, which I always think of as having a liberal mindset, it's really not OK to discuss sex or gender differences, which I think is really a strategy of liberalism that's backfiring in a way, because when I look at mainstream culture now from a feminist consciousness, I think things were better for women in the '80s or '90s. It was certainly a lot less exploitative than it is now. But one test that women outscore men on is looking at a group of objects and then looking at a second picture and knowing which ones were moved in relationship to other ones. Which is probably the reason that in general women are better at doing electronics assembly. So that was this other part, for me, about knitting this hat. A lot of what I do is detailed handwork. In the history of business and electronics manufacturing, this is something that is not always written about.

I also got upset at Bard when people were like, You're like a mad scientist with this machine! I was like, No, a mad scientist is someone making a nuclear bomb and having a sociopathic outlook. I'm totally a humanist! I built this thing because I didn't want to exploit other people. I'm not as concerned about this as I once was, but at one point that was a main motivation in building my own instruments. I decided I'm not going to use an instrument that was made by slave labor. Did I really get away from that? Well, no. Integrated circuits are made by slave labor and by a totally environmentally toxic process. So, I don't know.

It seems that you're building instruments that have a potentially long lifespan. You're outside that mentality of, you have to buy a new Power-Book every two years or else your computer's too slow to do the latest complex processes of digital audio.

That's what I like about synthesizers. It's more like a guitar; it's just like an instrument.

Once you have it, you can play it for a lifetime.

Yeah. And the sound may go in and out of fashion, but you can also find new ways to play it. That's what's going on now. The classical synthesizer technique in the early '60s was so top-down, like, *This output goes to this input.* It was this very scientific approach to sound, like, What are the fundamental parameters of sound? Volume, pitch, and timbre. What a joke that is! It has nothing to do with anything. [Laughs] How do you manipulate volume and pitch? And timbre they couldn't really figure out. The new trend, I think in part because of circuit bending, is that people are a lot more interested in chaotic patches, connecting

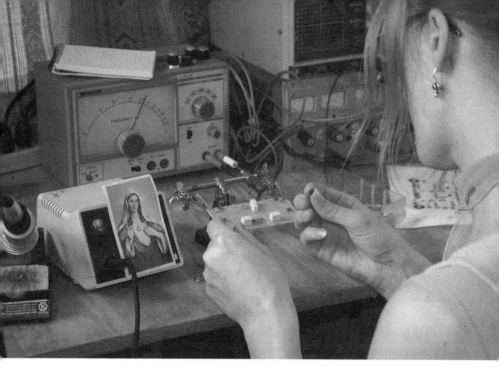

Jessica Rylan in her workshop, where the Virgin Mary is said to guard against shocks from the soldering iron, 2006. PHOTO BY ZACHARY PIPER.

active outputs together so you get these weird interactions between the power supplies of different modules. With circuit bending it's so much by chance, and it's usually done in a haphazard way so if you wiggle a wire a little bit it's totally different—all bets are off. It would be nice to be able to do more chaotic sounds or actions in a repeatable way, which is very possible. But it's hard to find the interesting chaotic sounds. It's like looking through a tiny pinhole at this infinitely big world, and then you move the pinhole a fraction of an inch and it's a totally different one! [Laughs] This really wasn't done in the past and nobody knows how to design it yet. It's complicated. They would always tell you with old synthesizers, Don't connect the outputs together! Serge Tcherepnin was very clear about that. But he's my favorite designer. There's really only three synthesizer designers that are interesting to me: Don Buchla, Bob Moog, and Serge.

Have you had access to the schematics of all of those?

The Serge ones are hard to find; I have eight of them that are on the Internet. The Buchla and Moog ones are really cool 'cause they're so old. All transistors, I love it. That's been a big inspiration. I started going back to using only transistors, just as an experiment, but I've been getting a neat sound that way too. I like music from the mid-'60s and I like the electronics design. They had nice colors: electronics enclosures were either powder blue or sometimes a chartreuse green that I love. And I really like the classic instruments, those early modulars, 'cause they were so beautiful. They'd use walnut for the cases; they were designed to be a nice thing to play.

What interests you about the Serge designs?

Moog and Buchla schematized sound in similar ways to early computer music, with pitch, loudness, timbre, and envelopes. Buchla had a different controller interface, but the approach to sculpting a sound was basically the same. Whereas Serge was more interested in long time frames, and in analog computers to get different kind of functions than just a sine oscillator or a simple envelope generator. The most interesting Serge module is this kind of magic thing, called the Smooth/Stepped Generator. You can run noise through it and it generates these neat fluttery patterns. You get these very reality-sounding time frames and repetitions, the kind of natural patterns where it doesn't repeat exactly but it stays within its range of motion. So that module I really love. Buchla had an interesting module too, the Source of Uncertainty. It's a low-frequency noise source to randomize timing information, and you can use it when a sound is coming in or out.

I recently saw a site about visualized noise textures, which was an important advancement for computer 3-D graphics, for filling objects with randomized textures. That was really interesting for me to look at, because it's exactly what I've been trying to think about with sounds. Like when you listen to rain, it's so different on different days. Some days it's big, fat raindrops that don't come as often; some days it's really fine mist and it's really smooth and constant; some days it's a mix between the constant *chhhh* with quieter, little drops that are steady, and big drops once in a while. That's what I want in a sound! How do you get there, to break up the timing information like that? It would be a lot easier to simulate, probably, using algorithms on a computer. I often think I should use a computer program to come up with equations to model that, and then build it electronically. But it's not my style! [Laughs] I just want to do it analog. I know what it's doing.

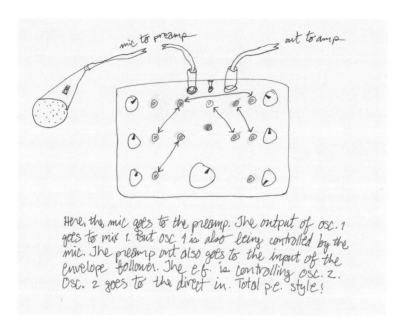

Here, the mic goes to the preamp. The output of osc. 1 goes to mix 1. But osc. 1 is also being controlled by the mic. The preamp out also goes to the input of the envelope follower. The e.f. is controlling osc. 2. Osc. 2 goes to the direct in. Total p.e. "style!

Excerpt from Flower Electronics Little Boy Blue synthesizer manual, designed by Jessica Rylan, 2006: "Here, the mic goes to the preamp. The output of osc. 1 goes to mix 1. But osc. 1 is also being controlled by the mic. The preamp out also goes to the input of the envelope follower. The e.f. is controlling osc. 2. Osc. 2 goes to the direct in. Total p.e. [power electronics] style!" COURTESY OF JESSICA RYLAN.

How do you resolve the issue of control in your synths and achieve the chaotic elements you're interested in? Are your synths structured so that you know what's going to happen, or is there a certain amount of instability in the system?

I do things in a really primitive way, like I turn a knob or I move wires around. With the Personal Synth, if I hold two cables in my hand, the hand is a bridge for the signal, depending on how tight I squeeze it. I just realized that recently. It doesn't always work, but in certain instances I can do a kind of fine control that way as the signal travels through the capacitor into my hand, across the surface of the skin. The tighter I hold it, the easier it is to get through. I also do a lot with singing, and having my voice control certain aspects.

What's been interesting to me is setting up really complicated patches on the synthesizer but then the voice goes through the patch in different ways, so that the direct voice signal right after the mic preamp is controlling the wave shape of an oscillator or its frequency. On the synth that I use mostly, there's also an envelope follower on the voice, which uses the amplitude information for controlling something else. Between the voice and the feedback through the whole system—the synthesizer through the speaker system getting picked up by the mic itself—when it's going through a complicated patch, you get a chaotic result. That's a really popular kind of sound right now. I really like that. But I wish the vocals were clearer, because sometimes it's hard to understand them. But some of my lyrics I'm embarrassed about and I don't really want people to know!

It's true that many of your pieces that incorporate voice and storytelling are processed to a point where it can be difficult to understand the lyrics.

I know, I'm sick of that style.

The pop musician in you is winning out?

Well, I got into that through popular music. It's a tradition that goes back to that song "Louie Louie." I mean, what are the lyrics to that? Who knows! And it was a big trend in the early '90s. I remember hearing rock bands that either mumbled a lot or screamed incomprehensibly, and there was no possible way to understand what the lyrics were. But the lyrics were very important, for some reason! But I'm sick of my stuff sounding so muffled and incomprehensible. I've been struggling with that. The next synthesizer I build will have a high-quality mic preamp in it, and I'm going to start using a condenser microphone. I want it to sound good.

Do you feel that the term noise is appropriate for your work? How do you trace the history of noise music?

I've been really into noise. And I think now is the appropriate time to ask these questions, because something changed fundamentally in the last two years. Noise is more popular now than it's ever been. There's a lot of debate about what "noise" means. Most genre labels are pretty contested, but noise is extremely contested, especially as it starts to get more popular.

In 1996, it got big in the U.S. because Relapse Records, which was a metal label, signed Merzbow and Masonna and they did a ten-city tour. Now, any popular noise band, the odds are that at least one of the members was at one of those shows. Brian Chippendale from Lightning Bolt was there; Wolf Eyes saw it . . . For this whole wave of people it was really important.

I think of noise as not being guitar-focused. To me, I trace aesthetically to Merzbow and the Japanese harsh noise style; and in Europe, to Throbbing Gristle and Whitehouse. But that's almost a different kind of music, more power electronics. I think modern American noise is kind of a mix: the combining of straight-up white noise or really thick sounds with power electronics, which was more focused on vocals but still really aggressive music. Also, the incorporation of a chaotic performance aspect or Dada elements. Many more people would trace it to Reed Ghazala for circuit bending. Making stuff from scratch is really difficult. Circuit bending is a lot easier and much more democratic, in a way. The materials are so cheap; you don't need special tools as much [see Ghazala 2005; Collins 2006]. But within the popular "noise scene" bands, there's a real emphasis on people building their own stuff, which can come from the art tradition too. In Europe, building your own things has a very different history. From the limited amount that I know about it, I would trace it back to Michel Waisvisz from STEIM building his Cracklebox, and to Gert Jan Prins or Voice Crack.

I'm interested in your ideas about "personal noise," which you've mentioned in other interviews. And related to that, how you've chosen names for some of your machines, like the Personal Synth, and what you mean by that.

I just like hearing new sounds. Sometimes I feel like a little kid. I like that excitement of hearing a new sound. The way that I like to play at home, late at night by myself on my synthesizers, is just really quiet and exploratory and long time frames, and not trying to have songs. It's really cool especially to have a synthesizer that's small enough that can sit on your lap, and you can just sit there and play it, and then you're like, *Whoa!* That was awesome. It just feels like a very comfortable way to work. I have a hard time naming things, but the Personal Synth is just the right size for a person.

But it's interesting, 'cause your book is specifically about women in experimental music, and I've only been talking about men! There are things within the noise and experimental music scenes that are really interesting, ideas about instruments and sound. But what is missing,

Jessica Rylan performing with the Personal Synth, 2006.
PHOTO BY LAWRENCE BRAUN.

to me, is content, and especially personal content. It seems trite to say that it's gendered, but it definitely can be.

When I think about early synthesizer music, the first works that come to mind are Pauline Oliveros's electronic works, and Eliane Radigue's works. And Suzanne Ciani is this really interesting cultural figure who, even though she was doing sound effects and commercials more so than music, had this very public "love affair" with the Buchla synthesizer! [see Pinch and Trocco 2002]. And of course Wendy Carlos had the first breakthrough synthesizer record, with *Switched on Bach*, which brought electronic music completely into the mainstream over-night. So it was really women who first learned to communicate effectively with these instruments. Though that's electronic music, not noise.

Well, historically, this tradition of noise and machines is really gendered.

Oh, it's super gendered. Noise really goes back to Futurism, which was actively misogynistic and nationalistic and racist. British power electronics music like Con-Dom, Grey Wolves, and Whitehouse was also pretty overtly misogynistic. Now, noise is popular with a lot with punk kids. It's basically what punk is now: young kids getting excited, being dissatisfied and idealistic too. It's a rebellion. A lot of these kids that are into noise dress in ridiculous clothes, they never do their laundry, and they smell bad. It *is* really countercultural at this point, where the models on TV are Beyoncé Knowles and Ashton Kutcher—these super gorgeous people that are just unrealistic. The contemporary noise scene is pretty progressive in a lot of ways; it's an interesting conflict with the past, reactionary political style. The Japanese tradition always used bondage and dismemberment imagery for their releases. I hate that stuff; I'm so glad it's going away. Whitehouse I can understand, because they're very sincere. The thing that really changed my perspective on them was some of the lyrics on the last album, *Asceticists* [Susan Lawly, 2006]. First, he's mad about some hipsters talking about the Internet—well, who isn't? Then, he's mad because he's trying to teach a little girl to read and she has the book upside down! It just seemed very familiar, it reminded me of my dad when my brothers and I were driving him crazy and he was overworked and stressed out. Not anyone's favorite part of life but something we can all relate to. So with their more misogynistic lyrics, whether it's right or wrong—'cause as a liberal I would say it's wrong—that's how they feel sometimes. There's a lot of guys that hate women, and it's not right, but it is a fact in society. I guess it's *authentic*.

So maybe that's what's personal about noise.

Sometimes it's offensive.

But there's an honesty in it.

What's so wrong about that? Art has gotten really politically correct in a certain way. Art is supposed to reflect what's happening at the time. But within the noise scene, it's cool that there's been a lot more women involved in it recently. Especially the last few years, as more younger kids get into it. That's really good, that the younger generation is taking all that history in but making it their own, and not feeling like they have to follow in a genre footstep.

: : :

Rylan's recent projects include the score for *Behemoth*, an intermedia dance work created by the Boston-based company Kinodance (2008); a cassette release featuring recordings of a 1976 Serge modular synthesizer (*Flight to the Ivory Tower*, Heavy Tapes 2007); and a CD with compositions on her synths and the Serge (*Interior Designs*, Important Records, 2007).

Part 4. Circulation and Movements

"Moving, grooving, connecting": this is how DJ Susan Morabito characterizes the energy in a dance club. It is an apt expression as well for considering how electronic music cultures are animated by the movement of cultural forms within them, and by the communities that organize around them. Electronic dance music gathers meaning through the movements of sounds, styles, DJs, and dancers across diverse and dispersed cultural spaces. Morabito notes how the reputation of the Saint in the early 1980s spread from New York City to her home city of Cleveland and motivated her pilgrimages to the Manhattan club to experience the scene for herself. Her professional advancement hinged on her movements within various club spaces to acquire necessary knowledge and music, and on the circulation of her name and reputation among club owners and managers.

DJ Rekha's work is constituted through transnational circulations. Her monthly Basement Bhangra parties mobilize communal celebrations of South Asian diasporic cultures in New York City. She regularly draws new talent in bhangra and British Asian music to the United States, and she also DJs abroad, often using her performances as fundraisers for social justice issues.

DJ Mutamassik likewise infuses her work with cultural and political consciousness, cultivating "incitefulness/insightfulness" among those who are moved by the rhythms. Her music references the eclectic array of styles she was exposed to growing up—from African to South American to baroque—and draws upon an assortment of records she has accumulated on her international travels as a DJ. Mutamassik foregrounds rhythm as a sonic metaphor for collectivity and Afro-diasporic cultural identity, in opposition to the "cult of personality" of the soloist in Western music traditions. Although she may DJ alone, with her "relentless rhythms from the immigrant sound sources," she brings with her a formidable crowd.

Jeannie Hopper's travels as a news reporter to Central America and the Middle East catalyzed her desire and ability to use radio for political communications. Turning her attention to underground dance music and spoken word scenes, Hopper began to celebrate the gathering of individuals who migrated from dispersed geographic locations to find solace in the New York City clubs. Her Liquid Sound Lounge radio show redistributes that sense of community over the radio waves to give it greater reach. In each of the following artists' work, sounds become movements—dispersed from a DJ booth, home studio, or radio station to stir bodies and politics in diffuse cultural spaces.

Susan Morabito

Susan Morabito, born in 1960, grew up in Cleveland, Ohio. She moved to New York City in 1987 where she felt she could best pursue a creative path as a club DJ. Since her first big break in 1991, when she landed a summer residency at the Pavilion in Fire Island Pines, she has played at nearly every major club in New York City, including Twilo, Sound Factory, Limelight, and the Palladium. She has performed regularly at high-profile parties for gay communities in New York City and nationally, including gay pride events; the Stonewall twenty-fifth-anniversary celebration in 1994; and Circuit parties, the large-scale dance events attended by thousands of gay men. In 2003, she was the first woman to DJ at the Black Party in New York City; she has also spun at several fashion industry parties and galas.

Morabito has cultivated a reputation for tasteful and versatile sets that bring together European progressive house, tribal, and underground U.S. house. She has released seven mix CDs, of which *Love to Dance* (Whirling Records, 1999) and *Pride* (Centaur, 2001) offer a good introduction to her style.

Susan was one of the most prominent club DJs—a kind of household name—in New York City when I became interested in electronic dance music in the late 1990s. We met for this interview at a cafe in the West Village in July 2006.

: : :

Tara Rodgers: What are your earliest experiences of music?

Susan Morabito: I had older sisters, which is so fabulous when it comes to being turned on to things. Because when you're eight or nine years old, you're not buying music, but *they* are. They were early teenagers, so they were listening to the pop of the '60s, things like Bobby Sherman and Frankie Valli and the Beatles. It was great, because I was exposed to—I want to say fun music—it was light, it was easy, it was silly. And then rock got very refined—Cat Stevens, Joni Mitchell, James Taylor, Carly Simon—and I *loved* that stuff. When I was in high school and started buying records, I liked all the rock like Jethro Tull, David Bowie, King Crimson, Roxy Music. I started buying all that stuff on record. I didn't know about dance music until I went into a gay disco in 1980. That's when I heard things like Boris Midney, Donna Summer, Abba, and I fell in love, you know? I walk in, it was the first gay club I was in. One, I was so thrilled because I was in a gay club.

[Laughs] Yeah. How old were you then?

I was twenty. You know deep down you're a little lesbian, but you don't know what that is. Like, I don't know what that is, except for Billie Jean King! [Laughs] You know? And, nothing against Billie Jean King, but here, I see drag queens and women and it's like, Oh my God, what is all this? This is really decadent and fabulous. Well, upon all that, I'm hearing what I considered *fabulous* disco music. You know, with the beat and the singing and all this orchestration, and there's people on the dance floor just celebrating, dancing, feeling. Moving, grooving, connecting. And it was like, This is fabulous. I was really impressed: Where's the music coming from? What is this? And I'm looking around the dance floor just in awe of all the homosexuals in one place—this is all new to me—and then I figure out, OK, the music's coming from a DJ in a booth. And I go up there and I watched him for a long time, and it amazed me how you could mix other people's music and create this journey. And the songs—the beats—matched. I didn't know what it was at the time, the beat-matching, but this DJ was telling a story with other people's music, and he was making people *feel*. So the music was like a link to their emotions.

In time, I realized, That's what I want to do. It took awhile for it to all come together. I didn't know what I wanted to do for a living. I thought I would be a radio DJ, but then when I found out that a radio DJ had a program director, and you didn't have the freedom to turn people on to what you wanted to, that wasn't very appealing to me. Because part of the fun was finding the music in the record stores, and then turning people on to it. So I started going to gay bars more, and I got to know a couple of the DJs. One in particular, I really liked his style. I'd hang out at that club all the time 'cause I liked what he played. I got to know him and I asked him if he'd teach me. And he said, Just sit here, shut up, and listen! He told me how records are structured, and I took that information, and now every time I listened to records I would do the counting. At that time, every time I listened to records I would pay close attention to how they were structured. They're basic, and how they're structured is how you mix them, how you beat-match.

So I started playing clubs in Cleveland, started playing a lesbian bar. I was a bartender first, and then I started playing records. I did that for maybe a year and a half, but I got fired from that job 'cause the women liked making requests, and I wasn't real happy with that. 'Cause, you know, I didn't want to be a human jukebox, it wasn't about that. The guy who owned that lesbian bar also owned the men's bar in the city, and eventually he gave me a job at the boys' bar, the smaller nights. I remember him telling me that I had potential. Now this was in my second year, maybe. Potential—I didn't know what that meant, really. Then he was telling me about a club in New York called the Saint. An all-men's club, membership only, five million dollar club. This is 1982 now, and I'm really impressed by this. My attitude was, they're not gonna hire a woman. And then he proceeded to tell me that there was a woman by the name of Sharon White who worked there. Sharon White was the first female DJ who broke into the male scene in New York, the first who had a large name and following. She really opened up the doors for all of us. She was popular and she was extremely talented. Now, for me, being twenty-two years old, by knowing that a woman already did that, that gave me hope. That made me realize it was possible.

So I started coming up to New York in 1984, visiting a couple times a year. Then maybe five, six times a year. I would come up to go to the Saint and listen to the DJs and dance. It was an incredible space. I can't describe it and do it any justice. We'll never see anything like that again. It was like the pinnacle of gay dance experience. It's definitely carved in the stones as part of our history. The Paradise Garage was equally on par: they were both extraordinary clubs in their own right, with a different vibe. What the difference was, the Saint played more of a disco-oriented sound, and also a dance-oriented rock sound, and was more white-boy based. Where the Garage was more black and

Susan Morabito. PHOTO BY DANIEL HANDAL.

Latin, and a mixture of everybody. Musically, it was more about soul and house. There definitely was a difference, but they were both spectacular dancing venues.

So I kept coming up to the city, going to the Saint, experiencing those DJs. I also realized that because it was open until the wee hours of the morning, sometimes into the afternoon, you could take music and bring people on a journey on a whole different level than I ever knew existed. Such as the "down trip." Depending on the DJ, the last three hours, they would really bring it down to like 110 beats per minute. And people would just shuffle on the dance floor. It was like wrapping up the entire evening to this slow, cuddly, emotional music. Wasn't pumping, you know? And that was really my favorite. I *loved* when it started coming down. Going to the Saint, I experienced that. You didn't experience that in Cleveland, or anywhere else. You don't experience it *anywhere* anymore. Maybe San Francisco. But it was a huge part of the New York dance scene, the journey including a down trip. Very, very important part of the evening. Not everybody stayed for it, but you'd have maybe four hundred people still on the dance floor for that part of the evening. Now, you bring it down, they run out!

163

What do you think has changed?

They don't want to go to that place emotionally; I think they're doing too much crystal. A lot of it's the drugs. Also, if the DJ doesn't educate you to it, how are you going to know? Most of the DJs today on the Circuit scene weren't a part of that era. I'm bringing my history to my dance floor—what I knew twenty years ago, still today. But on a minimal level, because the crowds won't allow me; they're not gonna support it.

So the Saint opened up a whole new world for me. I knew if I wanted to take DJing on the creative level I knew was possible, New York was the only place I could do it, *the* only place where I could take them on that kind of musical journey, and explore musically what I was capable of. Because for me, DJing isn't about playing things you think they wanna hear. If you do that, you're painting a picture with them giving you the colors. For me, it's knowing all the colors I have to choose from—the songs, the records—and painting that picture the way I want to, and hope they come on that journey with me. A huge part of the job is record shopping, and you are what you buy. That's part of your statement that you bring to the dance floor.

When you first moved to New York, you worked in a record store— which one?

I worked at Vinyl Mania [on Carmine Street in the West Village]. They used to have six stores on the street. At that time, all the DJs bought their records there. I worked in two different record stores in Cleveland—maybe three—and I knew if I came to New York, my goal was to work at Vinyl Mania and to play the Saint. I knew music, I loved music, and that was the store to work at. Within two weeks once I got up here, I got a job at Vinyl Mania. Which was great, 'cause it really exposed me to more music than I was exposed to in Cleveland, and it exposed me to people.

But I didn't make the Saint. It was hard getting work in New York in that field. It was very competitive. The woman thing did not help at that time. There were several men—club owners and managers— who told me later that they would not hire me at first because I was a woman. They didn't understand that a woman would get it. At that time, there were so few women. I saw more guys step over me for certain jobs. I was around longer, I was going to the same clubs, and certain people were getting jobs a lot quicker. So I didn't make the Saint because you had to have a reputation before you played there, and a good one. Just as my name started circulating—I was cutting my teeth, proving myself, earning a reputation, starting to scratch the surface—the Saint closed. I was really crushed. My roommate at the time said to me, You know, maybe you were meant to carry on the tradition. I guess in a way I was, because I did carry on that Saint tradition. After the Saint closed, in time, I started working on Fire Island a lot, which had been a springboard to the Saint. You made it out there, then the Saint was the next step. Eventually I played Saint parties—they have Saint At Large parties—for years.

You've played in nearly all the big clubs in New York. How have you seen the atmosphere around clubs change over the years, through different political administrations in the city, and different social trends?

It's changed a lot. I'm really grateful that I had the height of my career between '94 and 2000. That was my peak. I was really popular; I may have been considered one of the top three on the Circuit. I'm not considered one of the top three on the Circuit now, and that's OK. You're not going to be one of the top three on the Circuit forever. I'm grateful I had it at the time I did. I wish I would've had it in the Saint days, only 'cause I would've loved to have played that room. And the down trip was a bigger part of the evening.

But I think things really changed in 2000. It was almost like this psychological thing with the millennium. I think crystal started taking over. I think that the people who run the clubs, a lot of them in New York have no imagination. It became cookie-cutter, it became generic, it was the same template ad. They started catering to the young, which I kind of get, but I don't feel there was leadership. They didn't set the tone, they let the young set the tone. Is this marketing for clothing, or is this an art? Enough said. Bruce Mailman who owned the Saint, or Michael Brody who was the owner of the Garage with Mel Cheren—those guys were leaders who had a vision. And when you have a vision, creatively, there's a magic to that. I felt the magic over the years just started slipping away.

People's reasons for going out changed too. When I first started going out in the '80s and even in the '90s, you went out and you were celebratory. You were celebrating that you could be openly gay, that you *had* a place to dance. I think by 2000, there was entitlement: I have every right to be in this club, and how dare you search me? But I think that kind of change happens with anything. And I guess we all think our day was the best day.

I'm also interested to hear what you have to say about the presence of lesbians and queer women in dance music. The history of disco and house music has been marginalized for a long time, no doubt because so much of it was coming out of gay, black, and Latino cultures which themselves were marginalized or underground. But even in the histories now being written, there's just passing mention of how lesbians and queer women might have been part of those scenes, or developed their own spaces around dance music. The audiences you've played for in New York, you've played primarily for men, yes?

Right, yes. There's a couple reasons for that. The men will allow me to take them on a journey. The men will dance all night long, until the wee hours of the morning. The men are doing the drugs. Dancing is a tribalistic ritual. It also can be a sexual ritual. And I'm not saying women can't or shouldn't be a part of that, but the girls go out, and by two, three o'clock, they're going home! The guys will pay fifty bucks to go to a party. The women? Try to get ten. It's just a different culture. And I can speculate why, but it's just different. The bars in New York close at four. The majority of women don't even go until four. It's not a ritualistic, community, gathering-of-the-tribe, spiritual dance for them. Do you need drugs for that? I don't think so. What is it that makes the dance such a male-dominated thing? Going back in time on the ritual of dance, maybe the answer is there.

I've done some gigs at lesbian bars but I always got the same message from the owners: that house music didn't work there, that the women wanted to listen to the jukebox or hear something recognizable. I know several other DJs who've encountered the same thing, again and again. But against the stereotype, I know lots of lesbians who like house music!

You know, I think if you had a really groovy women's club—small, and done with vision and creativity, and it supported a DJ who wanted to create a journey—now granted, a journey that was within their liking . . .

Ends by 2:00 AM! [Laughs]

Well, you know who did it? The Clit Club [on West 14th Street]. I played the Clit Club a couple times. One time it wasn't that great of an experience, just an off crowd. But the other time, I got away with murder! And the girls went right along with it. If you think about it, I would go to another lesbian bar first and then go over to the Clit Club. The same women were there, but they acted completely different at the Clit Club. It was dark; they promoted more of a sexual, teasing, playful vibe. They had dirty movies downstairs, they had the dancers. They created that environment, and it brought something out in the women. If you create the environment, you know, music brings out certain things, it evokes certain emotions. So does lighting, so do the energy and the time and the setting. If you have this bar with the lights on, the women aren't gonna stay! You have to do something to provoke those feelings. I think if somebody set out to do that in a city that would support it, and had the vision, I think they could have a successful dance party at *least* until six o'clock in the morning, maybe seven. You've just got to set the tone, and know what you're doing, and know what it's about.

You talk about music being able to reach people emotionally. I wonder what it is that you're most attracted to in the music that you play; what qualities convey the emotions you want to convey.

Not one, because I am so versatile. I can play a White Party—happy, uplifting, light, gay pride—and I can play a Black Party—a lascivious, leather, sexual kind of event. So for these, there are basically two different kinds of music. I like happy house. I like dark and dirty. I like instrumental, I like vocal. It all depends on the mood and the party. But it has to be tasteful. As long as it's not cheesy. It's hard for me to describe cheesy. I like to think I go for a sophisticated sound. I like more natural instruments in my music regardless of the type it is. But on the other hand, apart from DJing, I listen to what I call "granola" music: acoustic guitar, pop/folk. I love that stuff. Different kinds of music bring out different feelings. I don't have one feeling, you know? So I don't listen to one thing. There's so much great music out there to pull from, regardless of whether it's dance. A lot to experience.

When you were asked to play the Black Party in 2003, you were the first woman to have that opportunity.

And only, I'll add. So far.

What was that like for you?

You know, here you have this leather-clad event, very lascivious, high testosterone level—high. And I led them on a sexual journey. Now, I'm a woman, and I did that, I orchestrated it, and I can get that without having to have a penis. It's a bit of a high! [Laughs]

How many thousands of people were there?

Six thousand!

So that's quite an achievement. [Laughs]

It's a little bit of a power trip! [Laughs] Yeah, it's really fun to lead 'em on a journey. DJs have an incredible amount of power. If you have an off night, they're gonna have a miserable time. You're on? Eighty or ninety percent of the dance floor will walk away having a memorable event. And that's really cool when you are on and you really pour your heart into creating a journey and they're right with you. There's this communal vibe, and sometimes we're all united.

It's a very rewarding job. It's given me back a lot. I make people feel, and sometimes think. I'll get e-mails from people expressing thanks for the way I've made them feel on the floor, and what I've given them spiritually or emotionally for a moment. And it feels great. It's a very give-and-take job, too. What you're giving to the floor comes back to you, and you feed off of it. That often directs me to where I'm going to go with them. 'Cause I never know what I'm going to do, it's all spontaneous. You never know, you're just feeling the vibe. If you're really feeling it, it works.

168

: : :

Since our interview, Morabito has continued to perform around North America, including gay pride events in Chicago and Montreal.

Rekha Malhotra
(DJ Rekha)

Rekha Malhotra was born in London and raised in Queens and Long Island. As a founder of the successful Basement Bhangra, Mutiny, and Bollywood Disco parties, she has been a primary catalyst of the South Asian music scene in New York City. The *New York Times* and *Newsweek* have recognized her as one of the most influential women of the downtown music scene and among South Asians in the United States more generally (Ryzik 2007; Sweeney 2002; Kantrowitz and Scelfo 2004). Through her production company, Sangament, Rekha has been instrumental in introducing new talent in bhangra and British Asian music to U.S. audiences, and she is frequently consulted as an expert on musics of the South Asian diaspora. She consistently combines music with community activism, using her events to raise money for human rights and other nonprofit organizations, or teaching DJ workshops for girls.

Rekha and I met through mutual friends in New York and participated on a panel together at the CMJ Music Festival in 2000, and she performed at the Pinknoises.com launch party in 2001. We conducted this interview at a diner in Brooklyn in May 2002.

∶ ∶ ∶

Tara Rodgers: How long have you been DJing?

Rekha Malhotra: That's kind of a relative question. Technically speaking, I became part of my DJ crew ten years ago, but I don't think I was actually DJing. It took me five years to actually start DJing, so I'd say about seven or eight years. I started with my cousins, they were boys, and I was booking the gigs, I wasn't playing on the tables.

What made you decide to start?

They left! I used to dabble, but I really put them forward, and then they left. Starting to DJ was somewhat circumstantial. Our roles were very gendered, like I was very involved in the music selection, and administrative duties. There were two of them, and they left one by one and moved back to India. The first one was really the DJ, he was really talented; he's still a DJ, actually. And it was fine—it was partly gendered, partly because he had an interest and a talent for it. Then when he left and the other cousin was there, you know, he was all right. But that's when I really got my hands on it, got started.

And the actual skill of doing it, was that something you worked out on your own?

Yeah, when I learned, it was very trial-error. I just feel like the simplest things, things that seem very obvious today, we learned very slowly and painfully. You know, there was no knowledge out there—this was pre-Internet, there was no written material, no documentation, no nothing—you have to learn from someone else. I felt like we were working very isolated. We decided, as a group of cousins, you know, kind of like siblings, to start a crew. Kind of like the Ramones—they had three chords, you know? I remember telling this family friend, who's older, that I wanted to be a DJ, and he was a DJ. And he was like, Do you know how to mix? And I'm like, What? I didn't even know what that meant. He's like, It takes a really long time . . . I was like, Whatever, I didn't even care, I'm just gonna do it. 'Cause I had a lot of faith in my musical tastes and musical knowledge, and that's really what it takes.

What music were you listening to?

I listened to everything. I had a lot of Prince in my life . . . I felt like I always knew what was going on musically, like with the hip-hop stuff, even before hip-hop was cool and trendy. Some Indian stuff . . . So all of that, I mean, I felt like I had a reasonable palette to choose from.

What made you want to be a DJ? Was it working the crowds, or presenting the music you liked to other people?

I was very excited about the music, and it was kind of like a family bonding thing with me and my cousins. We wanted to do something together, we wanted an activity, and we thought maybe we could make some money. We actually were inspired because we saw a lot of punk-

DJ Rekha. PHOTO BY NISHA SONDHE.

asses do it, and thought they did a really bad job, or thought we could
do this better, which made a lot of sense. And then before I knew it,
one of my cousins all of a sudden landed upon some hot gear. It was
like one minute we're talking about it, next minute, someone's selling
me a CD player and mic, and I'm like, OK, cool, that's it, done, we're
started! And I still have that gear I bought. It was a Radio Shack mixer,
CD player, tape deck, microphone, like good shit, you know?

*I know that you got interested in radio, along with community activ-
ism, while you were in college. Was that around the time you started
DJing?*

My activism stuff started way before I was DJing. And I think because
of that, DJing gave me more opportunities. I got to do a lot of fundraisers, community events; it got me open to a great crowd, a good
audience, and then I got involved in radio.

I felt like almost immediately, I became like this person who had to
speak about bhangra, like, ad nauseum, you know? It just started almost immediately—next thing I know, someone's writing their Ph.D.
and they need to interview a real person in the field, and it was me. It
was really interesting, 'cause I remember back then people were just
like slurpin' it up, because it fit all the metaphors people use—*It's*

created in the diaspora!—It's old, it's new! They just want to retro-fit their theories so badly. I helped them out so much!

But that still goes on, right? You're so much the point person on bhangra, for better or for worse. Is there a certain pressure with that, or is it frustrating that you have to keep regurgitating the same information?

It gets a little monotonous. I think I just take it as part of my work. It's like if you're an actor, and you do this great part, everybody knows you, and you're happy, too, that you did it. But you know that as an actor, you did many other things, but they're always gonna talk about *that*. And I feel sometimes the same way; I'm happy and I love it, but I don't want to get musically typecast. So I try to create other things, events that hopefully break that. But Basement Bhangra is the thing that people know the most.

And I also feel like there's other things in play, with the mainstream media—or let's just say the non–South Asian media. I feel like they want the ethnic story. It's not exciting for them if it doesn't have that. We had a very known lifestyle, music/trendoid magazine come to Mutiny, which I think is just a great party. And they came to Mutiny and they came to Basement Bhangra, and they wrote the story on Bhangra. And I just feel like it's not fair. I think it's an interesting statement, because it's deep—they want the ethnic story, they want the twist. And it has to be very obvious; Mutiny is not necessarily so obvious.

And to you, is Mutiny more musically exciting?

In many ways it is. To me, Basement Bhangra is just a fuckin' no-holds-barred, rock-on house party. You know, seriously. Work out and all that shit, you know? But Mutiny, you're gonna go and experience something. It is about dancing, but sometimes it's about listening. And I think that is exciting to me. And there's so many different people who DJ at that party, and so you're really getting open to a lot of different things, whereas at Basement, it's just me and Phil Money, and we have our ways.

When did you start Mutiny?

Fall of '97, six months after Bhangra. It was me and Vivek Bald [a.k.a. DJ Siraiki].

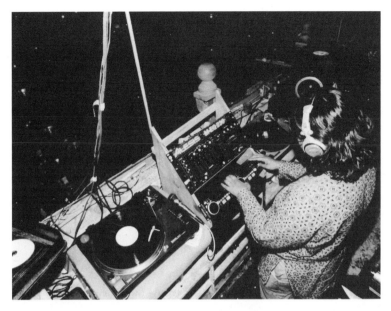

DJ Rekha performing in New York City. PHOTO BY NISHA SONDHE.

How would you characterize Mutiny musically?

Very hard to characterize. We used to say South Asian drum 'n' bass, and I don't even think that's true anymore. Electronic music is such a vast landscape. And I feel like we draw on electronic music in every form, and we put in a lot of South Asian influences, and that's where we go. Sometimes DJs will be doing a straight drum 'n' bass set, or you know, everyone's on the electro kick now. It can go in lots of different directions. It's very eclectic.

And as you start getting into your own productions, how are they evolving?

As an artist, I really have to assess my process and how I work. Production has become a real hurdle. I think the whole idea of producing something is very daunting, and I feel like the production work I've done, if it's an assignment, I can do it. And I still feel like it's just as creative an endeavor as if it was organically from my mind. Like I did this documentary, I did the music supervision, and I produced three music pieces for it, and it was great, I thought it was fine. It's an industrial project, so I'm not makin' any records off it; those pieces are very interstitial, they're not tracks, full-fledged; but it was great, I learned a lot. And that worked for me. And a little over a year ago, same thing—a movie producer needed two tracks, and I banged them out with a friend. One of them was very commercial-sounding. But I still had fun doing it, and even within that, you want to still get your essence across. So what if it's commercial; make it fuckin' banging. So I've been trying to formulate ideas more—I'm trying to create the assignment now.

But I do feel like over the years I've learned a lot more about production, and I have the concepts down in a way that I didn't have a few years ago. And now it's technically just about executing them. And I think, for me, a lot of it has to do with having somebody to work with. I do not enjoy doing it alone, and I need feedback. Like I can't DJ in my own head, by myself; I want the response. So when I started DJing Basement Bhangra, when I really became more serious about being a DJ, I worked with my partner then, Joy. And he's since moved on; I felt like we were a good team. And now I've made friends with this producer in Britain, and potentially we'll be doing some stuff together. Even if I work in the studio and he's engineering the stuff, I feel like, that's fine. It was really good 'cause I went there in January and I met with him and felt like he was talking to me seriously; he wasn't thinking I'm a dumb chick, you know? We were sharing information, and it felt really positive.

We've talked about this before, but the business side of producing events . . .

Runs me into the ground! Quote me.

You handle most of it yourself, right?

Yeah, it's two of us now. It's definitely eased the load up. But still, at the end of the day, it's the DIY problem of doing it all yourself, not having a tremendous financial backing—like no one's underwriting me; I am. You win some, you lose some. And you realize, when you do things in a business mode, things cost a lot more money. All of a sudden, it's like, how many press kits am I gonna print up? How much ink am I gonna go through? Shit like that, you know, it starts adding up. Things like you can't have downtime on your computer, or you can't have things break on you. You're constantly hustling. You know, people think it's luxurious that I have a car in New York City, but I fuckin' use that thing all the time. It's an investment, it helps me get a lot more done.

But doing all the business stuff must limit the time you have to work on music.

I think it's about the kind of energy you need to do that stuff, and I think it really saps me. Now that I have someone working with me who's very smart and doesn't need things spelled out, I think it's gonna free me up to work more on music.

I also want to figure out a way to integrate other things that I enjoy about being more of a creative director. I like producing shows. I do like breaking talent, I love doing it, I like being the first to do it in America and bring people over—that's exciting to me. So I want to keep doing it all, as much as I can.

I'm interested in getting your opinions on women and music technology—like why there are still relatively few women producers, although it seems like progress has been made with DJing.

It's great. We are making lots of progress. It's not a big deal anymore. It's not like, Oh my God, there was a girl DJ!—you don't say that anymore. I mean, I think it's about socialization, fundamentally. Even with my gigs, even though I work with very sensitive males, the technology and the gender thing, it's so deep, and it's so right there! I do workshops, and all I need is one guy in the workshop, and fifteen women, and he's up front and center! Did we do that thing together at CMJ?

Yes. [We participated on a panel of women who DJ and produce electronic music, at the CMJ Music Festival in New York in 2000. The event was promoted as an introductory workshop on DJing and production, particularly for women and girls interested in learning. But the audience consisted primarily of men who, when asked by Rekha, admitted that they were already DJs.]

Well, I made a point of asking how many people in the room were DJs, 'cause the workshop was explicitly about kind of a "101" survey of how to DJ, and I guess because they were DJs they were interested in the topic, but I really felt like . . .

It was more about testing our knowledge.

It was more about testing our knowledge than gaining anything. And I felt like I made it very clear there when I said: Oh, you just wanna know if we know what the fuck we're talking about.

Yeah, I think it's there, it's there a lot with all forms of technology, not just music and music production. I mean, I feel the way men share knowledge, share information, boast about knowledge—it's all part and parcel. And I think unless women are empowered more at an earlier age . . . Earlier when women are growing up, they do better at math; after a certain age, it drops off. Why? It's socialization, it's so cultural. And there's all these sexual, gender implications loaded with that, so if you are a women that's technically adept, then you have to deal with more stereotypes.

The one thing I try to teach in my DJ workshops is, I like to start with the equipment cased, and assemble the gear, do the setup, and make it as tactile as possible. I think that a lot of the hesitation is touching: touching equipment. You have to touch it! You can't be afraid of it; you can break anything, but you have to be able to not be afraid. It's a needle—it breaks, you buy another one.

But I think the gender stuff is still there; I walk into stores, or I go record shopping . . . it just doesn't stop. And because at my gigs often I am the promoter as well as the DJ, I totally get ignored as the DJ. They only see me as the promoter. Which, maybe that's just the trappings of being a promoter and a DJ. But I feel like there's never the credit due on the other end.

What are your thoughts on the gender politics of bhangra, both in the lyrics . . .

They're horrendous! They're terrible.

. . . and on the dance floor, when men often seem very much in control of the dance space?

Yeah, I struggle with that all the time, a lot. I don't know what to do about it. But I feel like in club spaces—and there are plenty of other club spaces that some of those issues come up, in hip-hop spaces and stuff—I think it's part of clubbing, it's part of life. There are those politics, and I think they're cultural, and I also think they're about men and women in dance spaces and what happens and what our expectations are; all of that, alcohol, part of the nature of clubbing can be that way. That's the way it is, and we try to do our best to deal with it.

Bhangra, in terms of the content and the lyrics, it's a pretty male-dominated sport. I see a lot of similarities with hip-hop, just in the way it's seen, consumed—all of that—valorized in the same way. What's the difference between the bhangra thug and the hip-hop thug? Not much difference. That whole style, there's a level of machismo attached to it. And the lyrics, a lot of them talk about Punjab, and this idyllic homeland that doesn't exist, a lot of it's just about dancing, wooing the women; it's about many things.

Do you see yourself doing this kind of thing, DJing, promoting . . .

Forever? Yeah. Fuckin' 'til the day I die. I hope it gets easier; it won't. I hope it gets more profitable; it may, it may not. I'm just really happy walking away, creating things. That's the ultimate high for me, to have a hand in creating something. Part of me wants to have my run doing DJ stuff, holding onto my own, but also running things from a more "creative director" point of view, bringing it back into community work. I think I'm in this phase now where I'm still building it, and after a point, I can build it enough so it comes back to me being able to really pick and choose what I do.

: : :

From 2006 to 2007 Rekha was an artist-in-residence at the Asian/Pacific/American Studies Institute at New York University, where she developed a radio documentary about bhangra. She also toured North America in support of her first mix CD, *Basement Bhangra* (Koch Records, 2007).

Giulia Loli
(DJ Mutamassik)

Giulia Loli was born in Italy to an Egyptian mother in 1973. She moved to the United States when she was five, spent her formative years in Rust Belt areas of West Virginia, Pennsylvania, and Ohio, and relocated to New York City at age twenty-two. As DJ Mutamassik, her live sets and studio productions combine traditional Egyptian and pan-African musics with hardcore and hip-hop beats, fusing rhythmic energy with political awareness. This sound is evident on her solo release *Masri Mokkassar: Definitive Works* (Sound-Ink, 2005) and *Rough Americana*, her collaboration with the guitarist Morgan Craft (Circle of Light, 2003; see also Moten 2008). In addition to these projects, she has worked with George Lewis, Butch Morris, Marc Ribot, and many other experimental composers and improvisers.

I first heard Mutamassik at Frank's Lounge in Fort Greene, Brooklyn, where I also performed between 2000 and 2002. We didn't connect for an interview until later but nonetheless had lively e-mail exchanges in February 2003 (when I was in Rhode Island and Giulia was in New York), and again in October 2006 (after I moved to Montreal, and she to Italy).

: : :

February 2003

Tara Rodgers: Has music always been a big part of your life?

Giulia Loli: Absolutely! My parents both loved to dance and were always blasting music around the house—mostly African, South American, and everything in between (James Brown, Jimi Hendrix, Muhal Richard Abrams, Chopin, Tarantella, Oumm Kalsoum). I started playing piano early and jumped around on sax, violin, and whatever else I could get my hands on. My older brother and I were big hip-hop fanatics until I was about twelve, at which point I started getting into other stuff. By thirteen, I was deep into punk rock, started really forming some strong political opinions (with guidance from my favorites at the time, Dead Kennedys). Simultaneously, I started really getting into classical European music, especially baroque music. I can still point to my influence in its mathematical, relentless rhythmicality, counterpoint, etc. This led me to study the cello at fifteen and join some punk-rock/experimental bands playing cello and drums. I was also always in various choirs from kindergarten to ninth grade singing the usual repertoire of Latin hymns, English madrigals, pop tunes like "Lean on Me," etc. Until now I've overlooked its importance in my musical development. I remember around seventh or eighth grade I really wanted to start singing the alto parts and the teachers were always keeping me as a soprano or mezzo-soprano. This pissed me off to no end. There was always that predilection for the rhythm section, but also harmony and its cousin—dissonance.

All through college, I also worked in the library in the music resource center. My job was to play people music, dig out parts of scores (not to mention mindless data entry). I was always a natural archivist. As early as I can remember, I would obsessively make loops from tape to tape of parts of songs that just drove me nuts—so good I couldn't get enough of them—that inner "spark-plug" going off every time. I'd sit there for hours doing that, happy as ever. In college, I was in a lot of bands and also had friends who invited me to guest on their radio shows. I started by playing cassettes of Egyptian folk music and reciting some absurdist political manifestos. Then I started DJing once I moved to New York in '95.

Why did you want to be a DJ?

In retrospect, it seems natural because of my music library days. (Funnily, one of the first records I ever bought back in the early '80s was "Last Night a DJ Saved My Life.") Mainly though, I was dancing every night in New York (mostly jungle parties—my favorite DJ was Cassien) and eventually I just wanted to hear what got me psyched. Also, I had just come back from a trip to Egypt before moving to New York and brought with me a suitcase full of cassettes. I was so overwhelmingly excited about this Egyptian dance music that I just wanted everyone to hear it. I was like a traveling salesman for this stuff. I was going around to each friend's house to play it to each individual. When I

DJ Mutamassik in her studio, 2006. PHOTO BY STUDIO SPIRIT.

finally got offered a spot at SoundLab in '95, it seemed like the most efficient solution for my obsession.

How did you choose "Mutamassik" as your DJ name?

I found it in an Arabic language book. It means many things . . . mostly "stronghold," as in someone who hangs on firmly to their beliefs (the extreme of this is fanaticism). To Egyptians, it has a religious or cultural connotation, usually a bit old-fashioned. For Saudis, it can mean a "holding" as in a bank or share "holding."

How would you describe the mix of music that you play? What musical traditions or styles do you draw upon?

Afro-centric breakbeat. Relentless rhythms from the immigrant sound sources. First-generation punk jaw electronic pan-African derivatives. Depending on what kind of night it is now, I'll interject all of my influences, from Sun Ra to punk rock to hardcore to hip-hop to jungle to dancehall to soukous to Egyptian baladi. I mostly enjoy hard syncopated beats. I really started very specifically doing jungle/

hip-hop mixes all the while mixing in Egyptian breaks as well. I would say I got my early chops from the hardcore jungle parties I was spinning at (Konkrete Jungle, Rumble Sessions, etc.).

Do you have favorite record stores or sources for vinyl that you've found either locally or on your travels?

I used to shop at Throb, initially, and then Breakbeat Science and Rock n Soul. I'm not motivated by much coming out in the stores these days as far as dance music goes, and I don't find the surplus cash to buy records with either. That usually gets funneled into gear. Lately, I'll go to Beat Street (for hip-hop and dancehall). I'll stop by A-1 sometimes to poke around for something really eccentric. But my favorite shops are in Paris and Brussels. They have African-Arabic stuff just busting out of the seams there. The Clignoncourt market in Paris is the best for older stuff. The old people selling dusty records on the side of the road, too. The promo vinyl people send me has been the best bet lately (as far as fresh and alive go).

181

For the tracks that you produce, what gear are you using? Any particular piece of gear that inspires you to create, and why?

I use Cubase VST, Akai S3000, E-mu SP-1200 and a minimum of outboard stuff (I like my Lexicon MPX-1), and a nice warm 24-channel Topaz board. I love the combination of MIDI and digital audio. I started on an early version of Cubase on the Atari ST1040, and the mistakes it would make would be awesome! I can't get that loose on the Mac G3 or G4! Of course, they can do a lot more, but are so uptight relatively. There's a lot of exciting soft and hardware out there . . . Now they're actually creating programs that simulate what it's like for someone to misuse gear—it's too easy. The beauty of technology is using it in ways other than the manufacturer's instructions. This is how DJing began (subverting the brainiac's invention in a brazen display of resourcefulness and artistry)! Technology is only a tool—so even if I might get ideas from a piece of gear, the inspiration comes from a source way beyond the gear or even the people who made the gear. Gear doesn't bring tears to my eyes (not even when I can't fix it).

What's your method for putting tracks together? Are you sampling from vinyl? Do you set out to make something in particular or do you mess around in the studio and see what comes out?

I started out strictly sampling from vinyl and cassette. My intention, at first, was to exalt these old, crusty Egyptian tapes, sort of remaster and remix them. Mix them with hip-hop beats to draw the musical dots very clearly. I felt that the first people that it would touch would be heads in search of cultural roots (re-education through music, in a way, because growing up in Ohio we never learned about the vastness and depth of African civilization, only the humiliation and savagery—truly scandalous) then it would just take its course. Now that I feel I've done that initial thing, I'm pretty aggravated with sampling (always some exceptions), but I feel a responsibility now to play stuff and record it myself. I've been recording percussion, cello, background vocals, rappers, guitarists, bassists, and getting into playing my own drum loops now on my trap set. This is the ultimate goal. Sampling can still be an amazing thing as long as one does something really new with it. For me, it was more of what was available at the time. Just making tracks by any means necessary. Now, I can't set out to do anything specific because the creative process makes me run off in so many different tangents.

What musical elements most inspire you—rhythm, melody, bass, texture, something else?

Rhythm, rhythm, rhythm. I didn't wanna have anything to do with singers or lyrical/melodic elements in the beginning. I was actually very antagonistic towards those elements because I was so fed up of the ratio of things . . . melody=foreground, rhythm section=background, which has so much to do with cult of personality and not with music. Or the tradition of the virtuosic jerk-off soloist, etc. I'm still rhythm-obsessed but I'm open to the fact of using the melodic in the same way that Egyptians do, actually . . . to counterpoint the beat, to make it pop out of the background and not the other way 'round.

How did you learn DJing and production skills? Mostly working by yourself, or working with other people?

DJing I learned by myself. Bought a pair of Technics from some teenagers from Staten Island who owed some party promoter dough. Locked myself in my bedroom for months upon months and hacked it out on my knees on the floor. Production came later when someone offered me to work in their studio because they saw the relativity of what I was trying to do with the Egyptian and Afro-American. They sat me

Excerpt from DJ Mutamassik's studio notebooks, 2006. "6.8.05 . . .
jam w/beats (Sa'aidi etc.) that you love (record them as base tracks)
then erase them & leave your track that is within that feel . . . 7/2/05
. . . again starts pretty, almost wistful—then as if storm 'out of the blue'
—dark & scary. (but you can see the storm cloud coming at you)."
COURTESY OF GIULIA LOLI.

down a few times for the basics and then let me figure things out. It
helped immensely to be working in an environment where there were
people who knew what was going on to ask for tech support.

*I've seen you perform a couple times at Frank's Lounge, but I hear that
you've been traveling around the world lately. What are some memorable performances?*

I just played in Dubai this September—that was a trip!—at a club
and in their Virgin Megastore in this enormous mall. Dudes walking
around in their dash-dishes (traditionally gulf garb) juxtaposed with
Arab Britney Spears look-alikes just staring at me trying to suss it . . .
like the Arab Las Vegas . . . very weird. But the club gig was great.

Local breakdancers that just went ballistic and couldn't believe some American-Egyptian was so on their wavelength.

Traveling is an awesome factor though. My favorite gig was in Brussels a few years ago at a free outdoor street festival. Those are the best, 'cause you get grandma, the kids, the businessmen, the freaks, the immigrants, etc. Clubs, in comparison, have become horribly banal as kids are so jaded and just wanna party and get sodomized by the bass (not all clubs of course).

I guess I've been pretty nostalgic about Paris, too. The huge North African community really gets my shit there (and I get theirs). I mean, it's like the Puerto Ricans and Dominicans in New York who have figured out how to "assimilate" (as much as the government will let them) and not let go of their cultures, and imbue everything around them with their flavor.

Cairo was mostly stressful to play in because they're very proud of their music (all surrounding Arabified countries look to Egypt for the hot, swinging style), so to accept anything else (especially some half-breed flipping it) is, needless to say, very difficult. But I felt it was very important to be there. I learned so much.

Stockholm was cool, other than a middle-aged Swedish woman demanding that I play some "real, Oriental music" in the middle of one of my sets and cursing my music as "not Oriental." Wow! The authority that critics give themselves! I guess she wanted the Sheherezade, 1001 nights, harem, genie fantasy.

So what makes a successful or satisfying performance for you? A good mix? Making people dance? Communicating some sort of message or vibe with your music?

One of the most successful gauges is when people are like: I've never heard anything like that before. Or even just seeing the expressions on their faces. Making people dance is great, but too easy. I'm more satisfied to flip their wigs a bit, make them see something in a way they hadn't thought about, and/or make them feel that thing that can't be described in words. Euphoria isn't quite it . . . that intangibly sublime quality of music that makes all feel connected to the greater pulse that runs the universe. Combining that with a cultural and political awareness (I'll mix in Jello Biafra playing the dual role of the U.S. secretary of war and Margaret Thatcher or a speech that I'll hack up by Charles de Gaulle or a hard beat with an Algerian rapper mixed in and out of an American rapper)—attempting interconnectedness, relativity, and an adrenaline rush. I guess you could call it incitefulness/insightfulness. It's like, OK, let's recognize these worldly issues that divide us and bind us all (religion, politics, race, etc.) so that we can then move on to inspiration. Music is so amazing like that because it can teach us about the world and things and each other and languages and cultures, and then transport us beyond that same "knowledge" into another sphere completely.

Do you feel that gender is a significant element either in your professional experiences and/or in how you express yourself musically?

No, although I'm sure there's some scientific argument that my ovaries and estrogen have something to do with something, but if that were the case, I would say then that I must have a high level of testosterone. I also think so much of it is how we've been socialized. You know, the stereotypes that girls sing and are melodic, and therefore melody is feminine, and rhythm is hard and belligerent and aggressive, and therefore masculine. But when you look at how many cultures the women have been making the drums and beating them as well, you realize that we're living in a secretive Masonic society or something that has tried to make official rules to some old invented game between men and women. I really don't think gender has much to do with my creative impulses. I know this to be true from my earliest memories of those impulses. There was and is something so incredibly pure and transcendental about art. It goes so far, way beyond hormones and tits and dicks and twats, quite frankly. I just stick to this truth that I knew when I was little and not get caught up in bullshit.

It's interesting that just based on my sound and name people have mistaken me for a man. I used to get a great kick out of it because I felt somehow that I had a very strong, present legitimacy in people's minds—more so as a man than a woman—now I realize how sad this truth is—what it says about how we think about sex. In my opinion, the more interesting people in the world are those who recognize both their female and male aspects. That's why I can't get with neither the self-pitying whining girly circles, nor the man-hating dykes, nor the gash-fearing fags, and especially not the "manly"-type pigs.

What are your plans for making music in the future? Do you think you'll be DJing, say, twenty years down the road?

I don't know if I'll be DJing in clubs in twenty years. I'm not super social. Operating in large crowds can be draining. I do love using the turntables more and more as instruments (punching them to play bass or percussion, tapping the needle head, etc.). My dream for the future is being more solid in the studio. Really having a full-on production company (albums/soundtracks, etc.), playing drums and setting up all my instruments to record (right now I only have one Shure SM58 mic). Also, combining my first discipline (visual arts) into the company—making album/book covers, etc. That's more where I want to be. Hopefully having the platform to get messages across. I find it increasingly harder to do work that doesn't address what's going on in the world. That's what is so shameful about the industry in general, all these people that are adored and followed all over the world (e.g., Puff Daddy, etc., etc., etc.) who have the largest megaphone to their lips and only take that opportunity to flaunt their wealth and shove more corrosive vomit (hookers, hookers, hookers; pimps, pimps, pimps) down their young fans' throats!

October 2006

You recently wrote a letter to a hip-hop magazine addressing the gendered stereotypes which operate in their depictions of music and technology, and the expensive gear and lifestyles that are promoted in commercial hip-hop. Do you want to discuss any of this here?

Yes, and isn't it funny that that's precisely the note our interview from 2003 ended on? And here we are three and a half years later and it almost seems worse than before. Worse, because if there are more women involved in the hands-on production side of things since 2003, you don't see it. You see much more pussy/$ slavery than skills.

I wrote that letter to *Scratch* totally enraged [see Golianopoulos 2006 and Loli 2006]. This is a magazine dedicated to hip-hop beat-making/production in the strictly "active" sense as opposed to the "passive" sense, and they're asking, Where's the female rappers?! What a dis to all the women out here busting our asses! I don't want to see women doing it just to see women doing it and go, That's progress ain't it? Think about the rationale of equality for minorities where the black woman becomes the CEO the same way the man did: through ruthless, back-stabbing, greedy Machiavellianism . . . and people applaud these conquests. I've been too disappointed time and time again with the type of feminist, affirmative action that allows opportunistic assholes or undedicated slackers to get over with minimal technical requirements. I know there are fiercely skilled women out there and I am excited and positive about that. What I've seen more of lately though is coquettes with drum machines or turntables or even guitars, which they barely know how to use (with no visible attempts at pushing past necessary learning curves). My three-year-old can tap out a hot beat on my SP (and sequence it!) better than some get-overs out here. No, I want to see women with the life or death FIRE a.k.a. Holy Spirit for this. For that matter, I want to see men and women with that.

The whole hooker thing is not just relegated to video hos and hookers who've made a career out of obvious sex antics anymore, but has trickled down as acceptable if not expected from everyone (pop and underground alike). The new feminist motto defending this seems to be saying: If you're not showing and shaking your tits and ass, you are not comfortable with your womanhood, therefore you are not "liberated." I'm not mad at nudity. What annoys me is when I feel like someone is working overtime to deliberately, stereotypically, desperately force seduction through manipulation of their sex. There are exceptions like Prince, from back in the day, who ignited some baffling and exciting gender mysteries in young minds. He was not doing the stereotypical male sex thing and he was a multi-talented force to be reckoned with. But being known for one's ass starts overshadowing whatever artistic talents one has (if any). It's a very limited game. It's also a pathetic start for the kids who it's aimed at. Like I've always believed, pop stars have a lot more influence on kids than politicians. And who is coming up next, if not the kids? Even though this debate seems to relate mostly to the commercial music world, everyone is affected. It's all a trickle-down from the over-consumptive, extreme capitalist imbalance without which there would be no Wahabis, Taliban, Zionists, Hezbollah, Christian Right . . . Extreme actions, extreme reactions . . . I cannot just nestle myself away into the intelligent arms of the avant-garde, making my high-art in peace ignoring the war outside.

There is a positive side to things getting worse in this technological "democracy" (albeit limited democracy) that we're living in as well. (I've always wondered if it needs to get apocalyptic, slash and burn, phoenix-rising-from-the-ashes style.)

187

The obvious positive to the technological democracy is that ANY-BODY can do it, explore, experiment, make it happen, put records out. Setting off creative bombs, empowering budding artists with the resources to become self-reliant.

The negative is that ANYBODY can do it, live their "fifteen minutes," role-playing in the noble threads of "artist," playing gigs, being on magazine covers, being the sizzling it shit, etc. You get the feeling that some people doing this electronic/DJ/digi thing are gonna wake up when they run out of hype and ideas and find their true or resigned calling as accountants or corporate computer programmers or something more "sensible" or at best, recognize that they're not artists or musicians and instead get involved in the business/organizational side of it, e.g., running a record label, programming festivals, managing artists, etc.

The world needs them too.

This artist shit is not for everyone.

As a result, a lot of tech-based music is being or will be demystified, unveiled off-to-see-the-Wizard-style. While critics/people were a bit worshipful of certain cutting-edge electronic music scenes in the recent past, as they get a glimpse into how the music is made and how much of the technology does the work, they'll become increasingly disenchanted. Perhaps even angry that certain individuals were taking advantage of their ignorance. And then, hopefully, there will be a cleaning of the slate. A purging of the hiding of the above-mentioned lack of ideas, vision, guts, etc., behind the veil of expensive gear and software. Inversely, the people who are pushing the technology in innovative ways will be more appreciated because the world will better understand what they've been up to in the lab all this time.

If the Fire is strong, it will come out through a spoon, a leaf, a four-track, whatever. It's not about having the "right" monitors to do your "correct" mix on with the "proper" compressor on your bass. King Tubby was dropping the whole damn Echoplex and recording that. Lee "Scratch" Perry was doing all kinds of acrobatic juju on the faders. It doesn't have to be about dub. You can apply that to anything, be you a doctor, artist, chef, mechanic, chemist, farmer, carpenter, geologist . . .

Which leads to the next point: the mystery and vagueness behind the term "producer." I was straight-up shocked to read this cover story in *Wired* magazine a few years ago on the "Super Producers" about how almost all of them have long-time engineers [Levine and Werde 2003]. I'm not gonna front and say I can walk into any studio in the world and rock their SSL mixing board overnight (but I can with time, and that's the attitude women and men have to have to break out of this bullshit). There are times when one is given opportunities to work in various situations/studios different from one's own and that situation or studio comes with the engineer(s) who knows that gear inside and out. Fine. But these "Super Producers" are being heralded as the most professional, creatively and technically proficient production masters of our time! And they've got this Wizard of Oz character really running the gear? When I was coming up learning to produce everyone I knew who was producing at the time was responsible for their tracks from the inception to the mix. The only thing most people had an engineer for was to master the finished tracks . . .

My new works are not heavy on other peoples' samples like previous work. If anything, I'm sampling my own drums, cello, accordion, percussion, etc., playing this time. A vital evolution. I've never been a formidable instrumentalist. Just able to speak my own language with what I know. Just being honest with everything that I come from and am.

: : :

Since our interview, Mutamassik has been working on a new solo album, *That Which Death Cannot Destroy*, and another Rough Americana collaboration.

Jeannie Hopper

Jeannie Hopper moved to New York City in 1987 from her hometown Milwaukee to pursue a career in broadcast journalism. As a news reporter for the Pacifica radio station WBAI, she covered volatile political movements in El Salvador, Nicaragua, Panama, and Palestine, all the while returning to the underground dance music scene in New York for relief from the intensity of her work. Eventually, she brought her reporting skills and impassioned spirit to the music community and founded Liquid Sound Lounge (LSL), her radio show that has run weekly on WBAI since 1993. It is a hub for the house and groove music underground. Everyone who's anyone has passed through the studio on her show; the long list of DJs and guests includes Little Louie Vega, Carlos Sanchez, Nickodemus, Sarah Jones, Cheb I. Sabbah, and Roy Ayers. LSL grew into a record label and promotion company, dedicated to breaking new talent and promoting the soulful music and spoken word Hopper has always championed. She also DJs at parties, notably the LSL semiannual boat cruises off Chelsea Piers.

In addition to LSL, Jeannie is now a station manager for WPS1 Art Radio, the Internet radio station of P.S.1 Contemporary Art Center, where she curates DJ Sessions and produces shows that showcase her interviewing skills as well as her musical knowledge. She has been a supporter of Pinknoises.com, performing at the launch party in 2001 and informing people about the site on WBAI. We met for this interview at her Manhattan apartment in November 2002.

: : :

Tara Rodgers: You're known for playing an eclectic array of soulful music. What first turned you on to this music?

Jeannie Hopper: When I was seven years old, my parents took me to the roller-skating rink, and I fell in love with the music there. At that time, you'd hear P-Funk, Rick James, Ohio Players, Grandmaster Flash, Sugarhill Gang. That was the early days of hip-hop, when it was first formulating. A lot of soul and funk was played there, and there was a lot of boogie-ing down and dancing. Really, music for me was just an escape. I always loved it. I went through listening to many different styles, from different roommates in college, friends that were into dancing, and friends that liked new music—which was bands in the late '80s like the Chili Peppers. So music was always kind of there for me. And my parents and grandparents are dancers; they do a lot of ballroom dancing, and different styles of couple dancing. My parents even competed, so dancing was always around in the family and I got to dance at an early age.

I get bored with one style, and my drive has been to get as much great music onto the radio show and into my club sets that was sent to me and really stood out on its own. That shaped my sound, and ultimately, on an unconscious level, turned into a style I'm known for.

How did you end up coming to New York?

I came here in '87 to finish my degree in broadcast journalism at Hunter College, and I knew I was going to stay. It was supposed to be a junior year in New York program, but I was like, No way! That's my in! [Laughs] I'd never visited here; I don't know why I had such a drive that I needed to be here. I had a lot of energy, and I knew that in Milwaukee I was not even tapping into it, because there just wasn't the outlet.

And how did you get involved with the music scene here? Was it through going out dancing?

The music scene here, it was a little tough. When you first come, there's the obvious things that are promoted to you, which you'd see easily. At that time, the Limelight was big, the Tunnel, Palladium; I think the first club I went to was the Cat Club. A lot of it was just being on a college budget, like, Wow, we get *a* drink with our entry fee! And then it was about trying to figure out where the other places are, because these places were just so mainstream; that's what they felt, they were so huge. I realized I like a little smaller, more intimate setting or something out of the ordinary.

I ended up at Sound Factory, and we found a lot of places on the Lower East Side. Save the Robots, which was an illegal after-hours party at the time. David Mancuso's Loft on Third Street, and another place called Hotel Amazon, which was a party in an old schoolhouse on Rivington Street. It was an empty building, and they would set up in the cafeteria, with the decks on these big cafeteria tables, swaying with the weight! It was wild. There was a lot of people from the neighborhood—Puerto Rican and Dominican—that would hang out in there, and such a hodgepodge of people from all over the city who knew about it word-of-mouth. And then the World, of course, on Third Street and Avenue C, which was a great club. Run DMC played, and Sinead O'Connor played there before she was known. So once I found those spots, you know . . .

But to get my big fix there was Sound Factory (the original one on 28th Street in Chelsea). Sound Factory was strictly gay. The bouncer noticed we'd come a couple weeks in a row, and was like, These girls, they haven't figured it out yet! [Laughs] He would say, You gotta come in with a guy. Just go down the street, hang out. So we would latch on to some guy down the street. To me, the thing about Sound Factory, it was *the* most phenomenal sound system. It was incredible. Nothing like it, that I'd ever experienced. And Junior [Vasquez] was playing very different then. The music hadn't gone any higher than 110, 115 beats per minute yet. Certain songs that I know were anthems back then—one of them, we used to think it was so commercial, so fast—I'll pull it out now, and I'm like, Oh my God, it was 110 beats per minute!

Also I found out about Shelter, which opened in '91. Once I found Shelter, that was the ultimate spot. Great sound system, but it was stuck to that soulful side. The crowd, too, was just a bit more underground. There was a lot of different sort of circles, or tribes of people that were hanging out there.

Were there DJs then whose sound particularly inspired you, or who you would consider an influence now?

Honestly, I was going to these places, I had no idea who the DJ was. I somewhat had an idea who the DJ was at Sound Factory because people would talk about Junior. But I really didn't know. I didn't learn 'til later who the DJs were. Later on I found out who David Mancuso was. Later on I found out that it was Romain, Smash, and Carlos Sanchez that were spinning at Robots. Later I found out that when I was going to the World it was probably a mixture of people like David Morales, Frankie Knuckles, and Larry Levan. And of course Timmy [Regisford] at Shelter. I still haven't been able to figure out who that was at Hotel Amazon; there's a couple people that switched off. But I did find out that one of the side rooms happened to be Andrea Clarke, who's on WBAI, she has a show, *Sister from Another Planet*.

It was a very cool time. I guess everything has its time, but right now, we're all looking around trying to see what's going to be next. A lot of those spots, what's important about them is that they lent themselves to culture being able to flourish and grow. And these sort of became movements, and became scenes, and became a style that then emanated all over the world. New York was really on the map for that, especially since the Paradise Garage, which I also didn't learn about 'til later, in that everybody was trying to emulate those days at the Garage. It's kind of sad right now, 'cause we're going through, as everyone calls it, the *Footloose* time! [Laughs]

Right, no dancing! [Laughs]

No dancing allowed. Which is just so absurd. We're gonna look back at this and be like, *Whaaat?* Can you believe that, that they told people that they couldn't dance? [see Katz 2000]. And it's *so* political, because getting cabaret licenses is very expensive, and only if you use the city's "recommended expeditor" will you get it faster, so I was told from one club's experience in going through the process.

Tell me how Liquid Sound Lounge got started.

I started volunteering for WBAI right away when I got to New York. I worked for a professor at Hunter College doing work-study in the communications department. I was really into TV and film, and that's what my goal was. But another woman doing work-study said, Have you ever done radio? Why don't you come up to BAI, they're doing this special day for women. It was a political satire, kind of skit show. So I went, thinking if anything, it'd be easy to put visuals to it, get a little practice on the audio side and putting a story together. But then I just slowly, really fell in love with radio. The idea of no images, and no preconceived notions. The idea of BAI, too, being noncommercial and completely paid for by the listeners, therefore giving the producers complete freedom on the air. There's no censorship.

This is so rare now in American radio.

And it's so raw. You know when you're tuned to BAI, it's got a certain sound to it. It's a very politically active station. In college, and even now, I was very politically active. I was obsessed with trying to get the truth out. In 1989, when I was twenty-four, I had an opportunity to go to El Salvador and that's when I observed firsthand how the commercial press operated in regard to what they saw and what was reported on, that if I pursued broadcast journalism in commercial media, it would be difficult to report the whole truth. And that was really hard to come to terms with. Especially because when you learn in school about reporting, you learn all these great stories about the muckrakers, yellow journalism, Edward R. Murrow, etc. So I went to El Salvador and subjected myself to some seriously harsh realities, and the harshest thing is the striking realization that it's not being reported on. And the media's right there, and they're all housed in the most expensive hotel, removed from reality. And the State Department comes to them, and gives press conferences in one of the rental halls in the hotel. Some journalists working for the commercial media, however, do try to reach the mainstream with the real story. But I learned that as soon as journalists start to touch on reporting things as they see fit, and the editors find them getting a little too off point from what the station wants revealed, the station sends the reporter off to another country so that he doesn't cause problems raising issues—i.e., reality.

After that I went off to Panama, and to Nicaragua for the first elections after the Sandinistas took over, and then I got into the Gaza Strip and the whole struggle of Palestinians. The first time I went over was when the first Gulf War had ended. I just ended up in these amazing moments in time, like meeting with the gentleman Dr. Haider Abdel Shafi, who became the head of the first Palestinian peace delegation, just when he came from a meeting with U.S. secretary of state George Shultz, and I could feel his emotions from that talk. In Panama I got to meet with [General Manuel] Noriega, and that was a trip, especially considering that a week and a half later the U.S. invaded. So it was a lot of political work that I did for BAI. And in the meantime, I was doing some radio theater work, doing different voices, doing a little bit of sound design and Foley. I kind of got burned out from the political reporting. By the time I was going to the Gaza Strip I felt really numb.

Just from stories, like kids being used for target practice, just for the hell of it. All that stuff, it all rushed back to me from El Salvador and the massacre that happened in Panama. It was pretty heavy. And I didn't like that I was becoming so numb.

During this time, from '89 until '93, I was in these [underground New York music] scenes and dancing, and that was my relief from all this heavy reporting. That's where I would kind of lose myself in the music and just give myself a mental vacation. And it was very important for me, every week, to dance. Especially Shelter. I would go there at like three or four in the morning and stay until four the next day.

Anthony Sloan, the arts director at WBAI, would go dancing with me. I said to him, You know what, we've got to bring this music and this scene, all these great underground things that are going on, to the radio. How people really find solace and a community in the clubs; how people find, when they come to the city, their surrogate family. People find this connection where, they all left places around the country or they felt disenfranchised here or there. It was like a big family gathering or house party of like-minded souls linked through the energy of the music and in a more communal setting. Those are the parties I was going to, and that's the side that I wanted to bring to the radio. And also all these great independent artists and record labels that exemplified the great music that I was hearing, who weren't being exposed on the commercial dial except here and there in late-night mix shows, or the midday mix with John Robinson [on WBLS in New York]. I had no *idea* what on earth I was listening to though, because the music was very faceless and nameless. . . . But I said, WBAI is community radio, and that's the whole point—to give exposure to a community that will gain greater reach through the radio waves.

So I brought up the idea that we should have a show that brings all these people together. I was also really worried that we wouldn't have a new listenership to carry on the legacy of BAI, and I was really driven to bring a new listenership. I know people's radio patterns, where if you don't like what you're listening to, most people are flipping through the dial to find something else. I knew that being in the middle of the dial, I would have this opportunity to grab people with the music. When I got back from my last trip to Gaza in '93, Anthony was like, OK, you have the show! I'm like, *What?* Then I was trying to figure everything out and get it on the air. And I hadn't DJ'd. That's the last thing I ever expected to do.

Jeannie Hopper. PHOTO BY JAMES PORTO.

How did you go about tracking down the music?

Oh, man. The only thing I knew to do was, I went to these clubs, and I had already gotten to know some of the people that ran these parties, 'cause they were used to seeing me. I was kind of talking here and there, and people were sharing: Did you get this record? This is where I get my records . . . So I trailed a bit of that information, and really that's it. It's this very word-of-mouth kind of industry in terms of finding stuff out. And I had cassettes of DJ mixes that people had given me, and so I went around and I would literally play the songs on my Walkman to the person at the record store: Do you know this? I need this . . . Literally, that's how the first music came together. Also at the beginning I would feature a guest DJ a bit more than I do now. Now I get so much product that it's difficult for me to have guest DJs.

I approach the show from a radio perspective, meaning: I receive a lot of product, I prioritize the product, I make sure that it gets on,

I give the information about it, and it's not so much that it's "the Jeannie Hopper show," or it's "a DJ mix by . . ." even though that's kind of what people perceive it to be. It's more of a magazine format radio showcasing more than just a mix of music, but also informative on all aspects of the scene. And it's turned into that I do play my DJ sets like I play on the radio, when people ask me to come and spin. For the first year or two, I wouldn't play out live in clubs. I started a party right away when the show started, but I didn't spin. I was like, No . . . I'm not a DJ! Even though, in the traditional sense, I really was—the term "disc jockey" comes from radio. Slowly my skills improved. I didn't have 1200s up there at BAI.

When I visited the studio you were talking about how old the equipment is.

Oh yeah. We have these digital-pitch, rosewood Technics decks. Those became the standard at radio because you can trigger things to start, so you don't have to turn around to start the turntable or the CD player. But back when I started the show, we had a really old radio board which had pots. So to cue, you basically knocked the pot down to off, and it goes into cue that way. So that was really tough. I couldn't even really mix, because once you knock the pot out of cue, you don't hear cue anymore. And also, there's a two-second delay. So it was challenging. But I'm glad that I learned how to mix on the radio that way, because it made me really play a song for what a song was, and find the natural breakdown, and then bring a record in and mess around with a cappella or ambiences to transition records.

I also worked with a lot of poets, so I would bring poets on the show. I had a lot of music, but I thought there wasn't a lot of thought-provoking vocals. It's still very difficult to find that. You really have to dig. And what BAI really is, is about messages. So to me, the poets were like the heartbeat of the street and what was going on. I would have musicians on too, and that helped to transition the records as well. Besides the show, I was doing a poetry event called Listen and Be Heard with Martha Cinader, a poet who was regularly on BAI and on my show. We did it at University of the Streets, on East Seventh Street, which was a very underground jazz jam spot. Then I created my own series at the Nuyorican Poets Café and Knitting Factory called Wordology + Mixology, focused on my style of matching prerecorded music, beats, and sound effects along with live musicians, in a way that complemented the poets. So in the early days on the show, I had Dana Bryant, Tracie Morris; and performances with Latasha Natasha Diggs, Sarah Jones, Ava Chin, Edwin Torres, the Last Poets, and more. It was like sitting in a hotbed of incredible talent, and now I've watched a lot of people break through and really flourish. It's exciting.

On the show, I took all the scenes I was in—I loved to go hear live music, I loved to hear something that's downtempo to midtempo, and I loved to hear something that's just straight-up house—and I brought all of that together, because those were my musical influences. And the thing that threaded all the music together was that it was soulful and had some sort of live instrumentation or voice. Something that gave warmth and a human soul to it. Or something that was just so freaky. I just love it when there's no category, when somebody's just goin' for it, 'cause that says a lot about the artist.

The show grew. I did weird overnight spots for a while. I was on the first time from three-thirty to six, Saturday night to Sunday morning. I even brought somebody over from a club to perform, and then they had to go back to their party. At that time, besides Shelter I was hanging out at Underground Network, this great party at Sound Factory bar on 21st Street. Little Louie Vega was spinning there, and he would let me come in the booth and just watch him while he was mixing. Really, what I feel that I brought to the show was an alchemy of all these influences from all these different DJs—again, I didn't know their names, I found them out later—that really made an impression on me. And of course it was about getting to know the music that they were playing. In other words, I didn't do it in a very linear way. Sometimes I find a lot of guys approach it that way. They get into this tech talk, like, That was done at such-and-such place, and you can tell that this equipment was used . . . For me, I got one turntable at a time, and my folks bought me a mixer. Slowly I pieced it all together. And because of BAI being very technically challenging, and having worked with a lot of older, analog equipment, it sort of trained me to deal with really crappy equipment. Sometimes I think people can get too out of control with all the new tech toys when there's so much that can be created from something that's so simple.

The ways that you reach people with this music are so different: over the airwaves versus in club spaces.

It's so different. I love radio, without a doubt. The beauty of radio is you can really just go out there. You're not in a club where you have to move a dance floor. You catch people in a real intimate setting: they're at home, they're in their car, they might be Rollerblading or roller-skating with their Walkman on. Especially over the last couple of years, there's a lot of people that know about the show, and now people are coming up to me. Whereas the beauty of radio, which I loved, was that I could keep my anonymity. But it's pretty incredible when people share their experience from the radio. Some, of course, love the house music, but that has also been around the longest and is a lot more understood. It's great too when I come across people that really love that I have this political content, discussions and interviews within the show. I'm always thrilled when finally someone calls and says, Wow, that interview was great. 'Cause I'm like, You know what, you all have to *learn*. You *have to learn* about these people! And you never, ever are gonna have access to this person unless by some chance you happen to be in the scene and you know this person.

The other thing with radio, compared to a club, is that it's not a destination. You're not going to go to a club unless somebody recommends it, and even that night that you go, it might not be a good night. Whereas the radio is always there for you to tune in when you want.

: : :

In April 2008, LSL celebrated its fifteenth year with a DJ performance by Jeannie Hopper and special guests at the BAM (Brooklyn Academy of Music) Café, the first of a series of parties around New York City celebrating the anniversary.

Part 5. Language, Machines, Embodiment

In many electronic music performances, gestures, vocalizations, and instrumental sounds are inextricably entwined with electronic sensors and digital processes. Electronic transformations of voice and language are the domain of the sound artist and poem producer AGF. She describes herself as "a brain person definitely / but also very emotional," and her work foregrounds both modes of expression. Out of frustration with the limitations of familiar language and a desire to be "free from meaning," she began vocalizing computer code. In these compositions, conventionally disembodied and rational phrases of code are infused with a poetics of desire.

In Pamela Z's work, the technologized body itself becomes a tool for manipulating language and narrative structure. Z combines spoken and sung passages—which are grounded in the ways her voice resonates through the bone structure of her face—with electronic transformations of her voice by the BodySynth system. The BodySynth consists of a series of sensors placed around her body that integrate with audio software and enable her to modify her voice with physical gestures. Among other compositional techniques, Z uses looped vocal phrases to reveal how a word can lose its meaning through machine-generated repetitions, or take on new meanings because precise repetitions enable human ears to examine it more closely.

Laetitia Sonami sometimes dreams of taking such symbiotic relationships one step further and having her Lady's Glove instrument grafted into her skin. Yet she enjoys the challenge of adapting her body to an external apparatus in performance, which she compares to the suspenseful choreography of a toreador and bull. Bevin Kelley, by contrast, appreciates that making electronic music is "not a physical thing." After years of toiling to contort her body to conventional practices of playing violin, she prefers that electronic music production be "brain only."

In full cyborgian spirit, Kelley is unafraid to pursue human affinities with animals as well as machines. With Kristin Erickson, she has developed an imaginary world of creatures whose names and pictures accompany some of their Blectum from Blechdom albums. Inhabiting such hybrid animal/alien characters (in the imagination, or sometimes in costume) imposes meaning on otherwise abstract musical projects. So, whether it is laborious or, in Kelley's words, "beautifully transparent," the interfacing of bodies and machines in electronic music facilitates play with the sonic materiality of language, the embodied production of knowledge, and expectations about gender in musical performance.

Antye Greie
(AGF)

Antye Greie, born in 1969, is a self-described "poem producer" who crafts music from her voice and electronic beats and textures, operating along the boundaries between sound-as-language and language-as-sound. She has been active as a musician since 1990 and first gained international attention for her work with the band Laub, which released their debut album on the Berlin-based label Kitty-Yo in 1997. Since then she has released solo albums under the name AGF and collaborated with artists including Vladislav Delay and Sue Costabile. Her first solo album, *Head Slash Bauch* (Orthlorng Musork, 2002), consisted of spoken and sung HTML code and software manuals woven into fragmentary post-pop song structures; her second album, *Westernization Completed* (Orthlorng Musork, 2003), won an Award of Distinction at Ars Electronica in 2004.

Antye was one of the first artists I interviewed for Pinknoises .com's initial publication in 2000, when she was just beginning her solo project. We have kept in touch in the years since, and conducted this second interview over e-mail in June 2005.

: : :

Tara Rodgers: Let's start from the beginning. Where are you from?

Antye Greie:
i grew up in halle-neustadt
a socialist utopia fake socialist dream city
built in the 60s artificially for workers
in east germany

Tell me about your early involvement with music. What music were you exposed to when you were growing up?

when i was small and innocent
the world including my parents brainwashed me with
schlager + blasmusic and all german folk i guess
russian folk as well and east german rock

when i became teenager
i started listening all kind of pop
bee gees beatles

my first groupie thing
freakin out on one person was john lennon
my whole girls room was covered with him

when he got killed i was wearing black in school
for ages

with 14 i got a guitar and i started playing
songs from bob dylan/lennon/all i could get

When did you start making music?

yeah with 14
i wrote songs in the school (mainly peace songs
humans rights etc)
and started a group

Did you have any formal music training?

not really
some voice lessons along the way
i am autodidact

How did you end up making electronic music specifically?

after playing in many male dominated rockbands
i was sick of it
having no control and influences in sounds
i started getting interested in electronic music
i was lucky
somebody sensed my talent

AGF in Finland, 2004. PHOTO BY VLADISLAV DELAY.

somebody gave me a commodore 64 and
a kurzweil keyboard

that was the beginning

when i could buy my first sampler akai 3000
and with atari i was a free person
to do and write whatever i want

it was sooooo exciting
and difficult with midi and shit

but i figured it
back then there was no internet and schools for this kind of thing

the laptop and home studio grew etc

You talk about this a bit in the lyrics to "Westernization Completed,"
but how have you seen things in Germany change within your lifetime?

And have these cultural changes affected the music that you make, or the professional opportunities you've had?

sure

dramatically

growing up in east germany was safe but very restricted
and computers / any object of consume
microphone etc was hard to get

and the travelling
we couldn't leave the socialist countries

it was most influential to realize
that the world is a place i can travel around freely
and it's so colorful

also when my country vanished
the internet came
so i kind of for a while escaped into that space
and updated myself

i don't know what would have happened to me
when the wall never would have come down
i guess at some point it would have become too small for me

What music currently inspires you?

lots of rappers and mcs from all over the world
i always look for original music

interesting beats with interesting vocalists and
things to tell and best is also innovative musical elements

it's hard to get

but also any form of folk
classical music
i like
i just discovered fado

some jazz . . . like miles, coltrane

Are there things going on in the contemporary electronic music and art scene in Berlin that are particularly interesting to you?

sure

but everywhere you know
people in the east . . . ukraine / belgrade
do nice stuff too
there is a special mood now

i know people all over the world doing amazing stuff
a city never really influenced that so immensely for me

there is a few brave and precious persons living in every city

I'm interested in the ways in which you combine code with poetry, particularly on the album **Head Slash Bauch.** *What inspired you to work with phrases of code in this way?*

it was the time i wished to use my voice without
expected content without saying things
i was so fed up being so judged by my words and poetry
and the limitations words have

i also realized that many people get offended easily
by my words and meanings and thoughts
and i thought it was a pity that within that music was unheard

i wanted to be independent on making opinions
stories attitudes messages
to not first reach peoples brains when you open your mouth

i am a brain person definitely
but also very emotional
i wanted to be free from meaning
in the end that created another meaning
which is nice

at that time i was reading a lot of manuals and learned html and
max/msp . . . so i was reading a lot of code and started to
re-design my daily use of words

falling in sleep mode and stuff like that

and also i wanted to test the processed voice
so i just read manuals and code pages into the computer
to check how it sounds
and it sounded amazing

i like contrast

when i was working with the scottish composer
craig armstrong he gave me a very emotional orchestral
piece to sing on

and everything i would sing emotionally would sound like björk
or so over emotional that i felt i need to do something which
    balances the beauty
so i read html code into the orchestral composition
and broke the code a few times into poetry

it turned out very strong

so i discovered the beauty of code on music and poetry

i think in the end it took the balls of me doing it
and craig to really publish it

later i performed this piece with huge orchestras
in barbican london or paris and brussels
me and the code and behind me 3 people
on ancient instruments

What do you enjoy about working with language as a creative medium?

everything

language is the most

it's very creative and in the end part of my main instrument
i am a singer and performer

that's my main skill i guess
with that i walk down different roads
it's interesting

i guess many things people do
have to do with their skills

if people make most amazing beats they most likely
have been drummers since 12

you know what i mean

i was reading poetry as a kid
and wrote poems in my whole childhood

poetry and lyrics were a big thing in east germany
you could express things deeper and differently
in a non-democratic society . . . via poetry

it's a skill too

Is "poem producer" your preferred description of what you do as an
artist? How did you start using that term?

i made the song
poem producer

i am a powerful poemproducer

and i needed a domain name

you have to be something i thought

i don't know what else makes sense to call me

e-poetess is nice too

but mainly it's not very serious :)

it's just annoying how other people name you
(glitch princess or electronic queen eeeekh)
so you better be faster . . . haha

Do you identify with the term "glitch" (or is that just a term that the
media puts on your music)?

i don't know glitch really
it's an american word

glitch [n.]
Haken (< —>) [m.]
Störimpuls von sehr kurzer Dauer [m.]

it's funny

... disturbing factor for a very short time

hahaha

i hope i am disturbing for a life time

;)

in general i am glad if people are creative with calling things

and i understand the need of media and promotion and distribution to find words to sell or people to communicate

it's ok

In your career, which has included working with bands like Laub as well as doing solo work and other collaborations, have you encountered particular stereotypes or obstacles because you are a woman?

well when i was still surrounded by rock musicians yes
but that's over since 10 years ago
since then i am pretty fine ...
i am glad more and more ladies are joining in
that's fun

boys are so competitive and sometimes not very open

girls you can meet them and be friends next day
not always of course

Do you consider gender to be an important aspect of your creative expression?

i wonder.

i guess i am a female
and it plays pretty much a big role

but i grew up in east germany where women were
totally taken for granted being equal

even it wasn't reality all over
cause women had to work double hard
have business life and family

but in my family actually there was a great amount of
equality between man and women
my father cooked every sunday for the whole family and
my mom was working 9–5
there was a career on both sides and so on

there also was no tits and dicks around in media
no pornography or sex sells shit at all
me personal stresses it out all this sex in public

i think sex is personal

i mean i am glad that the world is not prude anymore
and the word dick or similar words are every fifth second in the
    radio :)
or million of half naked asses in tv all the time. it's a personal
choice to switch this on

i like sex and i think it's personal

and i think east germans are known for having a lot of
sex and fun and kids etc

so i kind of grew up genderless

or it wasn't that important you know
didn't play so much a role if you are female or not
i mean of course when you became a teenager
and all this things happen to you

but before that
it wasn't such a training there to feel and look and be female
before you even have tits
we also didn't have products much
even you of course miss them all the time
in a way i am happy i didn't have them
cause it's like i was playing in nature with everybody i liked
and nobody had fancy things
we just had the trees and the old empty places

so i grew up as a human first

which is nice i think

same by the way goes for drugs

they haven't been there
i am glad about that

it's much better to decide the damage you do to yourself when ur
  adult

*Tell me about your process of composing a track. What elements do you
usually start with, and how do you work it up from there?*

i guess i start with some sort of sample/vibe
i found collected or built
often in rather max/msp based patches
then i import that into logic
set tempo and harmony . . . very simple

then very fast i sing / use voice
record many layers
and then process it

lately bass became very important

then i look what's missing
to make it taste good

sometimes
in the end to make people happy
i add melodies

PEOPLE LOVE MELODIES

i am ok without
but i see it's necessary
otherwise it's like you serve food
and it looks loveless or ugly

i have the theory
that really emotional happy expressive people
almost negate melodies in their work
and people who are very introverted and
hide a lot of emotions
they use a lot of melodies

;)

my small theory world ;)

How is your setup or process different for recording vs. live performance?

in studio i love to micro arrange things
like really compose very deeply
go over a song a couple of 100 times

live i am limited
i concentrate on singing performing
and making a good concert
means i touch people

What do you like best and least about the tools you are working with? About working with software vs. hardware?

i like the independence most
that i can create a personal sound alone

or if then in a collaboration

least i like the sound possibilities
the dynamic

when you listen to an orchestra in a good sounding room
100 individual good musicians highly motivated
and they create emotions and a sound which is so dynamic
it gets louder and louder and doesn't distort

that's what i am missing in digital production

and often the soundsystems you play in are limited too

but i am learning

Tell me about your collaborations with Vladislav Delay, your partner in life and (sometimes) music. How did you start working together?

we wanted to work when we met
he was looking for vocalists and i loved his music

then we fell in love
and then it took a long time to make an album
now it looks like we make it

it's not easy
but if it works it's the most beautiful thing to me

Also, I am curious about your experiences working with Eliane Radigue
in the Lappetites project, someone from an older generation in elec-
tronic music history.

she is beautiful
i am so grateful
that i had the chance to meet her
and work with her
i am very lucky

more on a human level
it was so inspiring

she is really cool and warm hearted and
i hope i see her again

it was crazy to have tea with her
and she was sitting beside this crazy huge arp synthesizer
and telling about her life

she made me do work on one ! single sound for 4 days
that was impressive

Tell me about your live work with Sue Costabile, and also the visuals
you have on your website (poem calligraphy/graffiti). Do you consider
visual elements to be an important component of the music you are
making, in live performance or otherwise?

sometimes

i like collaborating with humans i like
sue is one of them
she is amazing and a beautiful person
that's the main thing
she has an incredible technic and is very talented

i like to fuse our both works

live it's nice that the attention is a bit away from me
i have more freedom

unfortunately i don't see what she does in a live situation

the calligraphy is my thing
exploring poetry into different fields than music

the possibilities you have with music / music business
are limited

i don't like that

: : :

Following our extended e-mail acquaintance, Antye and I finally met in person at the HTMLLES Festival in Montreal, October 2007, where we both performed at the closing party. She lives and works in Berlin and often tours accompanied by her young daughter. Her recent album, *Words Are Missing* (AGF Producktion, 2008), shifts away from her earlier focus on poetry and language to explore silence and speechlessness.

Pamela Z

Pamela Z, born in 1956, is a San Francisco–based composer, performer, and sound artist who works with voice, sampling technologies, and live electronic processing. She combines operatic bel canto and experimental extended vocal techniques with spoken word, found percussion objects, and sampled sounds. She performs wearing the BodySynth, a MIDI controller created by Chris Van Raalte and Ed Severinghaus, that translates muscle efforts into MIDI data. With the BodySynth, she can use gestures to process her voice and activate recorded samples via Max/MSP software (Z 2003; Lewis 2007).

Pamela Z has toured the United States, Europe, and Japan, including performances at Bang on a Can at Lincoln Center in New York and the Other Minds festival in San Francisco; she has also received numerous commissions and awards, including a Guggenheim fellowship and the Creative Capital Fund. I first attended one of her performances at the LAB in San Francisco, when I was a graduate student at Mills. We met for this interview in October 2004 over brunch in Chelsea, the day after the New York premiere of *Voci*, her evening-length, solo multimedia performance.

: : :

Tara Rodgers: When did you first become interested in music and sound?

Pamela Z: I don't ever remember not being interested in music. I think I had my first public performance when I was five. I performed with my sister in a talent show in our elementary school, and we sang "La Cucaracha." And I was already using found objects to make sound. There were these little seed pods that would fall out of trees, and we were using those for maracas! As a kid, my father bought us a couple of those

Craig cassette tape recorders, and I figured out how to do overdubbing by bouncing back and forth between two of them. I would make these fake radio shows and do all the parts myself. And then I played viola in orchestra in elementary school through junior high, and sang in choir in high school, and from when I was in about fifth grade, I played guitar and was a singer-songwriter. I studied classical voice when I was in college at the University of Colorado at Boulder, and at the same time was a singer-songwriter playing in clubs. I made my living playing in clubs and cafes from the time I graduated college until I moved to San Francisco in '84. Towards the end of my time in Colorado, in the early '80s, I became interested in experimental music and electronic music, and processing my voice with a digital delay. And that was a huge turning point.

How were you exposed to experimental music?

I had a radio show on KGNU, a public radio station in Boulder. I really got a lot of my new music education from the music library there. I heard recordings of Ned Rothenberg and Laurie Anderson and Pauline Oliveros and Steve Reich, all these different people, and became really inspired by that. My first exposure to using electronics came when I went to a Weather Report concert and saw Jaco Pastorius play his bass through a digital delay. I think he was just using one of those little stompboxes. I went to a music store the next day and said, I want to do that with my voice, and I explained it, and they sold me an Ibanez one-rackspace, one-second digital delay. I took it home, and it literally changed my life. I mean, my poor neighbors! I was up all night, looping and playing with it, and by the morning, I decided I was going to change everything I was doing. I became really interested in repetition; it was my first real exposure to sampling. I had been trying to do more experimental work, and I somehow couldn't break through with the tools that I was using. I couldn't break through my old habits, and I couldn't find a new voice to do something different. When I started working with the delays, that was totally it for me. And delays have remained the mainstay of my gear, although now I'm doing it with Max/MSP.

When you were at the University of Colorado, how did you navigate the differences between your classical voice studies and your gigs as a singer-songwriter?

I was lucky. I had the only voice teacher on the faculty who wasn't like the others. A lot of them would not even let their students sing show tunes. They would say, You can only sing classical music, otherwise you're going to hurt your voice. My voice teacher was totally fine that I was playing rock in clubs, and didn't mind that I tried other things. He encouraged me. So in school I was singing all classical music and outside I was doing all rock and folk. And there was this dichotomy, where people in rock would say that my voice was too trained, and in classical, people would say: Don't sing that music or you'll hurt your voice! And it was through new music that I found out it was possible to combine all these different things, and there was no problem.

In Voci, *you implicate music pedagogy as a means of control—where voice teachers are effectively instructing you what kind of expressions are OK, and what's not. Is that coming out of your own relationship to your training?*

I do think it's really interesting that in Western classical music, when you study with a bel canto teacher, they're very interested in having you go after what's considered to be a correct sound—like looking for a certain tone color that is the right way to sing. And when you get involved in more experimental types of singing, or other, broader views of it, you find that there are all these other colors that you have and can use—and it's not right and wrong, it's just different colors. I appreciate the training because I appreciate learning how to really fine-tune a very specific way of singing. But I really also appreciate the freedom to combine that with other things. When I was making *Voci*, I realized that all of my experimental singing was self-taught, and the only training I have is very classical vocal training. I decided during that year that I would take lessons with non-Western singers, just to see how they teach. And it was so interesting to me that there were so many things in common. For example, they all taught about the mask.

Can you describe what that means?

People who don't sing always think that singing is all about the gut, but actually, a lot of the resonators are in your face. So to get a bright timbre and really project your voice, a lot of it comes from learning how to resonate through the bone structure in your face. It's about

using the nasal passages and things like that. A lot of singers will re-
strict the passage—close the inside of the mouth and get a thinner
tone that way. With bel canto, they really want you to get a dark, rich,
warm timbre—and they also want the brightness to come from the
resonators in your face rather than from restricting. They want you to
really open the back of your mouth and project forward through your
face. That's what the mask is about. And it was interesting that the
overtone singer and the woman who was teaching me Balkan singing
were also talking about the mask.

*Your work often explores the boundaries between sound and language.
I think of Pauline Oliveros's composition* Cross Overs, *where the instruction is to speak a sound until it becomes a word, and speak a word
until it becomes a sound.*

I do have a lot of that in a lot of my work. In my case, it comes from
found text or words being repeated through sampling or looping.
There's something about the perfect repetition of something that
changes it, because your ear begins to hear it differently when it gets
repeated over and over. When a human repeats something, it changes
with each repetition. But when a machine repeats something, it
changes with each repetition because the ear begins to listen to it.
In one piece called *Pearls*, at the beginning, I put a loop in the delay
where I sang, *Pearls, pearls! Pearls, pearls!* And that continued through
the whole song, and I sang and spoke over the top of that. I had so
many people come up to me and say, I love how you took that word
pearl and slowly morphed it to *peril*. They heard the word changing,
but it was the same loop—I didn't change it. I think when you hear
something repeat over and over again, with each hearing you hear another layer. You get to keep reexamining it, and your ear reconstructs
the timbral qualities. You hear different frequency layers within it, and
so it changes the color, it changes the sound of the vowel. All of this
is happening in your ear, but you think that it's happening in reality.
I find that really interesting. I have a lot of pieces where I have a word
or a short phrase that gets looped in the delay, and it begins to either
lose its meaning, because the repetition makes it stop sounding like
a word, or it starts to take on new meaning, because the layering of
it or the repeating of it gives the listener something to chew on and
digest.

Tell me about your choices incorporating various technologies into Voci—*objects like the cell phone and typewriter that mediate the voice and communication.*

In every piece I do, I incorporate technologies in a certain way. I have kind of a love affair with modern, high-tech objects, but I also like the simplicity and directness of mechanical things. And in my lifetime, I've seen so many different technologies come and go, technologies that were once very important and then just suddenly got replaced.

In *Voci*, it's all related to the fact that the voice itself is this technology that we use to communicate with, and a lot of times the voice has to go through these intermediaries, like a telephone. And now machines have voices. When machines first started having voices, it was like a *Lost in Space* monotone. But now, you've got the Macintosh voices, like Victoria—she's so full of angst! When I first heard her, I put the lyrics from an aria [from the opera *La Wally*] into Simple-Text and then hit Speak. And when she said, "Is regret, is regret, is sorrow," I thought, That's more sad than hearing a real person say it, you know? [Laughs] There's something about her that always sounds like there's some kind of distress in her voice. I don't know if it was intentional in how they developed it. But there is something there, to me, about how the machinery doesn't make it less human, it almost amplifies some qualities.

Right. You also make clear in Voci *the degree to which computerized voices are, on a daily basis, essentially telling us how to behave.*

Like when you call United Airlines, and it comes on and says, "I'm sorry, I didn't understand that. Try saying it to me this way." The voice recognition thing has gotten so good now, that it's a little bit confusing emotionally when you're dealing with it, because you start to want to treat it like a person.

Since we're talking about the interactions of humans and machines— when you perform with the BodySynth, your body is so explicitly technologized. Your muscle movements, through the apparatus, control how your voice is processed. When did you start performing with the BodySynth? And technically, how does it work?

Pamela Z in *Voci*, 2003. PHOTO BY LORI EANES.

I've been using it since the early '90s. I liked it so much, because I use gestures a lot anyway, and I wanted to be able to use samplers without standing behind a keyboard or using drum triggers.

The BodySynth has electrode sensors, just like hospital equipment. I put a little gel on the metal contacts, and then put the electrodes against my skin. I usually wear one on each arm, one on my shoulder, and one on my leg. The amount of electricity that's produced by the muscle is measured, and that's sent to a little CPU that turns it into numbers, and those become MIDI data. And that can be interpreted any way that you want to program the computer to interpret it. So it's like having continuous controllers in different muscle groups.

In Voci, *you also take on issues of madness and hysteria, even the history of madwomen in the operatic tradition. I wonder what your thoughts are on this.*

I thought about it a lot when I first started working with technology, and I began to realize that, for example, if I was ever on an electronic music compilation I was usually the only woman on it, and usually the only person using voice. At one point I became interested in people who do extended vocal techniques, wild and interesting things with voice. I wanted to hear men doing it, and I was having a hard time finding it. For the most part, in new music, the people who are well known for doing extended vocal techniques—and for processing their voices electronically—are women. And I thought, I wonder why that is? I didn't study it very deeply, I just came to conclusions based on some cultural things I'm aware of. Historically, women are socialized to use our bodies as a way of communicating with the world. And men are kind of uncomfortable in their bodies. Not in terms of doing physical things, or showing their strength—but basically, for them, they like to manipulate tools. Women tend to be placed in a position where they're expected to use their body in this public way. Like in the old tradition of jazz ensembles, you'd always have an entire ensemble of men, and then the front person would be this pretty woman. She was supposed to wear a really attractive gown, and what was she using as her instrument, but a part of her body. So somehow it's more acceptable for a woman to do something that seems like losing her mind, being wild and being crazy with her body or her voice, either as a dancer or a singer. While a man can be really wild and crazy, but he has to do it with a tool. He's got to buffer himself with something—a guitar or a saxophone—it can't be coming right out of his face, because that somehow seems like losing control. This is stereotyping, but it's sort of an analysis of why that is the stereotype. It's really interesting that women are a little more free to just be insane because we've already been accused of that! [Laughs]

And the flipside of that, which you point out in the essay you wrote for Women, Art, and Technology *(Z 2003), is that there are perhaps more women than people expect who are using electronic technologies, but they're left out of the history.*

Right, they don't get recognized for it, because people want them to do this other thing. People love it when a woman does wild things with her voice, so you can get famous if you do that because that's what they want you to do. [Laughs]

Also, especially when I first started doing this work, I found that the press—and largely it's men writing—when they write about a woman, they need to find a woman icon to compare her to. For me, it was always Laurie Anderson—Laurie Anderson's the number one—and then Meredith Monk or Diamanda Galás. I always got compared to one of those three people. What's really humorous to me is, I couldn't think of three people who are more different from *each other*, and yet I was always being compared to one of them or the other. And I don't mind comparisons if it's based in something. I admire Laurie Anderson, but she communicates with her voice in a really different way, and the sound of her work is very different from mine.

I think when these people look at a woman artist, they have developed a set of symbols, and once they see the symbol they don't look any further. It's kind of like the woman on the mud flaps of the truck that's the symbol of female form, you know? It's like: woman, music, electronics, doing something a little cerebral, arty—*Laurie Anderson!* OK, I've figured out how to peg that one, now I'm done. But when they're looking at the men's work, they ask, What is he doing with chord progression? How is he working with texture? They're actually looking at the work. I think it's the same thing when people look at people of their own race, they tend to see more specifics. But when they look at somebody of another race, they just have a symbol. And that's kind of overstated, it's not that all writers do it, but that's kind of what I've come up against with people making comparisons. It's human nature to want to make a comparison, because you feel more secure once you have a box to put something in. But somehow the desire to do it seems to be stronger with people who are "other" than yourself.

To continue on issues of race, a lot of the music critics and the people writing the histories have been white men, and experimental music as it's been constructed has been very white.

Things have changed a lot, but I remember a time when I used to walk into a club to play a gig, and the person working there would see me come in, and they'd say, Oh, you're the musician tonight, so what do you do—blues or reggae? That doesn't happen so much anymore. [Laughs] Even though it is a white male world that I'm in, that's changed a lot in recent years. And I feel, in a weird way, that it's almost worked in my favor, because people are so amazed that I do what I do. Because they never see a woman doing it, and they never see a black person doing it, so it's like I'm some kind of anomaly. But that's not so much the case anymore, because people of color, and women, are starting to get more recognition in the avant-garde field.

I visited one college where there are a lot of black people in the music department, but they're all studying really conventional, classical music. And among the people in the electronic music program, there are not very many people of color. And the school was trying hard to get the black people to come to my presentation, because they wanted them to see somebody of color doing something like this. At first I didn't get it, but then I got there and I realized how important that was. 'Cause all these black students were just not exposed to this stuff and they don't ever see anyone who looks like them doing it, so they figure it must not be for them. It was a reminder to me that there is a reason to target people sometimes.

I taught workshops at the LAB in San Francisco through the California Arts Council, starting in '93 or '94. The first ones I did were for at-risk youth. Someone said, Why don't you do one for girls? I didn't want to, because I didn't want to discriminate. But then I found that mostly boys would apply, and the few girls that came into the class would be really uncomfortable and shy. And I'd go around and ask everyone, Why did you take the workshop? And the girls would say, My boyfriend has a recording studio, and I feel really stupid 'cause I don't understand anything. And I thought, God, it's the '90s!

I had a similar experience when I taught a recording workshop to women last summer. When it was over, one of them came up to me and said, You just taught me more in an hour than my boyfriend's taught me in five years! It was touching, but also really disheartening.

Yeah! So then I was convinced that I should do it for women. I started doing it for low-income women, and I started getting all these applicants. I did it for several years. It wasn't just about technology, it was about sound art and performance. I taught everybody to use ProTools, I taught them all about signal-to-noise ratio, how a mixing board works, signal path, all of that. And it was just like you said—they were like, I've taken these classes and all the men gather around and they won't let you touch anything, or they make you feel stupid.

The other thing I've learned about men is that they have this problem where they can't *not* know technical stuff. And if they don't know it, it's so embarrassing for them, they prefer to lie and pretend they do know it. And that makes the women even more intimidated because the woman, if she doesn't know something, she just says she doesn't know it. If a guy doesn't know something, he pretends to know it. So they would get into these classes and think, The guys all know it all and I don't know anything. And the guys don't know anything either! They just pretend to know it, and sort of absorb it as they go along. The women I taught were so shocked that it could be taught in plain language, and they could understand it. And then I realized that there was a total need for that, to do something specifically for women.

: : :

Pamela Z's projects in 2008 included SoundWORK, a seven-week sound and performance workshop at her studio and Royce Gallery in San Francisco, a San Francisco run of her new multimedia performance work *The Pendulum*, and a solo performance for voice, electronics, and video at Essl Museum in Vienna, Austria.

Laetitia Sonami

Laetitia Sonami is a composer, performer, and sound artist born in France in 1957 and now based in Oakland, California. Since 1991, she has designed and built new gestural controllers for musical performance and composition. Her main instrument is the Lady's Glove, a glove modified with sensors, which allows her to use subtle movements of each finger to control sounds, mechanical devices, and lights in real time. She created the first one in 1991 for the Ars Electronica festival in Linz, Austria, and has developed four updated versions since then. With the Lady's Glove, Sonami has performed many works for voice and electronics, several of which use texts by Melody Sumner Carnahan as source material. Her compositions have been described as "performance novels," because musical form and textual narrative unfold and are transformed through her physical motions.

Sonami also makes sound installations that combine audio and kinetic elements embedded in ubiquitous objects such as light bulbs, rubber gloves, bags, and toilet plungers. Most recently, she has collaborated and toured with Sue Costabile, creating live films by combining sound, video, and kinetic elements in performance. Her work was often discussed when I was a graduate student at Mills, since she had gone through the same program in the late '70s and still lives and works nearby. We met for this interview in May 2004 at her home in Oakland.

: : :

Tara Rodgers: How did you get started building your own instruments?

Laetitia Sonami: It was really when I came here, to Mills College, in 1978. I first went to the Boston Museum School of Fine Arts. I was just seventeen and planned to study visual arts. They had two Putney VCS3 synthesizers, nice, portable, small synths. They did not sound that great, but they were not too expensive and were available. One day a friend said I should check them out, and I was like, Wow, what is that? I was hearing sounds that were very crude, but still there was this whole sense of magic, of electricity producing sounds in ways I could not fathom. I had learned the piano as a kid, but up to that point, music or sounds were not a preoccupation. So it was a surprise, discovering this whole new world and being mostly puzzled by the mystery, not understanding how it worked. I realized I didn't even understand how sounds were formed, how they blended together.

I went back to France, and I tried to go to the GRM [Groupe de Recherche Musicale] where they had a lot of electronic music and recording equipment, and they said, No, you have to go to the conservatory for two years. But I really was not coming at it from an idea that it was a continuation of musical ideas. I was interested in the technology and understanding sounds, and I didn't think I had to learn harmony to be able to do it. I can see why some people would, and expand their vocabulary with technology, but this was not my situation.

So that is when I met Eliane Radigue. A friend of mine knew the owner of a very experimental record label called Shandar, and she knew Eliane, and suggested I meet with her. After first meeting with Eliane, she allowed me to use her equipment (a wonderful ARP 2500) two, three times a week and see what would come out of it. We became very close friends, one of those friendships that change the directions of your life. She ended up letting me work there all year. Once a week she would leave—she just had a small place—and I would work, and then she would come back and we would talk and eat and listen. She knew I couldn't really do my work in France; it had quite a rigid system which required you to follow particular schools of musical thought. She was herself a student of Pierre Henry, and had encountered difficulties when it became clear that her music had nothing to do with that of her mentor. He was the great master of musique concrète, and her music was very subtle, with slowly evolving sonic spaces. So, to make a long story short, Eliane introduced me to Joel Chadabe. He had this incredible Moog studio at the State University at Albany, so I studied with him for one year. And then I came to Mills in '78, and ended up studying with Robert Ashley and David Behrman.

Mills had an incredible pool of self-taught builders, such as Paul

DeMarinis, John Bischoff, Frankie Mann, Rich Gold, and many others. They were building their own homemade, personal electronic systems. It was expected that you would build what you needed, or at least try! And I was shocked: build my own musical tools? It was definitely not in the European tradition. There you have engineers and artists, and there is a very clear separation. While here, definitely, the separation between engineers and artists, at least at Mills, but I think in California and America in general, is more fluid, so the feedback between art and technology is much tighter. So that was quite a sur-

prise. They showed me how to order a kit, put it together . . . I never got very good at it, but I got to be not scared at blowing things up! I figured then that you needed to know at least enough to do it wrong, and then people will always say, How come you didn't do it that way? And show you how to improve. But if you don't try, nobody will show you. It's like a car, if you show a guy your car, and you fixed something wrong, they're always going to try to fix it for you! So I figured with electronics, it would be a good approach. Always do something, and even if it's totally wrong, there will be ten guys saying, That's not the way to do it! [Laughs]

But I like building, and using my hands, even more now that we are so immersed in digital systems embedded in black boxes. I try to get students to do it, and people really like it. It is very popular right now, hacking, building . . . It's funny, one of the classes I teach is Digital Audio Systems, and one or two times a semester we build analog circuits. You would think with all this equipment, and all the things you can do with digital audio, that it would keep their interest. But nothing compares to building a little oscillator that goes *wooo-wooo-wooo!* People are amazed, because they can see a connection to this object that produces something unexpected. It is harder to do with a computer, where everything is out of sight. With a circuit, you still have this idea of a wire that goes to this, which goes to that, and then to this . . . There is a palpable causality that you don't understand, but is left to be deciphered, like magic.

When did you build the first Lady's Glove?

The first Lady's Glove was in '91. It was a pair of rubber gloves for a performance with Paul DeMarinis for Ars Electronica. The second one came soon after, and the third one, in '93, was much more evolved. The fourth one I used from '97, for six years. And now I'm using the fifth version, which I finished in December 2003. Bert Bongers, who was sponsored by STEIM in Amsterdam, built the last two versions.

The glove was first more of a joke, a kind of a social commentary on technology, but then it became an instrument. I've been trying to figure out at which point a controller becomes an instrument . . . I think that when you use or design a controller, and if you're just using it to push buttons or trigger things, it does not really affect the way you think of the music or how you write the software. You have your ideas and you're using a controller as an interface. Then I would not call it an instrument. I think it becomes an instrument when the software starts reflecting and adapting the limitations and possibilities of the controller, and your musical thinking and ideas become more a symbiosis between the controller, the software, and the hardware. I used to have much more of a distinction between the hardware, my sounds, the software, and the gestures—a sort of puzzle. Now I realize that my imagination is pretty much molded by the system I use. I don't think as much how will I adapt my ideas to the instrument, but I realize that the instrument has already influenced what I envision. So the Lady's Glove is more of an instrument now, good or bad.

And with it, sounds in a way are embodied through your gestures.

I think so. Recently someone asked me whether the system is imposing itself, or I'm controlling it. It's a little of everything. I sometimes dream it could be inside my body, grafted in the skin. But then, I would miss the awkwardness of an external apparatus, a mechanical system that the body's trying to adapt to, and the struggle that comes with it.

But I got a little tired of gesture controllers. I used to think: laptop performers, they never think about movement, they're so boring. But now I actually quite envy them, in a way. That ability to ignore an audience is very tempting to me. I'm always very aware of the audience, and of performance. On my dark days I feel like I'm just a glamorous waitress! [Laughs] This idea of service . . . There's this traditional, classical sense of performance as a way of offering a situation, and being aware of how the situation is being received. That's what a lot of performance is, especially if it also borders some kind of theater. Sometimes there's a side of it that slightly bothers me. Especially some of the more academic new music concerts, where people fall asleep. I had several of those in a row. I got to think that maybe I was somebody's

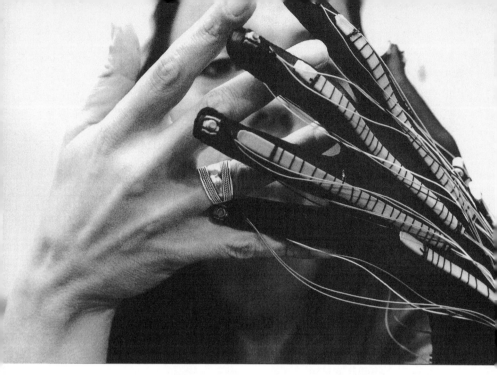

Laetitia Sonami and the Lady's Glove, 1999. PHOTO BY ANDRE HOEKZEMA.

waitress, here to entertain somebody so they can eventually go to sleep! So I went into other things like sound installations.

Then I saw this movie by Almodóvar, *Talk to Her*, and there's a woman toreador. It's funny, in my mind the scenes of her with the bull were a major element, but I went back to excerpt those scenes and I got at most five seconds. The tension between her and the bull really resonated with me—the gestures, the communication—and I felt really close to that idea. I thought again about performance, and what was it that made me watch her? You know, I'm a huge fan of John Bischoff's music, and he's working with a laptop, while on the other hand some people who use gesture controllers do not particularly interest me. So it's not really about creating some kind of embodiment of a performative action with electronics. It has to do really with the concentration, and the focus the performer radiates. That's when performance is beautiful. The intimacy that the performer presents to the public, and you witness this intimacy and you feel so fortunate. In a way the Lady's Glove allows a little of that concentration. So I went back with renewed excitement, and that is when I worked on the fifth version. I don't know how long I'll do it, it has been a while now, but it has been interesting.

You mentioned the social commentary of it. Can you talk more about that?

Well, at first, there was this huge interest in virtual reality systems. On the entertainment side, people were using the Mattel Power Glove. It was very macho, which now I enjoy more, but at the time I was like, Come on . . . you know? [Laughs] This whole idea of macho control of technology, which shows itself so well in wars. So I thought, mine will be a sexy glove, sexy and feminine—'cause I'm French, and it's going to be a French glove! [Laughs] But with jokes like that, you think back, and if you're on that same "joke" for more than several months, you have to consider that it may not be a joke but something you're really serious about.

231

I always was amazed at what technology can do. I often feel that it is a projection of our dreams, illusions, desires, and it reflects how we see the world. I feel you have to respect that imagination. To reduce it to very crude systems is somewhat disrespectful of our imagination! I never thought of this while doing it, obviously; it was only later on, while reflecting on my obsessions. And I think there was always a desire to do something that would really display the magic, and refinement (or crudeness!) of the electronic world, and how delicate it can be. It just can change. It's like air, like wind. They are only moving electrons, which can completely change things around. So this desire to play with the subtlety of it—as opposed to reduce it—was maybe more feminine, you know? I've been interested by the fact that women can be more interested in subtleties of sounds than men are. If one wants to make really rough, crude generalizations! Men have done really interesting works that are system-based, very interesting systems, structurally fascinating, but sonically a little poor! [Laughs] I look at the work that was sonically incredible, and it's often been women, but of course not all.

What sounds have you typically worked with?

It's changed a lot, and has also gone through a lot of phases. When I first tried to play with sounds I was so puzzled, so I would listen a lot to the environment, try to figure out how sounds came together. I was just blind in a way. So I would sit down and listen to sounds, and take notes: airplane comes, dog barks, etc., and just try to dissociate the various elements which made the landscape. A lot of the work I did was recording natural sounds and extracting from them. And then at some point, I got less interested with natural sounds; they became too familiar. So I became more interested in synthesis, and then it became more of a juxtaposition of abstract synthesis with sampled sounds, or the sampled sounds are processed so you can't really recognize them. I am interested in the juxtaposition of abstraction and iconic elements; there might be a voice or a breath, but it would happen at a time when the landscape is very abstract, so there is always this play back and forth between recognizable elements and abstraction. Lately I got a little tired of even using processed samples, because it's very hard to modify. There's only so much you can do, and you cannot take it apart that well. One new piece is almost all digital synthesis in Max/MSP, sending pulses through resonators and filters, filtering raw signals and composing new signals on the fly. It's allowed me to be a little more flexible, less predictable. We have so many possibilities of sounds.

It can be hard to choose.

It's hard to choose, but you're always attracted to a particular color or texture, and these attractions change depending on what you are going through, right? It's kind of like a bee with a flower. You don't know, but you just go and zoom to those particular sounds. And then you gather them over two, three months, and you listen to them, and they start telling stories.

When you perform, is it largely improvisational, or do you have compositional structures mapped out?

It's not so improvisational. For me it's really hard to improvise with the software I write, as opposed to George Lewis or other composers who make "listening" software that responds to events or musical gestures [see Lewis 2000]. In my solo performances, the sounds have been chosen, the mapping has been chosen, and the processes have been defined. In the piece I am working on now, I try to be much more fluid in the way things happen. But it's hard. Sometimes it becomes too random when I leave it more freedom. The way I've resolved the situation is with the use of templates. Within a template, I have a set of possibilities: which sounds can happen, which sound is mapped to which sensor, are there filters, resonators, DSP of some kind . . . I have the freedom to move between templates and play with all those elements, which allows for a dynamic remapping of the sensors and the sounds. That seems to work pretty well, wandering around within templates. The only problem I've found, because I'm very much tied to a narrative form, as abstract as it may be, is the tendency I have to go in a very strict order between templates. And usually, because of the way I think of music, the templates are pretty defined, mental spaces. With the new piece, I'm trying to know less, but I'm struggling with this fact that I really want certain things to happen. It's not like they're recorded, but I have a very defined idea of what I want to happen. It's really very precise, kind of surgical.

Do you make recordings of your performances?

Well, I'm supposed to, but I have many problems with CDs. First, I have so little time, and I'm more interested in the situation of performance, which I find quite magical. You're alone, but then you're with people for a half hour, one hour, and you create this moment, and then that's it—it's gone, and nothing's left, just the memory of the moment. Sometimes it's good, sometimes it's bad . . .

Also, what attracted me to sounds is their impermanence and fleeting quality. The idea of fixing sounds, and thinking of sounds repeating themselves outside of a context, is so much against what I like about sounds, that I'm having trouble thinking about recording—the idea of "objective" sounds adaptable to any situation or time.

And the other thing is probably a lack of confidence. The idea of commitment of any kind terrifies me—that you would have to commit a sound to a particular time. It's like, Oh, God, how do I know it should be there? [Laughs] So there's that, and then there's just so much objects already in the world. But I'm glad other people are doing it. And one day I'll do it. I go through these arguments so many times. I was talking with this really nice composer, and he was saying, Just think of it as documentation, we want to hear it! And I said, But there's a hundred thousand other people's music that they could hear, or they can also come to my concert. And if you can't come to the concert, well, you just can't hear it! For some reason, musicians got into this idea that everything you do has to be recorded. If you use a recording medium, fine. But if you're not, if you're doing performance, that is a very different situation.

: : :

Sonami teaches at the San Francisco Art Institute and the Milton Avery Summer Program at Bard College and was the David Tudor Composer-in-Residence at Mills College in 2007.

Bevin Kelley
(Blevin Blectum)

Bevin Kelley, born in 1971, is an electronic musician based in Providence, Rhode Island. With Kristin Erickson, she formed the duo Blectum from Blechdom in 1998. Their album *The Messy Jesse Fiesta* (Deluxe, 2000), recipient of a 2001 Ars Electronica Award of Distinction in Digital Music, is an outpouring of densely mangled samples, electro beats, and synth splashes; it references pop and electronic music traditions only to turn them inside out. The duo split in 2001 but regrouped in 2007 and began work on a new record.

Blevin Blectum's solo work—including *Magic Maple* (Praemedia/ Bleakhouse, 2004) and *Gular Flutter* (Aagoo, 2008)—extends this collage form further into the realm of sound design, away from the more lyrical and pop elements in her collaborations with Erickson. Blectum also performs in Sagan, a group that includes J Lesser, Wobbly, and the video artist Ryan Junell. She works as a sound designer and as a licensed veterinary technician specializing in avian medicine and canine rehabilitation.

I followed Bevin's work with interest since she attended the MFA program at Mills a few years ahead of me, and we had mutual acquaintances there. We met briefly for this interview in December 2004 in Providence, on a night when each of us was doing a gig; Bevin revised the transcription via e-mail in November 2006.

: : :

Tara Rodgers: When did you start playing music?

Bevin Kelley: I didn't start out doing electronic music. I was started on violin when I was four. I didn't choose it. My grandfather's mother had a violin. She was a music teacher, so they had this decent instrument in the family. I was the first great-grandchild in the family, so they were like, You're gonna play *this* instrument—here you go! [Laughs] I was pushed really hard to be a violinist. It took me a long time to get to where I had the guts to disappoint people and quit violin and start over. I quit violin and started making electronic music when I was twenty-five, in 1996.

When did you and Kristin Erickson start working together?

In 1998, in Oakland. She was an undergrad junior when I started my first year as a grad student at Mills. I was using cheap portable samplers and she was using a slow old laptop. We were both strangers to the area, so we started a weekly event called the Globule in the space under the Concert Hall. If you open a door, there's a dirt floor there and a triangular room—the reverse of the sloping seats in the Concert Hall above it—really dingy, really dirty. There was a vent that would come on sporadically and blow dirt and dust everywhere, a sandstorm in the middle of an electronic show. I ended up wearing a dust mask half the time. There were piles of things that had accumulated there over the years; it's an old building. There was a huge stack of sperm donor informational packets from a seminar in the early '80s, which we would give out as party favors. We weren't really supposed to be in there but, to their credit, the faculty turned a blind eye to it. We put on the Globule with our friends and fellow musicians Will Fry and David Vazquez. So if there was somebody in the Bay Area who we wanted to hear or meet, we invited them to play. That's how we met Mike Martinez and Danielle Damasius who used to run Deluxe Records, they put out our first CD; and Josh [Kit Clayton] and Sue [Costabile] who put out our first 12-inch.

The naming schemes and imaginary world of the Blectum project and album cover art—how did those come about?

We were working backstage doing tech for concerts at Mills. We had to be quiet backstage and couldn't talk, so we'd have a note pad. I drew something, and Kristin would be like, What's that? I'd say, It's a Snaus! She'd say, I know what it does, it bites people's toes off! I'd draw another thing: What's that? It's a Mallard! That's a sick Mallard . . . that Mallard wants to experiment on the Snaus. And that's a Bee Grub that wants to sting the world. So that was how it happened. I think if you're collaborating with anyone, especially in music because it's abstracted, if you have a plot or a creature it gives you a unifying theme and a constraint. Sometimes it can be specific to sounds, but even if it's not, it gives you a character to inhabit.

I think I work better under constraints, especially equipment constraints. I had one crap sampler for the first two years me and Kristin worked together, and we did all our editing in ProTools Free on one of her old G3 computers. ProTools Free had only one shot of "Undo" in it, so you had to be careful how you edited! Or make good use of your mistakes. If you have a severe constraint and you're forced to get the best you can get out of something, it's good. I've never been into having all the perfect gear, and having the studio set up perfectly. If I attempt to do that, I never get anything done. So it's better if I don't have much to work with and I just have to work with something crappy. What we did wasn't really the aesthetic that the Mills music department was going for. Not that they're heavy-handed—they're accepting—but in schools there's always some sort of sound that's more prevalent than others. What I got out of being at Mills was an excuse to move back to Oakland, meeting Kristin, and access to equipment.

I wonder if you identify at all with punk aesthetics. Sometimes critics make that connection when they're writing about people who use crappy equipment, when in fact you may be coming from a totally different background.

I didn't identify myself as punk or listen to much punk music, except Nina Hagen if she counts. Although I guess I've always been basically anti-establishment; capitalism is gruesome, copyright is fucked up, the music business I hope will implode soon, etc. I started off using all crappy equipment not for political reasons but because that's what was available to me. Thankfully I got hold of a laptop in 2001 and have used a mix of quality and stupid equipment since then.

Other than the forced violin thing, my background would be electronic music (Wendy Carlos and Kraftwerk when I was a kid, and dance music of one kind or another later on) and weird radio plays (Jack Flanders and Jim Copp/Ed Brown), and science fiction. I started to DJ long before I bought equipment, because between the records at the radio station in college (WOBC in Oberlin) and friends who had records, you could do it for free. There was actually a lot of multi-turntable, freeform experimental stuff going on at Oberlin too. It was the first time I had seen that, and the first time I had heard acid house, early Warp records, house music coming out of Baltimore, New York, and Detroit, early Aphex Twin, early Black Dog, even Altern8 megamixes; that was in '89, '90, '91 or so. And then more Detroit techno; Dan Curtin in Cleveland, which wasn't too far from where I was; and my friend Morgan Geist, who I went to school with, who now runs the Environ label and puts out my brother's music (my brother records as Kelley Polar Quartet).

So I thought I'd rather make music than practice all day! Making music and DJing was a lot more interesting musically and socially. Up 'til then I spent way too much time alone, practicing, feeling frustrated. I knew I didn't belong in musical academia. But at first I didn't have any equipment or plan to get out and start over. It freaked me out to spend all my money on gear! I didn't make much past rent for a long time and the first thing I bought was a Roland S-330 sampler for $300 and it terrified me to spend that much. Then when I went to Mills, I bought another, a very bad, yet flexible, portable and functional Boss "Dr. Sample" SP-202. A comical name that attracted ridicule (some affectionate, some not).

What do you like most about working with the tools you work with now?

I enjoy that it's not a physical thing anymore. Playing violin, at least for me, if you don't have the right fast-twitch muscles, you can pretty much work on it forever and you're not gonna get it. I don't really understand violin and what makes you good at it or not, which is part of the reason why it was so frustrating for me. I'm not super coordinated, and past a certain point I'm not gonna get any better at an instrument that you have to be that physically skilled with. So, to me, the electronic stuff is beautifully transparent.

I manipulate samples until I hear something I like. I don't always have a preheard sound idea in my head and then force samples/sounds/edits/sequences to conform to that in reality. It's more like, I dig around and find something that grabs me as interesting or compelling or out of control, and pull the pieces out and put them together. I appreciate that I don't have to contort my body and do it X hours a day or else it's gonna go away. I want it to be brain only. I sometimes feel expected to go be a singer and dancer and incorporate my body somehow—and I don't want to! [Laughs] I use my voice sometimes, but I don't want to be a singer! All that emoting, it's tiresome. Guitar face, violin face, laptop face . . . not a fan of that. It's maudlin and at the back of my mind that there's something emotionally blackmailing about an audience, like they're needy and demanding emotionally, and the performer has to emote and satisfy them. Not always, though—sometimes it feels more equal with less of a divide. Usually in small clubs amongst friends.

If you really love playing an instrument and your burning desire is to master the technique, if that's your thing, that's your thing. If it's not, it's really bad to try to force it to be your thing. I think that happens sometimes with electronic music people; they don't think they're a "real" musician unless they've mastered or incorporated some physical instrument, which I think is a shame. What use is music that revolves only around having "chops" and being "good"? Why feel obliged to wrap your body around some anachronistic sound vehicle? And on a related tangent, I don't think you need to be able to build the computer to make good music with computers.

Do you run into the expectation, when you perform, that you need to be doing more than just playing a laptop?

Yes: expectations to be entertaining and glamorous, which are after all understandable. Some shows you can tell people are thinking, You're gonna change into your costume, right? [Laughs] Nope . . .

[Laughs] Which would be unthinkable if you were a guy.

Yeah. As with anything else, expectations and interpretations vary greatly according to gender. Even on the academic side, I think there's some sort of expectation that if a woman's making music, she should be using her body and dancing, if she isn't playing an instrument. Where if it's a guy sitting with a laptop, it's like, He's a serious composer! A woman sitting doing that, it almost doesn't compute: What do I do with that? She can't be a serious composer. Why isn't she using her body?

When me and Kristin stopped working together, I did some projects with Ryan Junell doing video (sometimes live, sometimes pre-edited) and me playing music live, as a way to keep it interesting. Because playing with someone is of course much more fun and interesting than playing alone. The video then sort of branched into also including a costume sometimes, usually a not very glamorous costume

Bevin Kelley performing at Centre Pompidou, Paris, 2006.
PHOTO BY VINCIANE VERGUETHEN.

(me and Kristin often wore costumes as Blectum from Blechdom—a two-person pair of pants attached by a stretchy fabric column of musical farts, and a dual-person pair of footed pajamas with multi-colored arms and fake-fur fuzzy underarms and crotches). One I've been wearing lately is a cardboard horse/alien that my friend Fausto Caceres made. I saw it hidden in the back of his studio and asked if I could wear it. I was reading a bunch of M. John Harrison books at the time, and it looks like one of the recurring things in his books *Light* and *Viriconium*: part–horse skull, part–alien, part–old Welsh custom. At an interview at a show when I was wearing the horse costume, I was asked, Do you have a problem with your femininity?—maybe because it covers up my face, although my face appears in the video. Or maybe because me and Kristin have gender-ambiguous stage names, and because neither of us is going for an overtly straightforward sexual glamour, being more into Snauses and Mallards than clothes or something. For awhile we held out some vain hope of not being identified as a "girl band" and tried to keep our gender a mystery. That didn't last long; we weren't masters of disguise.

Along those lines, tell me about your experience at Ars Electronica in 2001. I think it's interesting that you showed up on that radar, but then had some bizarre reactions to your work.

One judge was a fellow San Franciscan, so I think he rooted for us and snuck the Blectum from Blechdom album in there—the first one, *The Messy Jesse Fiesta*. And I think they were trying to not have it be such an old-school academic festival, they were trying to get new people and new sounds. They tell you in April that you got a prize, and you don't know which prize you've gotten until you get there and you do a show. It's actually on Austrian TV. It's very surreal. We went up at the end with all the people, and we were the only girls. We tied for second prize. The top three are cash prizes, which was good, because I got laid off and I needed the money to move into a new apartment so it was totally perfect timing that I got this lump sum right when I needed it.

One of the other winners, Markus Popp, basically writes software, so he was giving sort of a corporate presentation. We had some slides prepared, but it wasn't a slick presentation. The show was running late, and since we were projecting from the computer, it shut down and we had to restart the whole thing and the projector. So it took a few minutes for us to do that. I have to emphasize that this was not a technical difficulty of our making, and that it had absolutely nothing to do with music, music software, or our ability to use computers! Kristin does some pretty amazing work in Max/MSP and I thought that came through in our talk, we had slides of her patches which are cool looking as well as highly functional! So after, in the question-and-answer, some guy was like, I see California girls like to be fucked by their technology! His meaning and tone indicated that we were inept with our gear, and that we enjoyed being inept. We were like, That's really odd that you got that out of what we were saying, that's the only thing you got out of it. It was because we had taken those few minutes to restart everything. So, I am a stickler about having everything run perfectly and effortlessly, because I hate that—if you have any problem, it's usually attributed to the fact that you're a girl. Even if the power goes out or the building falls down or something, some people will interpret it as clearly, You are a California girl who likes to get fucked by technology! But then we got another question like, Can you tell me what happens when a Mallard turns a Snaus inside out? Somebody playing along with the story. So we got one totally clueless question, and one insider-joke kind of question, which was kind of flattering but kind of bizarre also. At Ars it was mostly really welcoming, but weird. The show itself was good, really nice sound, a fun time.

Music is one thing, but it's worse if you're working at some corporate sound job. My last boss told me that he hired me so he had someone to make the "girl sounds."

: : :

Kelley toured Europe in 2008 and has been collaborating on an opera with the writer/librettist China Miéville.

Part 6. **Alone/Together**

Women who make electronic music routinely balance goals of individual achievement, collaboration, and musical community. The project studios of the artists in part 6—which they assemble at home, or design for easy portability— indicate that a certain level of privacy, self-possession, and means for material possession prefigure and sustain their artistic output. Yet individual efforts are balanced with various types of collaboration. Le Tigre's production method combines private experimentation with group contribution and feedback. Both are necessary to the resulting work. As Kathleen Hanna observes, electronic music collaborations differ from traditional rock setups because individual ideas have more space to thrive: "There's something about being in your house or the studio by yourself . . . being able to feel like no one's watching you and you can make crazy mistakes and erase it, and we'll never know . . . And also the process of being able to share that, even though it's not done, with somebody else."

Bev Stanton began her solo electronic music project in order to avoid the unreliability of bandmates. She has found middle ground as a remixer, which allows her to collaborate with other people primarily by working with their music as files on a computer. In this format, unpredictabilities are more technical than social. Furthermore, Stanton's uses of software instruments and online networking have facilitated collaborations with local musicians in a wide range of genres, and interactions with an international community of software designers.

Keiko Uenishi—like so many electronic musicians who work out of a shared living space or apartment building—has developed many of her sound projects late at night after work, within the private listening space of headphones. Her performance practice, however, centers on the Share events that bring together many individual artists for spontaneous group performances. Riz Maslen's process is somewhat the reverse: she has moved away from sampling sounds off records to establish an informal bartering system among friends who play instruments. With her portable studio, she makes recordings of collaborators in far-flung locations and returns home to piece the material together on her own.

From these examples, we can envision the "split screen" of electronic music mentioned by Le Tigre's Johanna Fateman: on one side, the person working alone late at night in the home studio; on the other, an ensemble cast of characters who are present on the recording or in live performance. While some artists in this section may forgo identification with feminism, their strategies to mix the productive aspects of solitude and cooperation, of individualism and community, provide a useful orientation for a contemporary feminist politics.

Le Tigre

Le Tigre (Kathleen Hanna, born 1968; Johanna Fateman, born 1974; and JD Samson, born 1978) is a feminist electronic music and performance art group founded in 1998. After Hanna released her solo record *Julie Ruin* (Kill Rock Stars, 1997), she teamed up with Fateman and the video artist Sadie Benning to put together a live show; the material they developed in collaboration became the band's first album (*Le Tigre*, Mr. Lady, 1999). Samson toured with them as a roadie and technician and became a full-fledged member of the band when Benning left the project in 2000. Le Tigre released another album on the independent label Mr. Lady (*Feminist Sweepstakes*, 2001) and brought their work to a broader audience by signing with a major label for the release of *This Island* (Universal, 2004). Their lyrics engage feminist and queer histories and politics; for one example, "Hot Topic," a song from their first album, proclaims a litany of artists, activists, and writers who have inspired them. They have also advocated personal empowerment and political consciousness among their fans by writing on their website about issues like sexual abuse and coming out as queer.

I first communicated with Le Tigre when they posted a question on the Pinknoises.com message board, and I sent them a response. Soon after that, I contributed a track to their *Remix 12"* (Mr. Lady, 2001). We did this interview at a cafe in Manhattan in November 2002, which was the first time the four of us met in person.

: : :

Tara Rodgers: How do you describe your music? And tell me about how you started making it.

Johanna Fateman: It's hard to describe because we don't have that much distance on it, but when Kathleen and I started making music together it was after she had put out the *Julie Ruin* record, which was a home recording project that was sort of minimal, with a drum machine and sampler and keyboard. At that time we both had the kind of samplers where you just hit the button and play the sample; we weren't sequencing samples at all. Working together, we started to figure things out, like how to use more than the preset beats that we had on our drum machines, and how to sync up beats that we had on different drum machines, and it just kind of evolved from there. And JD joined the band, and she has different skills. She's learning how to use Reason, and Kathleen and I haven't used computers to make music until a few weeks ago.

Kathleen Hanna: I did a little bit on Reason but then realized I wasn't very adept at it and kept wanting to go back to the MPC again. For our new album we definitely don't want the whole record to sound like we made it on Reason, or like we made it all on the MPC. We're really into whatever we can get our hands on at the time, utilizing it to create the sounds that we want to make. If one piece of equipment isn't doing it, we'll try something else. We also have the goal of technical innovation for each project; we're really goal-oriented. We don't have crazy goals, like we want to do it all, but we want to learn ProTools so we don't have to rely on an engineer to help us sequence stuff or reorganize stuff in the last minutes. 'Cause you always want to reorganize stuff a million times, and I don't wanna have to sing parts over and over and over because we're using a linear tape process. We wanted to go nonlinear so we could sing the part once, and sit there for three days and figure out the perfect structure, and then go into the studio with a nice mic and sing it once with that fresh feeling that you don't have when you've sung something twenty times. We had the goal where we wanted to learn ProTools for that, and we have. Each record we have the goal of learning something new. Like the last time it was learning how to save something on the MPC and use the MPC more in the recording process.

People often describe your music with terms like "post–Riot Grrrl" or "electroclash," and I wonder how you feel about this—how you see your music as fitting in or not fitting in with other kinds of rock or electronic music.

Fateman: Well, I think we'd like to fit in! [Laughs]

Le Tigre, 2004. PHOTO BY DANIELLE LEVITT.

JD Samson: With the "real" electronic music . . .

Fateman: Obviously we don't sound like electronica, or dance music, or most electronic genres. But it's kind of frustrating that we're still kind of in this rock genre, even though we don't have a lot of peers using the technology that we're using, in that world. I think a lot of people who listen to our music and buy our records and come to our shows are not necessarily aware of Riot Grrrl bands. Probably our most hardcore fans are people who are from that scene, or know bands from that scene, but because our sound is a lot more poppy and danceable, there is this other audience that is into our music.

Samson: After shows some people come up to us and are like, I never really listened to the words and I only liked the music, but now I'm so interested in the politics; and you get the other half who are like, I'm really into the politics, but the music is so interesting, I've never heard music like this before. So it's kind of this half-and-half thing. Everybody's there for a different reason, and that feels very good. It's really nice when people say, I came here for the music but now I'm learning about the politics.

Hanna: Sometimes it is frustrating in terms of not getting press in electronic music magazines. I've felt like we're not taken seriously in that world or something. I don't know what kind of test you have to pass, or how you get your records into certain record stores. But I do feel like we should be reviewed in electronic music magazines. Part of it may be that our label isn't geared toward focusing on advertising in those magazines, or sending them stuff to review, and people haven't heard of us in that world. You know, people can be really genre-closed.

Every so often I'd like to play a show with other electronic acts that don't necessarily have anything to do with our politics, I think that's fun, and I think it's fun to play with rock acts. But I think it's really great to be classified in terms of ideology too, sometimes. Like some of our most successful shows, I think we'd all agree, have been where there's been a feminist rock act, a feminist hip-hop act, us as the electronic act, and even a folk act. And that's really great because it shows the diversity of feminist music. It doesn't all have to sound the same, it shows there's a huge range of feminist women making music and it's not just one style. Just because maybe in the media, the only openly feminist bands are Sleater-Kinney, us, and people from the women's music genre, people have a tendency to think that's all that there is. But we've seen on the road that there's a lot more going on, and I'm honored to be put in that spectrum.

It strikes me that electronic music is very much a do-it-yourself culture, like there's this understanding that anyone with a decent computer can make tracks. But the magazines still enforce this ideal of slick production. So it's do-it-yourself, but in a way that upholds traditional production values, which is sort of a double standard. With you guys, sometimes your music tends to be more edgy.

Fateman: Kathleen and I, a while ago, went to this panel discussion . . .

Hanna: I was totally going to say the same thing!

Fateman: It was about "the loop." It was four or five guys, all white, all in their early thirties, probably. Well, not all white . . . definitely all men. But what was more striking, was that what they had to say was so homogenous. It was pseudo-theoretical stuff about finding flaws in loops, and finding the glitch, and making patterns out of glitches.

Hanna: It was really fetishized.

Fateman: It really struck us that, when men make mistakes, it's fetishized as a glitch . . .

Hanna: Something beautiful.

Fateman: And when women do it, it's like . . .

Hanna: . . . a hideous mistake.

Fateman: Right, it's not considered an artistic innovation or a statement or an intentional thing.

Samson: We're even going more towards the edginess with not really working with an engineer as much as we have in the past. 'Cause it's been kind of difficult working with somebody who's telling you that they want it to be smooth. It feels really good now to be in complete control of what's gonna come out.

Hanna: So we're going even more into the glitch theory in the future. It was really interesting, though. My whole first record was about the glitch and the mistake and the hiccup, and turning that into art. And there was kind of this thing where, God, you didn't ask any women to be on this panel? That seems really weird, first of all. And second, we live in New York, and they flew these people in . . .

Fateman: And apparently we were available that day, because we were there! [Laughs]

Hanna: It reminded me of those really expensive fashion designers who make these clothes that look like you're homeless, and how totally offensive that is. You know, if you're homeless it's not this totally entertaining thing, like, Oh, look, my clothes are made of rags! So many people making electronic music don't have the money, or the desire—or sometimes a combination of both—to make their stuff sound completely seamless and pristine, and there's no point of entry. It's just so insulting to have people who have all this expensive equipment and access and they're like, Yeah, I was recording my five-thousand-dollar computer being unplugged over and over, and then making a loop out of it, because it was this really fascinating sound, making a crackling noise. And you're like, We have crackling noise on our record 'cause we were using 8-bit samples!

Fateman: I think also, the economics of it aside, to be in electronic music magazines, it seems it's not necessarily about how slick the production is; it has to be formalist music. If there's glitches in your music, and that's what it's about, then that's what it's about. Glitches in your music, *and* political lyrics—it's almost like the fact that there's this content in our music, and the primary content isn't that it's electronic music. It's almost like that's why it gets ignored.

Hanna: Also, we're not exactly wearing little tiny hot pants, and we don't have our legs oiled up all the time.

Samson: Have you seen that Peaches and Princess Superstar are on the cover of the next URB [issue 102, February 2003]?

Hanna: Which is great, Peaches is fucking rad. But she also looks really good in the hot pants!

Samson: She should be on the cover.

Hanna: She should, 'cause she looks good in the hot pants. If I had a magazine, she'd be on the cover in hot pants.

Fateman: When Björk was on the cover of URB [issue 87, September 2001], I totally bought it because I thought, When has a woman been on the cover of this magazine? Björk doesn't make my favorite music or anything, but she totally produces her own music, is really in control of how the production happens, is a ProTools engineer, does all this stuff herself, and is obviously really in charge of her own work. And the quote they picked out to blow up was something like, "Men make beats and women sing!" It was totally taken out of context from this whole article that was all about how she makes her own music. It also seemed like the whole article was trying to justify why Björk was on the cover, like, most people are going to think Björk doesn't belong in this magazine. It's like, why not? But these electronic music magazines, they're no worse than their equivalent rock magazines. That's why stuff like Pinknoises is so important; if there's gonna be a supporting culture for women to make electronic music, it's not gonna be by us getting our foot in the door at a magazine!

Hanna: It's not indicative of a positive feminist community around electronic music.

Fateman: Yeah, exactly.

Hanna: Besides, Pinknoises actually works! I love that you can e-mail a question and other women can help you with an answer. I feel like that interactivity is really, really crucial, 'cause you can feel so alone when you're doing this kind of music, and especially feeling like, having to go to the male expert over and over can be really humiliating, and you're like, why aren't there any women I can ask these questions to? And maybe there's not that live next door to you, but there is on the web, and I think that's really important.

Can you talk about how you conceive the visuals and music for your performances? Do these processes happen together?

Samson: It kind of happens all at once. All three of us are visual artists as well as musicians, so I think it's really important for us to involve some kind of visual art in our shows. Last time, we all worked on the videos, and we did some by ourselves and some together. We also collaborated with some other video makers. It was really hard, though.

We did nineteen videos in six weeks. Like we were saying before, we're really goal-oriented. We didn't even have a camera; everything happened so fast. We had a deadline, we had a goal, and we did it.

Fateman: I think a really good way to learn to make music or videos or anything is to make up a specific project with a deadline, and force yourself to figure out how to do that specific thing. I think sometimes people learning to use ProTools start reading the manual, and they're like, OK, this is how I do fades! But you don't need to know how to do a fade until you want to fade something! You know what I mean? Just record something! Just make some simple project that isn't super-fancy. If you just jump into it and have a finite thing you're working on, you'll learn. We learned how to use FinalCut Pro in a weekend, because we just . . .

Hanna: Had to. I think that's also a really important thing for any kind of marginalized artist who's been constantly told, You're stupid, you'll never be able to figure this out, this is for magical special people who come from the magic mountain . . .

Fateman: Or go to college for it.

Hanna: Or they've been blessed with some sort of technological know-how. I mean, definitely women fall into the category of, You can't do math, you can't do technical stuff. There's that kind of stereotype. For me, that can really lead to, when I'm doing a project where I have that voice in my head that's like, You don't really know what you're doing, you're faking it! You're not *really* an electronic musician . . . That means that I could sit there and work on a song forever and ever and ever and never finish it, because it's never gonna be good enough. So I think we've all found that it's helpful to say, we're gonna do this record, or this song, and this is when it's due. And that's it. There's no fuckin' around. It's not perfect and it doesn't have to be perfect. If you look around the world, nothing would get done if you waited until your project was totally perfect. Although it is nice with this record, we're chilling out, we're writing it as we feel like it.

Fateman: It's gonna be perfect this time! [Laughs]

Samson: For me, I could never finish something, so it's really good to be able to give it to Jo or Kathleen. Everybody together, I feel like we can make a decision as the three of us.

Hanna: And electronic music is so great in terms of being able to pass stuff off to each other. Like I'll take an MPC song as far as I can go, where I really like some elements but I can't take it any further, and I give it to her, and she'll send it back to me way better. Like the "Keep On Living" song, that was one where I was stuck. I gave it to JD, and she knew what to do with it and made it better. "FYR" was the same way; I gave it to both of them—here's the concept, here's the music as far as I've gotten it—and they came back with a complete song. That's the amazing part about collaboration, especially electronic collaboration, is that we're a group, but we each really get to thrive individually. In a typical rock setup you don't get that as much, because you're all in the room practicing together. There's something about being in your house or the studio by yourself, learning these things on your own time, coming to your own conclusions, and being able to feel like no one's watching you and you can make crazy mistakes and erase it, and we'll never know, and get to as far as you can get. And also the process of being able to share that, even though it's not done, with somebody else. That's something about electronic music that's really different from rock music, that's good.

Fateman: That's another thing: I feel like my best "art brain" sometimes is happening at 3:00 AM when I'm alone, eating candy in the middle of the night and working on music. Sometimes that's a really big joke to me when I listen to our music, 'cause it sounds like all three of us playing a live show. I think of the live show and what we do onstage, but I also have this split screen that's just me alone in the middle of the night! There's this part of it that's really live, and us all together having fun, and this part of it that's totally a crazy person alone. And I think we all have that, in the music.

Who inspires you?

Fateman: I just read this book about Laurie Anderson, who's had this really long career, full of multimedia art. I like the idea that you can have multiple lives as an artist: you can make a couple records, you can do a couple performance art things, you can make sculptures, and just keep doing that for fifty years.

Hanna: I'm really into Yoko Ono, kind of nonstop. She's someone who, a lot of crazy stuff has happened to her, and she still approaches the world with a lot of joy, at least in her public speeches and performances. There's so much intelligence and joy, and it's not separate. It's not like joy is this thing over here that's bodily, and intelligence is thing that's really mind. She's about bodily intelligence. Plus, she kind of invented the music video, and she was the first punk-rock singer—what's not to love? And I'm really inspired by some of the women we've met at Michigan Womyn's Music Festival, which we've played for the past two years. And especially the women we've worked with doing sign language, who've translated our lyrics into sign for our performances. I'm really inspired by signing, and what it means in terms of language and musicality.

Samson: I've been really inspired by my friends. Specifically, I just went to see my friend Sam Miller play. She plays country music. She just played in New York the other day, and it was so inspiring to me, 'cause she sings about all these really interesting butch situations. It's very new, the things that she's talking about, like love for other butch brothers—it just kind of blew me away watching her onstage. It's so different than anything I listen to usually, but it's also something I'm *so* a part of, in terms of our ideologies and our politics and our feelings and our hearts. I'm really inspired by feelings right now!

: : :

Le Tigre went on hiatus in 2007 but has been busy nonetheless: Hanna has volunteered at the Willie Mae Rock Camp for Girls; Fateman and Samson have started a new DJ, production, and remix team called MEN; and Fateman now owns a hair salon in the West Village.

Bev Stanton
(Arthur Loves Plastic)

Bev Stanton was born in the Bahamas in 1966 and grew up in the United States. Based in the Washington, D.C., area, she has independently released over a dozen CDs as Arthur Loves Plastic—a name she chose after her cat's fondness for plastic grocery bags. She is also a sought-after remixer for artists in diverse musical genres in D.C. and beyond. Some of her most acclaimed work (i.e., *Troubled*, Machine Heart, 2006) has been in collaboration with the vocalist Lisa Moscatiello, whose soaring alto complements Stanton's electronic grooves. Arthur Loves Plastic has won over a dozen Washington Area Music Awards (WAMMIEs) in the Electronica category, and was once selected as editor's choice for music in *Washington Blade*'s "Best of Gay D.C." Her work has also been licensed to appear in the background of TV shows including *Access Hollywood*, *The Oprah Winfrey Show*, *American Idol*, and numerous cable programs. Three Arthur Loves Plastic tracks were featured in the Geico "Caveman's Crib" website.

Bev was one of the artists I interviewed by e-mail for the first publication of Pinknoises.com in 2000. Since then we've met periodically, including for a gig she organized with the First Ladies DJ Collective in 2003. We conducted this interview at a D.C. cafe in July 2006.

: : :

Tara Rodgers: Tell me about your background making music, and how you moved from playing in bands to doing your solo project.

Bev Stanton: I started doing the guitar band thing in high school, mostly influenced by the Smiths, R.E.M., and the Cure. We went through so many dysfunctional people that after a while it just made sense to use machines more. You know, there's less drama. When I first started, back in college, they only just started putting MIDI inputs on things. This was probably 1986, '87. So it was very new. I had a Korg DDM-110 drum machine, and I wouldn't mind if I had one of those now, 'cause it would be quaint, but at the time it was a little hokey. And you had to do tape transfer, record on a little data tape recorder to save. So it was a real pain in the ass.

But we went through a bunch of people, and then finally after the third implosion we ended up just using drum machines and sequencing a lot. At the time, you had lots of drunks yelling at you when you played out live doing that. Eventually, we had some kind of equipment failure, and the band decided to go back in more of a guitar direction in the mid-'90s. Meanwhile, I did electronica as a side project, 'cause I really liked a lot of the house music that was coming out at the time. That project got signed and the band didn't, so after a while I just sort of did my own thing. So I've been doing the solo project about twelve years. I feel like I've shifted gears a lot during that time, because I started out doing a lot of sampling—definitely more dance-y, more house-y—but over time, I had different people to work with, and different tools to work with. I think there's a lot of technological determinism to your sound. And I think working with really cool vocalists shifted the emphasis away from doing sound bite-y stuff, to really trying to write songs more. The latest thing that's influenced my direction is software synths, 'cause your palette just expands exponentially.

In our last interview about five years ago, you talked about how you were still holding on to your drum machines and synths from the '80s.

Oh, I got rid of them! I sold a lot of stuff on eBay, and now I'm using a lot of software synths. It makes sense from a space standpoint, and sonically, when I work on something, if I want to tweak it, I can go back a month later and I'm right where I was before. And there are just so many people out there that are putting out really cool stuff for a very reasonable price. There's this guy, H. G. Fortune, out of Germany. I got in touch with him recently 'cause I was using his software, and I sent him some tracks, and he linked me on his web page. To have that kind of contact with the people who are producing the tools, you wouldn't have had that back in the old days. I wouldn't be calling Yamaha and saying, Oh, I really like your synth! [Laughs]

The Internet has added a whole new dimension to what I do as well. Being able to use shareware, being able to connect with people and trade loops. And a lot of bands are more used to the whole remix concept, so people come up to me instead of me going around asking if

Bev Stanton with cat in home studio, 2006. COURTESY OF LORI THIELE.

they want a remix, and chances are they have the material all ready in a format I can work with; I don't have to go grab it off tape. There's been so much that's happened over this time that's made it so much more interesting, and a lot easier, like labor-saving stuff. But at the same time, I'm glad I knew it how the old way was, 'cause it makes me appreciate it more. I went back to playing bass, and I was thinking, there's no way I'd be able to balance these projects if I was still having to go out from a CD player into a 12-bit sampler and go through all these ROM cards to find sounds. You know? It just took a lot more time to do stuff, and now I can have more things going on at once. I mean, not to sound like an efficiency expert at a corporation, but I can go back to something I did a month ago and pull it up. I used to have to work in so much more of a linear fashion, but now I can indulge my obsessive-compulsive disorder and really get into changing the levels. Whereas in the old days, you had your mix up on your mixer, and you couldn't touch it after you were done with it.

Right, or you had to write down the settings of all the knobs.

Yeah. I feel like it gives you a lot more freedom. It can also be misleading, because you never feel quite done with something when you've got that mindset. You know, you could just keep going on something for a long time.

I wonder if you feel that anything is lost in this new process, in sound quality or in your way of working?

Well, initially when the digital stuff started coming out, it sounded really brittle to me. But now, I upped to 24-bit [bit depth], and sometimes there's a certain warmth that's lacking, but generally what I do is, I'll record everything digitally, and then I'll take it to a guy who's got all the really good tube gear and have him master it. And I think it brings back a lot of the warmth. Because if I didn't have a decent recording device anyways, I might get a lot more warmth if I had the keyboard, but I'd also be getting a lot of hiss too. Now it's just different, it's cleaner. And I don't miss tape!

Do you still incorporate a lot of sampling into your work as well?

Yeah, but I think one of the downfalls of sampling is, it's really nice that people are coming up with combinations you would've never thought possible, but at the same time, it really does make everything derivative after awhile, to some extent. For the remixes I did with Lisa Moscatiello's album, to me, it's special because somebody played something for her, and I'm the only one who's using it. It wasn't just me infringing someone's copyright, I was doing something I was allowed to do, and it was something that nobody else had. I liked that.

I've had choices like that in recent years where I've collaborated with people and had access to their material. I feel better when I know the person, 'cause I can ask them if they like what I did with it, or offer to trade something for it rather than just take it.

Yeah, and it's also collaborative without having to organize a practice or do all that pain-in-the-ass stuff. That's been one of the most satisfying things I've done over the past years, is doing the remixes. Because it really puts you in touch with some of the bands that are around, and puts you in touch with the scene. I've always liked working with local people because especially in an area like D.C., there's no real sense of "scene." You have all these people in different genres who don't know each other, and the press tends to promote this sliver of bands and you'd think that's all that's here. But there's really a lot of award-winning people around here, people that have Grammys. The remixing has put me in touch with people in all these different genres, like pop and folk. So it's been nice in that way. And it's inspiring too, 'cause sometimes if I'm not completely miserable, it's hard to get inspiration on my own. It helps to feed back off of someone else's angst. I do good stuff when I'm completely miserable. But when I don't have that to deal with, it helps to have these collaborative things going on.

You work with so many different people, but the material that comes out under Arthur Loves Plastic has a distinctive sound. It's still your sound, even with different collaborations.

Well, I like to feel like I have a sound, but by the same token, when doing the remixes I don't like to be really cookie-cutter, and I don't like to feel like I'm just slapping my groove underneath someone else's work. I really like to take it apart. I have various levels of deconstruction. Sometimes I really, really like the song and I want to be like the fifth Beatle and just throw things on there. And then other times, particularly if you have the more poetic singer-songwriter types—where the word-to-melody ratio is pretty high—I tend to be a little more deconstructive, because it's sort of at odds with how electronica works. And sometimes when you get source tracks you find stuff that didn't quite make it through the mix that is really cool. Or sometimes the last bass note will be the best note that's played, 'cause it's got that finality to it. I like capturing things like that and throwing them all over the place.

It's so different when you listen to tracks all stripped down and by themselves.

Particularly with women's voices, there'll be a lot of breathiness and nuance, and especially if they're singing in an indie rock band, you can't hear that in the mix. But then when you get the source track, you find it's a whole different vocal. And sometimes there's certain words that were pretty incidental, but when you take them out of context you can take it down a whole new avenue. So I love doing the remixes, it's the most fun stuff I do.

Sometimes I've done musical odd jobs, like somebody wants a loop. Like this folk guy called me and he wanted a loop on something, and

I just put something in there and it worked. I kind of like that, being sort of an ambassador to different genres. That's the most rewarding thing, is working with other people. But the irony of it is that being an isolationist is what propelled me into doing the electronic stuff to begin with. It's kind of gone full circle in a sense. Maybe it's just that I don't like working with people when I have to sit in a room with them. [Laughs] But if they're on the computer—if they're files—that's fine!

That's a really interesting mix, because you have the isolation of time in your studio, but the social aspect of networking. And it seems like gigs come out of that for you, too.

The DJ thing, for me, it's not an end in itself, it's a means to an end 'cause it helps me promote stuff that I put out. Sometimes I feel like you can really be in a vacuum when you're working by yourself. So what DJing has enabled me to do, I have to listen to a lot of different music and find stuff that fits in with what I do, and it's been a really interesting exercise because it makes you think about how your music fits in with the rest of what's out there—or *doesn't* fit in. And I don't really think it influences what I do too much, but it certainly puts things in perspective.

I'm interested in the presence of lesbians and queer women in electronic music history, as well as the presence of dance music in lesbian spaces. What are your thoughts on this? Have you performed in many lesbian bars and clubs?

No, 'cause the music sucks! [Laughs] I've performed and had a lot of lesbians show up. It's a really weird thing, because most of the lesbians I know have really good taste in music, but it's not reflected in public spaces. I guess there's that whole "granola ghost" that follows the scene around. But I've never really understood that. And the thing is, you go to all these lesbian spaces where the music's sucking, and all you talk about is how much the music sucks. So I don't know who imposes this rule on us . . . One of my friends was a DJ at a lesbian bar around here, and she had to really dumb it down, to the point where we would go out to try and support her, and we'd be like, Oh my God, what's *happened* to her? [Laughs] But she was havin' to do it, she'd kind of smirk while she was doing it. I don't know what it is. Definitely the lowest common denominator is in effect.

In terms of networking and putting your music out there, you've always been quite self-sufficient in many respects, especially in developing a strong presence on the web.

I think the self-reliance arose from having a label go bankrupt and then realizing that signing a contract wasn't the answer. This was back in '96. I don't know when I was first able to start selling the things online, but there was MP3.com initially, and that went away, then CD Baby's been really great, 'cause they get a lot of their own traffic. Now I have stuff available through FLAC, which is the audio codec which doesn't diminish the sound quality. It doesn't decrease the file size that much, but with broadband, it's just enough to make it OK for people to download the whole thing. So I've been making stuff available that way, and on iTunes, and CD Baby. I'm finding that the iTunes is starting to overtake CDs now.

The thing that's been really nice is the podcasting. Instead of sending a bunch of CDs out to radio stations and have them wind up in a big cardboard box somewhere, I can e-mail links to MP3s and put audio up on these podcast-safe networks, and I can do searches and see if people are using it. Probably less people are listening to the different podcasts than would be listening to a terrestrial station, but it's so much easier, it's just a matter of e-mailing things out.

Right, and in terms of costs, you don't have to pay for a mailing or give up copies of your CDs.

Yeah, and with some of these portals, people can find you more easily, link to you more easily. It's good to stay abreast of things because in some ways it's more challenging to keep up, but on the other hand, it's more rewarding. And I find that interacting with people's really different now with blogs. I switched my website to where I have a blog on the front end, and I think people really like that personal touch. And then you have people following you without having to send e-mails out and pester people and spam them all the time. 'Cause I think people don't really read e-mails so much anymore. But if you keep a blog updated, people are still able to keep up with you and it's less effort. You can have everything right there. It's about ten years I've been doing the online thing. In some ways it hasn't changed too much, but in other ways it's really a lot different. You just have to stay on top. But I like it because you don't have to be a scenester to get out there.

Which I like, 'cause I hated that whole thing where you had to hang out in clubs and be networking and all that.

You feel like you can get that same networking online?

Yeah. It's sort of more suited to my personality that way.

You've placed some tracks on TV shows too. How did that happen?

I did some CD production library work, which I didn't like so much because you have to imitate other people. You do a minute or two minutes and you don't really know where it's going to be used. You get the check and you see that some Joan Lunden special used you, but you don't know what track it was. So I don't really hear the stuff in context. The one or two times that I've actually seen it used, it's been a little disappointing. One time I bought a DVD of a Discovery Channel special because I saw that I was on it. It was all this really exciting footage of this building being built, and then my music was used for the scene where the workmen had drunk too much the night before and were hung over! So now I don't run out to see; it's like, I made the money, I don't really care! But it's basically recycling stuff I've done, and that's how I make money to buy gear, and I write that off. So it's zero balance, and I get to do what I like doing.

: : :

Arthur Loves Plastic continues to make music and earn accolades: *Beneath the Watchful Eyes* (Machine Heart, 2007) won the Washington Area Music Award for Electronica Album of the Year, and a new CD, *Brief Episodes of Joy*, was released in April 2008.

Keiko Uenishi
(o.blaat)

Keiko Uenishi, mostly known as "o.blaat," is a Japanese sound artist and a former curator based in New York City. Her performance name derives from a Dutch word used in Japan that refers to a substance wrapped around medicine to conceal its bitter taste, which ultimately dissolves inside the body. True to this principle of dissolving, she has often interrogated and worked to displace the performer's presence on the stage. Her works are formed through experiments in restructuring and analyzing one's relationships with sounds in sociological, cultural, and/or psychological environments.

From 1999 to 2001, she curated the electronic music series [electroluxe] at Tonic in New York, which she described as her "personal research" for investigating nontraditional presentation formats. At these events she also created various versions of "opening ambience"—for instance by wiring contact mics to the cash registers, coat check room, and ping-pong table and racquets—an environmental situation that implicated the audience in constructing the sonic atmosphere of the venue.

She expressed an aversion to conventional rhythms, which stemmed in part from her background as a tap dancer. Unsatisfied with experiments in conventional tap dancing, she began making sound art as means of incorporating tap concepts with more avantgarde methods of performance. Her original performance setups included an "electro tap-board effecter," a floorboard she developed from textured pieces of plastic, wood, and metal she culled from shops on Canal Street, rigged with contact mics.

Around 2001 she shifted her work to the laptop, quit curatorial projects, and started to serve as part of the volunteering host team at Share, a community and forum for creative minds and a regular and open multimedia jam (Davis 2002). Uncurated and self-organized,

Share has expanded into more than eighteen cities worldwide through the efforts of an unaccountable number of people.

Uenishi has performed extensively in many countries, solo and in collaboration with other artists. She was an artist-in-residence at Harvestworks in New York City (2001 and 2004) and at Binauralmedia, Nodar, Portugal (2007). Her CD *Two Novels: Gaze/In the Cochlea* was released by the Portuguese label Crónica in 2004, followed by several compilation releases.

Keiko was among the first artists I interviewed for Pinknoises .com's initial publication. She was instrumental in introducing me to other artists in New York, and helpful when I was organizing the site's launch party in January 2001. We have kept in touch in the years since and met for this second interview in July 2004 in Manhattan.

: : :

Tara Rodgers: In our last interview, about five years ago, we covered the era when you were using your tap effector. Since then, you've shifted away from that.

Keiko Uenishi: Yeah, I don't use the tap-board anymore. It lasted about two years. Towards the end of it, I thought I'd done almost everything I could do with that setup. I wanted to explore other possibilities, soundwise. I was thinking about maybe computer. I was also doing experimental interactive pieces with only contact microphones, and I thought I could do a lot better if I used a Max/MSP program. But I had no knowledge; I didn't even have a proper computer. So a grant from Harvestworks in 2000 came in really at the right timing.

When I started studying Max/MSP, it was late summer of 2000, and even after two months I still had no idea how to use it. I felt really down about it. Ikue Mori gave me a tip. She started using it a little earlier, and she was already performing with it, so I started consulting her: How did you start it? It's so deep and vast, it seems like it will take years to grasp the concepts. And she said to start by doing it until Tutorial 12, and then jump to an example and open it up, and fool around with the sound. So that's what I did: opening up examples, changing stuff, modifications. And that made me think a lot better and understand a little more. So that was the beginning.

Right after that, pretty quickly I started doing some touring with a Max/MSP program. At the very beginning, I was still combining it with the tap-board, because I wasn't quite fully sure of shifting entirely to computer. Eventually I quit altogether using the tap-board, because I wasn't doing it for presentation sake, it was just because I didn't know how else to make sound. Once I started to be able to make sound only with computer, I thought, this is handier, I don't need to drag anything, or spend expensive car fare anymore, I can just carry a shoulder bag and come over. And also, the tap-board was too theatrical; everybody wanted to see it, and that was tiring me a lot. Now, I'm sitting down; it's a really boring performance presentation. I was excited about that—no longer, nobody's interested in watching me! [Laughs]

We've talked about that before, how you prefer to disappear from the stage. What sounds are you working with now? Do you still incorporate field or location recordings?

Not very much. I used to, with cassette tapes. Now, I feel like my tones are shorter and shorter, some of them less than a second now. Ten seconds is the most I use, and ten seconds is really long. I stopped using longer ones, so I really don't need so much variety. I already have hundreds of banks. And maybe once a year I do a refreshing; I dump what I have and make new banks. There's a lot of demand and interest in field recordings, but to me, the source of those sounds is too easy, it sounds too obvious.

You prefer it to be more abstracted?

Yeah, I didn't want the source to sound so obvious, because it so obviously leads you to think of something specific. If I do it, my interest is more about the sound which is not rooted to some original source. It's more that I'm interested to *misunderstand* the source. Sometimes I don't switch on the radio or listen to CDs in my daily life. I just listen to my room sound, my roommates walking by, I listen to every single thing. So my ear is really experiencing field recording all the time in my mind. And sometimes, I misinterpret some sounds I hear, as if I heard something else. And that kind of experience is more interesting for me.

In Max/MSP, are you working with synthesized sounds, or sampling?

I like both, if it's used well. Some of the samples I'm still using are from the period when I made sounds with the tap-board, so some of the files have really bad sound quality. But in my theory, crisp, clear sound is really attractive, but at the same time, really bad-quality sounds assembled together with those crisp, clear sounds—it makes some depth, like a three-dimensional feel. I think it's interesting to make compositions like that.

That's interesting, to mix resolutions to achieve depth. It's similar to the idea that music that's entirely digitally produced has a really clean quality, which can become more complex when you introduce something acoustic or analog.

Sometimes people add nice reverb, or analog compression when they're mastering. When I was working on finalizing my CD production, we tried many different things. However, somehow the method of adding compression didn't suit my original sound. It just didn't work out properly. Everything sounded much thicker, and a little distorted. I really have thin sounds, which to some people sounds too flat, like it needs more thickness. But I thought, well this is a different piece now. I don't want it; I want the thinness preserved. So I came back to the zero point.

Your CD is in two parts; I'm interested especially in the title of the second one, In the Cochlea. *What is this about?*

The first part is collaborations, and the second one is called *In the Cochlea* because it's all my solo work, and it's all composed with my headset in the middle of the night. That's when I'm working, and everybody else is sleeping, so I can't use speakers. Usually it's like the least recommendable thing to do; it's better to use speakers, but I didn't have spare time—daytime—to blast in my room. So I'm always sneakily working, not sleeping, in the middle of the night. Some of the tracks are really intense, so I added the caution to the CD: This is made for headset, however, be careful! Do so at your own risk.

Yeah, the conventional wisdom in audio engineering is that you should monitor in speakers, but increasingly so many people are doing most of their everyday listening in headphones.

For *In the Cochlea*, it doesn't mean that you can't listen in speakers, but certain effects—especially in those really bothering pieces, the ear-ringing pieces—if you listen in headphones, you not only feel the sound with your ear, but physically you feel the bone vibrating. The cochlea is a part of the ear, but it also gives you the feeling of balance. It's a very important portion of our body. And when I was making this with headphones, I felt this intimate feeling: the sounds and just yourself. But also, it was about the physical intake of sound, how we hear.

But it's of course a result of what I had to do, because of the situation I was in. Pretty much every single place I've lived in the past three years, I always needed to use the headphones 'cause I was sharing an apartment in New York. You know living in New York. We just have to be very careful when you're working with sounds. You can't always blast the sounds, there's a lot of limit.

Also, I think the process of composing is different, when you're working in headphones for a long period of time. When I do that, it's somehow more mentally intense.

Yeah. Mentally, you lose yourself into it—it's such a feeling. There's nothing to disturb you from it. I could go for many, many hours without sleeping, working with my headphones on!

Tell me about your curating projects, and your involvement with the Share events.

[electroluxe] doesn't happen anymore, unfortunately. I really don't have the energy anymore. It takes so much time, and I always did it with my own funds. I kept losing money, and I don't have a big income. I did it eight times, over a two-year period. It got bigger and bigger and I thought, I can do it and a lot of people want to see it, but only if I can get some sort of support. But I'm not running a not-for-profit organization, so there's no way to continue it. Some other people from other countries said, I can't believe you can't get government support. Those people, even if they are not-for-profit, they can get government support—but not here. There was also another fact, that a lot of people wanted to play, but not a lot of people wanted to work or organize.

In 2001, Share started, and I quickly fell in love with it. It's an open jam, without a sign-up board, without anybody who's controlling you. You just come in, and plug in and play. We'll help you, but we don't control you. It's a sharing experience, everybody bringing in whatever they want to play.

Keiko Uenishi with her laptop, New York City, 2004.

It was co-founded by Daniel Smith [a.k.a. NewClueless], Rich Pan-
ciera [a.k.a. Lloop; We™], and Geoff Matters [a.k.a. geoffGDAM]. Daniel
is a guru of multichannel systems. He configured everything. He's also
an engineer for speaker systems, so he knows inside out the configuration of speakers, and how to make audio sound great in different
rooms. I've been hanging out with these people from the very beginning. We built so much hardware, including long snake cables, so
wherever you sit down you have a box to plug in. It's really fantastic. I
learned a lot about soldering!

In New York City, it's every week on Sundays. It's ever expanding,
and a really loose community. We don't have any name tags, or who's
what, and that's the spirit we are trying to keep up. When they actually came up with the name, I thought, that's it, that tells everything!
This is the answer I wanted. I really got into that, and started seeing
that this is really the ultimate format of presentation, because finally
there's no apparent stage. Everybody's sitting around everywhere, and
you just start performing whenever you are plugged in. Then nobody
knows, sometimes. We have no idea sometimes, who's playing now.
'Cause everybody opens their laptop, some people are probably checking e-mail, and some people are just explaining stuff, and people are
chatting with you while you are playing: So what's going on? What are
you doing? And it's really not uptight, so people don't feel offended if
people talk with them. There are visual people too, jamming together.
We are using networked Internet and streaming out too, so people can
check it wherever you are.

When I started really getting into it, I thought, I don't need to
do any curation anymore. This is it. People are coming in, and some
of them are fantastic, much better than you could imagine curating
when you book a show. I thought, as long as Share is running, this
is just fine. It's different from karaoke; it's karaoke in a different format. This is something you create and you do it. There is no given
format. You simply come in and you play, and you encounter people
with a completely different kind of format and approach, and you play
together with people. And that is such a magical thing. We are not
controlling anything, we let all the localized people in the huge room
control it. They have to be able to hear themselves very well, otherwise
they start blasting out and it starts distorting and becomes chaos. But
as long as it can be controlled volumewise, for monitoring, then everybody can listen. Once they can hear what's going on, they can analyze

what they can do, so naturally they start collaborating without being told what to do. It's all about trusting humans, you know? And how much you can trust is related to how much you can do. I love it; I've never seen anything like this. Hearing some artist doing an unbelievable performance or concept is one thing; that's great. But then, this enormous amount of people who I don't even know and it's hard to remember all their names—they all can do amazing stuff. People know, any Sunday in New York, they can come over, and they do so. Some of them become spontaneous volunteers. So that's another reason I don't do [electroluxe] right now. I think helping Share is a very important thing for me.

You've said that you started curating [electroluxe] as your "personal research," to connect with other artists, and it seems like now you're getting that with Share.

Also, it was all about experimentation on presentations. Experimental electronic music—it's so boring, some people say. Notoriously, people who perform with a laptop are just sitting down in front of it, they don't even move and it's not fun to look at it. I thought it was completely wrong to present them onstage. Like, what is the point? So I wanted to shuffle around how to set them up, how to run the night, how people can have fun, and how much variety there is in the so-called electronic and experimental music that is happening. With some shows, the presentation tends to be really stiff: like this area is the performance area, and everybody tends to gaze at the performer and it becomes a one-directional thing. I wanted to scatter the attention to everywhere. I wanted them not only paying attention to the performer but to look around at what else is going on, because audio experience is such a thing. And unless people are told to walk around a room, they don't usually do it; they still want to see a performance. That's the tendency. It's probably human nature. So what I did was work for scattering: move them up and down, to different rooms, with the stage ever shifting around, offstage, side stage, onstage, backstage. It just moved around a lot.

But again, back to Share, it doesn't have *any* stage. It has three rooms, and people have no idea where to look at! [Laughs] So that's the ultimate, perfect situation. So that's happening every week, we don't need to prepare or curate. It's really easy. [*2006 update from Keiko*: In 2005, we moved it to a bar called Mundial with two rooms, bar room and lounge, but the jam concentrated in the lounge room for most of the time. Then in 2006 we had to move it again to a new venue called Reboot at 37 Avenue A in the East Village, where there is only one big lounge-y room but lots of breathing area. Downtown NYC has seen lots of changes and nonstop gentrification in the past ten years. East Village area has been experiencing so much pressure from community board—which is extremely residential with well-off young professionals, police, and fire department. Not only Mundial, there are lots of bars and clubs getting pressures to make the neighborhood "residential friendly." With moving around venues, the configuration and atmosphere changes, which is interesting, but hopefully we won't need to move it for a long while! We've always wanted to stay in a bar/lounge space since it makes Share encounter an unsuspecting general public who's not necessarily interested in coming to an "art event."]

From your experiences performing and curating, what are your thoughts about the politics of gender in the sound art scene?

I don't know, gender-oriented curation is sort of a hype, I guess. In Europe, there are some people who try to do theme-oriented festivals. I still am not really clear about putting only women in electronic music together and doing something together. I really want to see more women naturally fit into regular festivals, not putting "only women" together. It's like admitting we're minor—come on. So let's see more mix in the regular festivals. I really want to see interesting art that *happens* to be done by women. Sometimes I hear, You're in a good position, because each of the festivals wants a woman, one or two, so even if you are not on par, you have a better opportunity. Come on! That sounds like a really negative opinion. I want to be just a human being doing really decent art, decent sound. Not like, You're a girl doing electronic music, you're unusual, please come! That's not cool. Even some labels doing women-only record labels, I can't imagine doing it. What you are doing with the website as a reference point, you have all the information there so people have access to it, and your archive is running for a really long period of time without changing, and that's really precious. So I appreciate it. But curation-wise, it's not exciting for me to do gender-specific events or festivals.

Around this area, I'm known as a girl who makes music. But recently, when I sent out my CD, some I contacted first by e-mail, including this guy in London. He said, Well, actually, I should tell you, I saw your performance when I was visiting New York last year. But I didn't say hello. I was actually very surprised, I had heard of your name and was thinking you were a German guy or something! [Laughs] So it works, my moniker.

Was gender neutrality important when you chose your moniker?

No, but it's a part of it. I wanted to blur the idea of whether this name should be belonging to a woman or a man. 'Cause "o.blaat" can be anything, I purposely chose a name that doesn't sound girly. Everything about the concept of "o.blaat" is melting and disappearing.

: : :

Uenishi was an artist-in-residence for computer music at Brooklyn College in 2006–2007 and has pursued a master of science degree in integrated digital media at Polytechnic University, Brooklyn, New York. Her projects in 2008 included *vivre, vibrer,* a new site-specific, interactive installation in Antwerp, Belgium, and a collaboration with Merce Cunningham Dance Company and the composer Takehisa Kosugi at Dia:Beacon.

Riz Maslen
(Neotropic)

Since the mid-1990s, Riz Maslen (born 1965) has been a prominent
figure on the electronic music scene in the United Kingdom and internationally. She has released recordings as Small Fish With Spine
and under her more enduring alias Neotropic, including three albums
on the Ninja Tune imprint Ntone: *15 Levels of Magnification* (1996),
Mr. Brubaker's Strawberry Alarm Clock (1998), and *La Prochaine Fois*
(2001). In 2001, she founded Councilfolk Recordings with Paul Jason
Fredericks, a label for releasing their own work and that of like-
minded artists. On her more recent recordings for Councilfolk and
Mush (*White Rabbits*, 2004), she has drawn on collaborations with
other musicians to create ambient, postrock soundscapes in her dis-
tinctively introspective style. She is strongly influenced by film and
has turned to filmmaking to include visuals in her live performances.
Her music itself—which combines found sounds, thoughtful orches-
trations, and contemplative cadences—gestures toward cinematic
representations of places and moods.

When I began producing electronic music in the late 1990s, Riz was
the first woman I heard about who was producing her own tracks. I
first interviewed her over e-mail in June 2001 for Pinknoises.com,
and we met for this second interview in March 2004 at a cafe in London. When we finished talking, she walked me over—with a short
detour through a record store—to her friend Kaffe Matthews's studio, where I'd scheduled another interview the same day (included in
this volume). Riz revised the transcript of the interview in November 2006.

: : :

Tara Rodgers: Where are you from?

Riz Maslen: I'm originally from the West Country, about 100 miles away from London. We moved a few times but my teenage years were spent in a little village called Kempsford on the Wiltshire/Gloucestershire border. My dad worked as a civilian on an American air base. Kempsford is right on its perimeter.

Tell me about your earliest experiences with music.

My dad's a music lover, but not a musician. He was listening to a lot of rock and roll . . . Black Sabbath, Yes, Electric Light Orchestra, and the odd Beatles record. My mum was into Supertramp, Neil Diamond, and John Lennon. I was into all kinds of music from an early age, and learned flute from eleven years until about seventeen. I loved the idea of being taught how to play an instrument, but found the classical thing a bit boring. We often had to be in the school band or orchestra, which I found a bit tough. Could never really get to grips with the idea of working with sheet music. Seemed like a very different scene to what was happening on the streets, and what music I was daydreaming about at that time. But I can't knock it, 'cause it's where I got my musical grounding. I think discipline was the best thing I got from that, 'cause it is definitely the foundation of any craft. You'd come home from school, do your homework, practice for two hours, and after that? Talk to myself about how bloody ridiculous it was compared to AM radio. I was always very conscientious about that. I was also in a few bands when I was in school playing bass really badly and trying to be the front person. Which at that time I didn't want to be. As much as I wanted to be in a band, for sheer sake of providing a slot—bass player, keys, etc.—I was more interested in the gadgetry and functionality of connecting the dots to put it all together and record in a studio.

And at a certain point you left school. When was that?

I left school as soon as I could, at sixteen. Bloody hell it was tough for me. I just didn't feel like I could fit in, and subsequently got bullied for it. So I decided to travel around the country. Went and lived in squats and hung out with a lot of crazy/interesting people, who had more of an impacting presence than that of a glum old town out in the middle of nowhere. I learned a lot from being around older people, all that comes with being younger and hanging out with cool arty folk who listened to Joy Division, Throbbing Gristle, and Cabaret Voltaire.

Riz Maslen, 2008. PHOTOGRAPHY BY WWW.SAMFISHER.TV.

When did you move to London?

I've been in London for many years now. When I moved here I was basically meeting people through friends and finding out if anyone had studios, or if they needed some help, and I ended up working for a friend of a friend who wanted someone to help them out from time to time. Hamish [McDonald], the guy who ran the studio, was doing a lot of reggae and hip-hop at that time, and for me it was a great learning curve, and my real first introduction to music production, using computers and drum machines along with live instruments. I got to see how you'd record live drums and know which mic is best for which part of the kit, to get that all-important sound right. I had only really used four-track tape recorders before, which was pretty basic stuff.

I got to finally try and record, sample, and work with various bits of kit, and mostly just experimented with sound, trying out various recording techniques I had picked up while observing Hamish. In the same building was Reinforced Records, who were doing lots of drum 'n' bass at that time, and Future Sound of London had their studio downstairs. When they moved in, I had no idea who Future Sound of London was, but I found out that one of the guys was Humanoid [Brian Dougans]. So I ended up cornering him one day in the kitchen and asked him how he composed that track and said how much of an influence it had had on me. That bassline was killer!

The first time I walked into their studio I was like, Oh my God, this is amazing! Their studio was like a huge spaceship, with all this amazing equipment everywhere. They were so lovely and so supportive of me in my early days; both Garry [Cobain] and Brian encouraged me to experiment even more with sound manipulation, and to not be afraid of pushing the envelope. Through them and through working with Hamish, I got the confidence to really believe I could do this for myself. So I decided to get a small bank loan and set myself up with a really basic studio. I got an Akai S1000 and an Atari running Cubase, and a basic second-hand mixing desk, and just learned from there. I had an idea where I wanted to go with my music, if somewhat naively, at the start of my journey. For a good few months I shut myself away and became my own bedroom hero and just started writing, finally getting together a good body of work I was sure I was ready to send out to labels.

At what point did you start DJing?

On and off I've always done it, spinning tunes in the bedroom, playing mates' parties, and buying records from an early age. It's always been a fun thing for me to go out and play my favorite records, and even to this day I still love being turned on to new and interesting sounds. My time spent signed to Ninja Tune was a learning experience and a good fit with what was happening at the time. I felt like I was a part of a community that all had a like-minded agenda in regards to promotion and creating a fan base. This of course transcended into the music I tended to spin and through that came the exploration of new styles. It has also allowed to me to travel the world in support of my art, and I feel blessed that I have had those opportunities to experience so many different cultures.

Was there a certain point in your life when you knew that you wanted to be an artist or a musician?

I think I've always wanted to do something artistically based. We always had music humming through our house when I was growing up. Growing up in a community where folk weren't used to seeing anyone of ethnicity—my mum's mother was from India, and there weren't any black people in the village where I grew up—I got bullied at school for being a bit different, and this possibly drove me even harder to do something with my life to escape from a place I felt I wasn't welcome. I've done nine-to-five jobs, and I still do now, just to survive. I've worked in cafes and bars, and I teach music technology part-time to young people. Which I really enjoy doing because I feel like I'm giving back to my community, and offering an alternative to drugs and crime, especially in some of the poorer boroughs of London. A lot of the young people feel disaffected and don't necessarily have the money or the opportunity to go on to university. I still sometimes have to pinch myself, when I go out and play when there's a whole roomful of people who have come to see you.

Where do you teach, and how old are the students?

ADFED, which is Asian Dub Foundation's education program, set up by the founding members of ADF as a way to help and encourage young people to have a facility where they can come a learn to produce their own music. It's based in Tower Hamlets, East London, which has a real diverse population from many different cultures. The students range from fourteen years upwards. Some of them may have been excluded from school, or from various youth groups. It's about their experiences and how they can express themselves through music and word, and we try and get them away from thinking there is no hope, when in fact there is plenty of hope, and music can offer an alternative to hanging on the streets selling drugs.

There's an older generation of composers like Pauline Oliveros and Eliane Radigue, but in the dance music scene, you were really among the first widely known women producers. Have you experienced a certain amount of recognition for this?

I think for anyone, recognition for your work is welcomed, and yes, I have had people come up to me and express that they love what I do and I've had nice things said in the press. I guess when I first started out there weren't so many women out there that were visible. I just enjoy the fact that I can do something I love, and that's enough for me. Everything else is a bonus. I've met a lot of great female musicians, all of whom have contributed to the electronic scene. I met Kaffe Matthews a few years back and have worked with her on various projects. I have seen her live, and loved the way she could manipulate sound and create these great landscapes. And it was great for us to bring together two very different ways of working and creating something new.

Why do you think that there seems to be comparatively fewer women in the field?

Ten years ago I think when computers were just really starting to get their shit together, not everyone had access to them. Now I think it's become a lot easier just by the way we live our lives and how more dependent we are on our gadgets! Kids are so savvy from an early age; I am constantly surprised by what they know.

I still get a little sad when I see how women are portrayed in the media as objects as opposed to talent, however cute they may be. Making it all the more difficult to come across as a positive role model. But I'd like to think it's changing bit by bit, and we do have great women who are able to express themselves for who they are and not based on what they look like.

That's one thing I've always liked about you, that you seem to dress how you want and let the music speak for itself. Did you ever find in your career that you were pressured to do differently?

No, I've always been very much in control of me, and my image. I have a very strong personality and tend to do it my way. I'm very aware of that. As I've gotten older I've begun to understand it more. So when you start growing as an artist, there's a confidence issue as well that hopefully grows as you do. I love to wear high heels and feel sexy, but it's about me at the end of the day, and it's about my music. We aren't all blessed with perfect features, and I think men possibly have a better time of it, and aren't subjected to the same scrutiny women are. I think that's so much more relevant in the pop scene, as opposed to where I am and my contemporaries are. We don't necessarily have to compete in the same arena, but I think there is struggle for women in all fields of their work, so it's often the case of overcoming many struggles and learning from them. All you can do is believe in what you do and keep remembering that, whoever puts you down.

I think that women can confront competing assumptions—either that they aren't technically competent, or if they are, then they don't fit some people's ideas of what a "woman" is.

I think men and women work very differently, and our approaches may be counter-clockwise to that of anyone we may work with. I've worked with both men and women, and the tendency I feel can be down to men knowing what the latest piece of gear is, religiously reading some magazine reviewing a piece of equipment, or knowing its entire workings by reading the manual. That's cool too; I guess I'm just more interested in having a go with discovering how things feel and allowing the moment unfold itself. I've always had to deal with technical situations and was made to feel like I wasn't important or didn't know what I was asking for, but overall I've had more positive experiences than bad ones.

Tell me more about your process of making music.

I first started off in weird little bands at school and, even after leaving, I continued until I released my first Neotropic album in 1996. I experimented with using various lo-fi recordings, mainly using four-track recorders layering guitars and vocals with a friend of mine under the guise of Shrine, which I think really did turn me onto the technology side of things. After moving to London, and working with Hamish and learning the art of sampling, it was a case of using a mixture of found sound recordings I collected and samples from all kinds of sources, learning to manipulate them through the sampler, or processing it through effects. Still a process I use today, as I just love that idea of pushing a sound in all directions!

I tend not to use samples these days; it's more me sampling myself. I create my own textures and soundscapes, and have a lot of fun doing it. I can spend weeks recording sounds from the guitar and processing them . . . It's like putting all the ingredients into one big pot and stirring it up. I do a lot of preproduction. I'm kind of working in the same way as you would with film: preproduction, getting all your assets together, and then the shoot.

I think film has influenced me even from when I was a kid, being inspired by the way sound and moving images work providing atmosphere and space. I have been inspired by filmmakers like Stanley Kubrick, Alfred Hitchcock, and David Lynch, who've always pushed the boundaries not only with their films but the way they use sound and music. Lynch has this way where he brings a sound in by adding a totally uncomfortable edge. I like that dodgy feeling of certain sounds that you wouldn't necessarily associate with certain scenes; it almost feels a bit disjointed and kind of leaves you wondering why he did that.

Workingwise, I don't really have a formula; it's all down to the way I might feel on a particular day. Some tracks just come quickly and others take a slower route. I can get quite brutal in my critique and ditch a song without giving it a chance. But then I can often stumble on these little gems every now and then and rediscover them.

So I often have lots of little tracks on the go, and they tend to be works-in-progress. Particularly with this album, I've had a lot of these tracks sitting around for ages in a raw form and then I've gotten them back up, and I'm like, I think it's time to work on this now, it feels right. On *White Rabbits*, I went and worked in Minneapolis for three weeks and worked with a lot of people there, recording drums, guitars . . . Everybody I worked with was so receptive. And I love the community, where there's a real network of cool musicians—most of these guys aren't just doing their own stuff, but play in two or three different bands. There's a real mixture on this album, but it has a lot more guitars and live instrumentation compared to what I have done in the past, which kind of harks back to my teenage years.

Your last album was going in this direction too. I think of you as an electronic musician, but listening to your albums with acoustic instruments, one wouldn't necessarily know.

I listened to the first album the other day, and thought, Wow, it's such a big change. You can hear there's something similar in the way I put them together, but I think I've grown as an artist and you can definitely hear that. There's been a lot more playing involved; and I'm very much from that school, 'cause I've always been in bands and played, as opposed to relying on technology. I've come full circle with some new knowledge I didn't have in the beginning, and now I have the facility where I can use them both. There are now a lot of artists out there who are writing their stuff in their bedroom and they sound like a whole band. I love that element that you can never tell now whether it's been made in some big, fancy studio, or if it's just made in someone's bedroom or basement. I think it's fantastic that you don't need loads of money to make music.

You've been working in this realm for ten years or so, so you've seen a change in the technologies, from the hardware samplers you started with to all the software tools available now. Do you have favorite things that you've discovered along the way?

It's very hard to keep up; because you know how fast technology moves now, particularly software. When I first started out I could not afford a new Macintosh and opted for the tough and resilient Atari, which was a great place for me to start. It would only be time before I made that transition from the old to the new. I would love to be able to keep up with the newest laptop or piece of software, but I have learned to work with what I have and it serves me pretty well. Of course I do need a new machine the more I move into live audio, thus needing a faster machine to cope with it. Whereas before, I'd be running sixteen channels of audio and it would be fine. But now, I'm using a lot more, and I'm using more than one program. I use Rewire a lot, so I'm using Reason slaved with Cubase. It's a case of learning to bounce tracks down and freeing up that all-important RAM.

My work is more and more about working with various musicians and collaborating, and I then take everything away and piece everything together. It's not so much the sample element these days but working with raw material and shaping it. Sometimes it's a case of, I ring a mate of mine who plays cello and ask if they fancy coming over to my place to try some stuff out. I've got a great collection of friends who are all so talented, and it's fantastic having those resources. What we tend to do is all help each other out: If you can do this on my track, I can do this on yours. It's great when it's not always about money, as hard as it can be at times. So right now I'm trying to build on a community, which you don't really get here, unlike in cities like Montreal and Minneapolis where there is very much a community of musicians where they all pull on each others' resources. I do love technology, and I try to feed into it as much as I can. But you do get to the point where you're just trying to keep up the whole time, and it does become quite frustrating when you can't always buy the latest software or the latest piece of technology. I like the fact that my home studio can be scaled down and made portable which for me is such a great way to be. Over the past few years I've just done that . . . packed it up and gone traveling with it.

∴ ∴ ∴

Since our interview, Maslen returned to school at the University of Westminster and earned a foundation degree in multimedia, graduating with distinction in July 2007. In 2008, she released a new album, *Whiter Rabbits* (Council Folk), featuring remixes from Lady Husk, Hipnotica, 10sui, and others; she is also signed to Squid's Eye Records. She continues to teach music technology to young people in many boroughs of London. She advocates "the encouragement of more young women being involved in production, especially from those minorities that would not necessarily get the opportunity." She describes it as "one of her great passions" to pass on her knowledge and skills "in the hope that young people will have an opportunity to be heard in a positive light, through music."

Glossary

For more detailed explanations of these concepts, see Huber and Runstein 1997; Roads 1996; Truax 1999.

1200s: Technics SL-1200 series of turntables, originally released in the 1970s and since established as the unofficial industry standard for club DJing and turntablism

accel-decel (accelerando-decelerando): a gradual speeding up and slowing down of musical tempo

acoustic: a sound or instrument that is not amplified or mediated electronically

acoustics: the study of the production, effects, and transmission of sound waves; also used to describe how a spatial environment affects sound

algorithm: a set of procedures for accomplishing tasks, usually carried out by a computer. Algorithmic music composition involves writing a computer program to generate or process sounds based on specific parameters and step-by-step processes

amplifier: a device that boosts signal level by increasing its amplitude

amplitude: the "level" of a sound, perceived as volume; shown as the distance above or below the horizontal axis on a graph of a signal's waveform

analog: a continuously variable quantity. An analog audio signal has continuously variable amplitude and frequency values; an analog circuit provides a continuous output as a response from its input (as opposed to the discrete steps of digital values)

ARP: one of various synthesizers designed by Alan R. Pearlman from 1969 to 1981

attack: the first stage of an envelope; ranges from the beginning of a sound to its peak amplitude

attenuation: reduction of the amplitude of an audio signal

band: a specified range of frequencies (see also *equalization* and *filter*)

bank: in a synthesizer, sampler, or computer, a storage location that holds a large number of individual sounds

beat-matching: a technique used by DJs to synchronize the musical tempos of different songs playing simultaneously on two turntables; achieved by changing the playback speed on the turntables and/or manually moving the records

bel canto: an Italian style of vocal performance that emphasizes purity of tone

bhangra: a traditional form of Punjabi music and dance that has also been hybridized with other music and performance traditions, including hip-hop and club music

bit depth: the level of detail at which digital audio represents an analog signal; a higher bit depth (i.e., 24-bit compared to 8-bit) results in a clearer, more accurate representation of the sound

broken beats: rhythmic patterns in which repetitive structures are disrupted and/or reconstructed through techniques of sampling, editing, or improvisation

Buchla: an electronic musical instrument designed by Don Buchla; usually refers to one of his voltage-controlled modular synthesizers from the 1960s and early 1970s

buffer: a section of RAM that temporarily stores data

capacitor: an electrical device that stores electrical charge, holds and releases it as necessary; used to maintain a consistent flow of electricity

central processing unit (CPU): the main processor in a computer, which performs calculations and coordinates hardware components

chance operations: the incorporation, often systematically, of random elements or indeterminacy in music composition

channel: a path along which electrical signals travel (see also *mixer*)

circuit: an electrical device that provides a path for electrical flow (see also *integrated circuit*)

circuit bending: a creative technique for rewiring the circuitry of a low-voltage, battery-operated electronic device (such as an ordinary toy that makes sound) to produce unconventional or unpredictable sounds

close-micing: a recording technique that involves placing a microphone very close to a sound source in order to maximize the input level of the sound, and minimize nearby sounds or ambient noise

codec: software or other technology for compressing or decompressing data

compression: a process of reducing the dynamic range of an audio signal by boosting the softer parts and limiting the louder parts; also refers to a method of reducing digital file size by removing data, using algorithms that identify redundant or unnecessary information

contact mic: a microphone designed to physically touch the object producing sound; the resulting audio signal derives primarily from mechanical vibrations of the sounding object rather than from sound waves in the air

control rate: in real-time audio synthesis programming languages, variables can be handled at different rates; a programmer can specify that certain nonaudio variables (for example, an envelope generator) be processed at control rate, rather than sample rate; this enables more efficient computation

control signal: in synthesis, a signal used to modulate another

controller: a device that outputs MIDI data, such as a keyboard or joystick, often used in live electronic music performance. A *continuous controller* transmits data steadily over time (versus a *switch controller*, which turns a device on or off)

convolve (or convolution): a signal processing operation equivalent to filtering the spectrum of one sound with another

crossfade: in audio mixing or DJing, a transition during which one sound or element of a mix fades out, and another fades in

crystal radio: a simple form of radio receiver, prominent among amateur radio enthusiasts beginning in the early 1900s, that requires no battery or power source, only the power received from radio waves through a long antenna

Cubase: a MIDI and digital audio software application developed by the company Steinberg and first released in 1989

cue: in DJing or mixing, a signal that is fed to headphones or monitors for purposes of testing the sound before it is played over the main loudspeakers

decay: the reduction of a signal's amplitude level over time

delay: a signal processing device that stores a signal for a specified time before releasing it to the output

diffusion: the distribution of sound across multiple channels or speakers in a space

digital: a method of storing, processing, and transmitting information as a string of binary digits (0 and 1). In digital audio, an analog signal is periodically measured at a standard sample rate and converted to a stream of binary values for storage and manipulation

digital signal processing (DSP): audio signal manipulation carried out in the digital realm (often refers to digital *effects*)

diode: a device that allows current to flow in only one direction

drum machine: an electronic device, usually controllable by MIDI, used to generate or play back percussion sounds and rhythms

drum 'n' bass: a genre of electronic music characterized by broken beats, a fast tempo, and prominent basslines

dynamic range: the difference between the quietest and loudest levels of a sound

Echoplex: an analog delay device that uses magnetic tape for recording and playback, manufactured by the Maestro company in the 1960s

effects: any form of audio signal processing, such as reverb or delay

electroacoustic: a diverse genre that typically refers to music made with a combination of acoustic sounds and electronic technologies and played back over loudspeakers, often composed with particular attention to spatial aspects of sound

electromagnetic induction: a process of producing an electric current by changing the magnetic field near a conductor (a device designed to transmit electricity)

electron microscopy: a technique that uses a beam of electrons to illuminate a specimen, and has a very high magnification power

embouchure: the manner in which a player applies the mouth to the mouthpiece of a wind instrument

envelope: the shape of a sound's amplitude as it changes over time. In sound synthesis, an *envelope generator* creates an envelope with specific contours, and an *envelope follower* detects an input signal's amplitude variation over time and produces another control signal that resembles that shape

equalization (EQ): a process of boosting or attenuating various frequencies of an audio signal

extended techniques: unconventional methods of singing or playing musical instruments

fader (or *slider*): a linear control for adjusting audio signal level or other sound parameters on a mixer, synthesizer, or other device (see also *potentiometer*)

feedback: any process by which an output of a system is returned to its input, affecting the subsequent output

filter: a device or technique for affecting the spectrum (and thus, timbre) of a sound by attenuating certain frequency bands while allowing other bands to remain unaffected. A low-pass filter, for example, attenuates higher frequencies and allows frequencies below a specified point to pass through

FLAC (Free Lossless Audio Codec): a digital audio compression format that retains the information (and thus, sound quality) of the original data file, as opposed to "lossy" formats like MP3

four-track: a device (typically a cassette recorder) for recording and mixing sounds on four separate tracks

frequency: the rate at which an acoustic sound source or electrical signal repeats one cycle of positive and negative amplitude; measured in Hertz (Hz), or cycles per second (see also *fundamental*)

fundamental: for sounds that are made up of complex tones of various frequencies, amplitude, and phase (all sounds except for a sine wave), the *fundamental* is the lowest frequency among this complex, and is perceived as pitch

glitch: a sonic artifact resulting from malfunctions of digital technologies, such as CD skipping noises and digital distortion; also refers to a genre of electronic music that foregrounds these sounds

granular synthesis: a process of producing acoustic events by assembling massive numbers of individually formed sound grains of minuscule duration

harmonic: a frequency of vibration that is an integer multiple of the fundamental

house: a style of electronic dance music emerging from African American and gay clubs in Chicago in the early 1980s, fusing musical elements of 1970s funk and disco with newer music technologies, including MIDI synthesizers and drum machines. Subgenres include acid house (characterized by repetitive rhythmic structures, and the distinctive timbre of the Roland TB-303 bass synthesizer); tribal house (featuring layered drum and percussion patterns), and progressive house (known for its complex progressions of melodies and basslines)

hydrophone: a waterproof microphone designed for recording underwater

infinite impulse response (IIR) filter: one of the primary filters used in DSP applications; a process in which the output of the filter is routed back through its input repeatedly and potentially infinitely

installation: a work of art presented in a gallery or other exhibition space

integrated circuit: a miniature device or "chip," made of material such as silicon, that forms the basis of contemporary electronic devices; combines in one small device several components like transistors and capacitors that were previously separate

isolation: a recording technique that seeks to separate a sound source from extraneous or unwanted noise

isorhythmic: a method of music composition that uses recurring rhythmic patterns as a formal technique

just intonation: a tuning system based on the harmonic series, in which frequency ratios are related by whole number ratios, instead of on the octave system used in standard keyboard tunings

Logic: a MIDI and digital audio software application originally produced by the company Emagic, now released by Apple

loop: a phrase of audio that is repeated (often a *sample*). A *loop point* refers to the start or end point of a loop as set in the editing process

mastering: the final stage in the preparation of recordings before mass duplication

Max/MSP: a graphical software environment for music, audio, and multimedia, produced by the Cycling '74 company

microphone (or mic): a device for amplification or recording that converts acoustic sound waves into electrical signals

MIDI (Musical Instrument Digital Interface): a standard adopted by electronic music equipment manufacturers in the early 1980s to enable control and synchronization of different synthesizers, sequencers, and other devices. MIDI does not transmit audio signals but rather digital data "event" messages, such as pitch and volume information, that provide instructions for a synthesizer or other instrument to use when generating sound

mix (or mixdown): the process in which separate audio signals are combined and balanced; volume, EQ, effects, and spatialization can be managed during this step

mixer (or mixing board, console, desk): a device that receives and combines audio signals from separate channels; offers control of volume, EQ, and panning, and routes combined signals to directed destinations (such as analog tape or CD-R)

modular synthesizer: a kind of synthesizer consisting of separate modules with different functions that can be connected to each other with cables to form a patch

modulation: a process by which any parameter of sound or audio signal is varied systematically; for example, amplitude modulation is a periodic fluctuation in a sound's level, perceived as a tremolo effect

monitors: speakers used for mixing in a recording studio; can also refer to speakers placed onstage for musicians to hear themselves in live performance

Moog: one of many synthesizers designed by Robert Moog

motive: a pattern that is repeated in a piece of music

MPC (MIDI Production Center): one of several sampler/sequencer models manufactured by the Akai company, known for its touch-sensitive pads for creating rhythm patterns, and popularized in hip-hop production beginning in the 1980s

multitrack recording (or multitracking): a method of recording in which multiple sound sources are recorded on separate tracks, simultaneously or at different times, and played back and mixed together into a coherent entity

musique concrète: a genre of music, developed and named by the French radio engineer and composer Pierre Schaeffer in the late 1940s; music composed by assembling and manipulating recorded sounds, especially environmental and other sounds considered to be nontraditional in music composition

NAND gate: one of the basic building blocks of digital circuits that performs logical operations

noise: a term often used to describe the unwanted portions of a signal, like hiss or hum. The musical genre of noise makes creative use of these conventionally undesirable aspects, focusing on textural, dissonant, and distorted sounds

nonlinear: a form of digital recording that relies on RAM rather than a tape medium

object-oriented: a style of computer software development that is based on how objects in the world interact with each other

operating system (OS): the software that controls all other programs on a computer system

oscillator: an electronic device or software process that generates a periodic waveform, which is heard as a specific tone or frequency

overdub: in multitracking, the recording of a new track to be layered with previously recorded tracks

overtone: any frequency component of a spectrum that is not the fundamental

panning: placement or movement of a sound to a specific point in the stereo or multichannel field

parametric EQ: a kind of equalization processor that has controls for frequency, bandwidth, and gain; allows for very precise control of equalization

partial: a frequency component of a spectrum that is not an integer multiple of the fundamental

patch: a specific sound setting of a synthesizer or similar device. The term originated with early modular synthesizers, where cables were used to patch separate modules together. It has carried over into the software realm, so, for example, one uses the term "Max patch" to describe a particular software configuration that generates sound or other events in that program

phase: the relative position in the progression of a wave's cycle (for instance, the peak or low point of a waveform), where a complete cycle is 360 degrees

pickup: a magnet wrapped with wire used to convert acoustic sound (like the sound of guitar strings) to electrical signals

plug-ins: self-contained software programs that can be used to extend the capabilities of a primary software system

potentiometer (or pot): a variable resistor used to adjust the level or other parameters of an audio signal on a mixer, synthesizer, or other device; typically refers to a rotary rather than a linear control (see also *fader*)

power electronics: a subgenre of noise music that is described as being more synthesizer-based and lyric-oriented than other genres of noise

preamplifier (or preamp): a device used to amplify a weak signal, such as that of a microphone, before it reaches the main amplifier of a system

processing (or *signal processing*; see also *digital signal processing*): a general term for functions used to manipulate or enhance analog or digital representations of signals; includes processes such as compression, equalization, and filtering

ProTools: a software- and hardware-based audio and MIDI recording system, developed by the Digidesign company

psychoacoustics: the study of relationships between sound, auditory perception, and psychology

quadraphonic: recording or playback of four channels of sound, distributed through four speakers

quadrivium: the four branches of learning at medieval universities, including arithmetic, geometry, music, and astronomy

RAM (random-access memory): a type of computer storage used by programs to perform tasks while the computer is turned on. An integrated circuit allows data stored in RAM to be accessed in any order (versus mechanical storage media, like magnetic tape, in which data must be accessed in a fixed order)

real-time: events that unfold in the present, or information processing that occurs so quickly that it is perceived to be instantaneous

Reason: a software workstation manufactured by the Propellerhead company, including synthesizers, samplers, a drum machine, effects, and other audio tools

recursion: the ability of a computer program to call itself (a process of self-referencing within the program)

remastering: a process of creating a new master version of an older recording, typically by reducing hiss and noise

resistor: an electronic component that resists the flow of electrical current

resonator: a part of an instrument, body, or other object that vibrates, amplifying and affecting the perceived timbre of the sound waves interacting with it

reverberation (or reverb): the continuation of a sound as reflected waves in an acoustic space after the original sound source has stopped; also can be simulated digitally

Rewire: a software system for transferring audio data between different computer programs, developed by the Propellerhead company

ring modulation: an effect resulting from the multiplication of two audio signals

ROM card: a device that stores information in read-only memory; the contents can be accessed and read, but not changed

sample: a segment of digital audio (see also *loop*, *sampler*)

sample rate (or sampling rate): the frequency at which an analog audio signal is measured at discrete intervals (like snapshots) for conversion to digital information. A higher sample rate results in a more accurate representation of the analog source; the standard sample rate for CDs is 44.1 Kilohertz (kHz)

sampler: a device for recording, processing, and reproducing segments of digital audio

schematic: a technical diagram that explains how a circuit functions

semiconductor: a material, like silicon, that can conduct electricity under some conditions but not others, making it useful for controlling electrical current; the material used to build computer chips

sequencer: a device used to record, edit, and play back MIDI data

Serge: a modular synthesizer designed by Serge Tcherepnin in the 1970s

SH-101: a small, monophonic bass synthesizer (capable of playing one note at a time) produced by the Roland company in the 1980s

shift registers: in electronic circuits, a series of storage locations across which data shifts with each clock cycle

signal: an electrical representation of a sound wave in the form of alternating current; an electrical audio signal cannot be heard until it is sent to an amplifier and speakers, where it is translated into an acoustic audio signal

signal path (or signal flow): in a mixer or other electronic system with several components chained together, the direction of movement of the signal from the output of one component to the input of the next, and so on, until the end of the chain is reached

signal processing: see *processing*

signal-to-noise ratio: in sound recording or transmission, a measurement of the desired signal in comparison to the undesired noise; a favorable ratio is one in which the signal is clearly distinguishable from the noise

slider: see *fader*

Smalltalk: an object-oriented programming language developed in the 1970s

sound design: the process of creating sound effects or other sonic elements in a film or other soundtrack

sound-on-sound: a feature of some multitrack tape recorders that allows a previously recorded track to be transferred to another track at the same time a new track is being recorded

spatialization: the perception of sound in a space, or the process of working with sound to affect its perceived location in a space

spectral analysis: examination of a sound's spectrum, often for purposes of creative transformation or imitative synthesis

spectrum: the frequency content of a sound or signal, which contributes to a sound's perceived timbre

stereo field: the full range of perceived space encompassing left and right channels in a stereo (two-channel) audio mix

subharmonic: an integer fraction of the fundamental frequency. The harmonic series consists of integer multiples of the fundamental; the subharmonic series is related to the fundamental frequency by ratios (1/2, 1/3, 1/4, etc.)

SuperCollider: an open-source programming language for real-time audio synthesis

synthesis: the electronic production of sound via analog or digital means, without using any acoustic sound source, made possible through the analysis of parts of a sound wave

synthesizer (or synth): electronic instrument designed for sound synthesis (see also *virtual synthesizer*)

timbre: tone quality, often described as a sound's color or texture; determined by how a sound's spectrum or frequency content changes over time

time-scale: the time interval that is roughly equivalent to the duration of a particular process. For example, the time-scale of a musical gesture corresponds to the time it takes for that embodied action to occur, like your hand strumming a guitar. If the resulting sound is recorded and played back by a computer at another speed that no longer corresponds to the initial action, it could be described as having a different time-scale than the original sound

track: the path on a recording medium (such as magnetic tape) that holds recorded sound; also refers to an individual unit of music (i.e., one song on an album)

transistor: an electronic device that controls the flow of electricity

transposition: changing the key of a musical composition

tube: an electronic device with a system of conductive strips arranged in a glass or metal container. Amplifiers and other equipment with tubes were mostly phased out in the 1960s and 1970s in favor of solid-state (semiconductor-based) devices, although tube gear remains popular among some hi-fi enthusiasts and musicians for its perceived "warm" sound quality

turntablist: an artist who works with one or more turntables as a musical instrument, generating rhythms and textures that extend beyond those that occur with the ordinary playback of records

UPIC: a graphics tablet input device for a computer, designed by the composer Iannis Xenakis in 1977 at the Center for Studies in Mathematics and Automated Music in Paris. Xenakis used the UPIC system to control computer music with hand-drawn lines and shapes

variable speed: a feature on some recording devices that allows adjustment of recording and/or playback speed

video tracking: the process of following moving objects with a camera linked to a software system

virtual synthesizer: a software synthesizer, which typically emulates the design and features of a hardware synthesizer

voltage: a measure of the pressure behind electrical flow

voltage control: a method of altering the signal passing through a device, such as a synthesizer or amplifier, by introducing a change in voltage at the device's input

Wacom tablet: an interface for inputting information to a computer by moving a pen on a tablet, made by the Wacom company

white noise: a sound or signal made up of all frequencies within the audible range at equal intensity; many wind or water sounds are similar to white noise

women's music: a musical genre and culture created by and for women that emerged in association with second-wave feminism and other social movements in the 1970s

Discography

This discography represents a wide range of genres and practices in DJing, electronic music, and sound art. It is by no means exhaustive; using this information as a starting point, one could find many more recordings by these and other women. I asked the artists I interviewed to recommend which of their own recordings represent their work well, and which recordings by other women they would like to include. Most artists responded to both requests, so this list consists substantially of their input as well as my own. The sound artists Carrie Bodle and Anna Friz also made recommendations. For the most part, this is experimental and underground music that circulates outside mainstream distribution channels. I rely on the following stores to obtain recordings like those listed here:

Aquarius Records (San Francisco, Calif.),
   http://www.aquariusrecords.org/
Bleep.com (online only), http://www.bleep.com/
CDeMusic/Electronic Music Foundation (online only),
   http://www.cdemusic.org/
Forced Exposure (online only), http://www.forcedexposure.com/
Other Music (New York City), http://www.othermusic.com/
Twisted Village (Cambridge, Mass.), http://www.twistedvillage.com/

One Hundred Recordings by Women DJs, Electronic Musicians, and Sound Artists
(Compact disc format unless otherwise noted)

AGF. *Westernization Completed*. Orthlorng Musork ORTH 18 CD, 2003.
Alice and the Serial Numbers. *Obit*. AliceMusic, 2003.
Allien, Ellen. *Stadtkind*. BPitch Control BPC 021 CD, 2001.
Amacher, Maryanne. *Sound Characters (Making the Third Ear)*. Tzadik TZ 7043, 1999.
Anderson, Laurie. *Big Science*. Warner Brothers 3674–2, 1990 (1982).
Anderson, Ruth, and Annea Lockwood. *Sinopah*. Experimental Intermedia XI 118, 1998.
The Angel. *No Gravity*. Supa Crucial Recordings NLR-39008–2, 2001.

Apache 61. *China Syntax*. No Immortal NO EP 002, 2002. 12".

Arthur Loves Plastic. *Pursuit of Happiness*. Machine Heart MHR2006alp1, 2006.

Babin, Magali, and I8U. *Peak*. Independent BI 01, 2003.

Barron, Louis and Bebe. *Forbidden Planet: Original MGM Soundtrack*. GNP Crescendo PR-001, 1995 (1978).

Blechdom, Kevin. *Bitches without Britches*. Chicks on Speed Records, COSR 009 CD, 2003.

Blectum, Blevin. *Magic Maple*. Praemedia/Bleakhouse PRAE CD B01, 2004.

Blectum from Blechdom. *The Messy Jesse Fiesta*. Deluxe Records DLX 007 CD, 2000.

Block, Olivia. *Pure Gaze*. Sedimental SED CD 026, 1999.

Brazelton, Kitty, and Dafna Naphtali. *What Is It Like to Be a Bat?* Tzadik TZ 7707, 2003.

Calix, Mira. *Eyes Set against the Sun*. Warp CD 150, 2007.

Cardiff, Janet. *The Walk Book*, by Mirjam Schaub. Cologne: Verlag Der Buchhandlung Walther König, 2006. Book with audio CD.

Carlos, Wendy. *A Clockwork Orange: Wendy Carlos's Complete Original Score*. Produced by Rachel Elkind, remastered by Wendy Carlos. East Side Digital ESD 81362, 1998 (1972).

Chavez, Maria. *Those Eyes of Hers*. Pitchphase PP CDR 04, 2004.

Chicks on Speed. *Will Save Us All*. Chicks on Speed Records COSR 001 CD, 2000.

Cinader, Martha. *Living It*. Produced by Jeannie Hopper and Sabine Worthmann, with remixes by Sub Dub and BoC. Liquid Sound Lounge LSL 213–1, 1997. 12".

Colette and DJ Heather. *i-OM Mix Series: House of Om*. Om Records OM 219, 2006. 2xCD.

Colleen. *Everyone Alive Wants Answers*. The Leaf Label BAY 31 CD, 2003.

The Coup (with Pam the Funkstress). *Pick a Bigger Weapon*. Epitaph Records 86720–2, 2006.

Derbyshire, Delia. Various tracks on BBC *Radiophonic Music*. BBC REC 025M CD, 2002 (1968).

Electric Indigo. *Six-Track Reworks 2*. Remixes by Miss Kittin and Acid Maria. Indigo 005 EP, 2004. 12".

Elias, Hanin. *In Flames*. Digital Hardcore Recordings DHR CD 22, 2000.

Endo, Nic. *Cold Metal Perfection*. Geist 015 CD, 2001.

Fe-Mail. *Blixter Toad*. Asphodel ASP 2033 CD, 2006. 2xCD.

Friz, Anna. *Vacant City Radio*. A2Z, 2005.

Fullman, Ellen. *Body Music*. Experimental Intermedia XI 109, 1993.

Gardner, Alexandra. *Luminoso*. Innova 662, 2006.

Gosfield, Annie. *Burnt Ivory and Loose Wires*. Tzadik TZ 7040, 1998.

Granny'Ark. *Resurgo*. Zora Lanson Label ZoLaLa 001, 2004. 12".

Greenham, Lily. *Lingual Music*. Paradigm Discs PD 22, 2007. 2XCD.

Hand, K. *Detroit History, Part 1*. Tresor 168 CD, 2001.

Heart, Heather. Featured on *Sonic Groove Defined: Frankie Bones, Adam X, Heather Heart*. Instinct Records INS-583–2 CD, 2001.

Honda, Yuka. *Memories Are My Only Witness*. Tzadik TZ 7703, 2002.

Hutchinson, Brenda. "Long Tube Trio." *Mini-mall*. Tellus CD 027, 1993.

Kemistry & Storm. *DJ-Kicks*. Studio !K7 074 CD, 1999.

Kermani, Elise. *Solos for Air*. Ishtar CD 301, 1999.

Klein, Judy. *The Wolves of Bays Mountain*. Open Space CD 15, 2004.

Kubisch, Christina. *On Air*. Die Schachtel DS 3, 2004.

Kuttin Kandi. "Bongo Bop." *Turntable Essence*. Hip Bop, 2001.

La Berge, Anne. *United Noise Toys: Live in Utrecht '98*. X-OR FR 8, 1998.

The Lappetites. *Before the Libretto*. Quecksilber 10, 2005.

Lesbians on Ecstasy. *Lesbians on Ecstasy*. Alien8 Recordings ALIEN CD 051, 2004.

Le Tigre. *Le Tigre*. Mr. Lady Records MRLR 07, 1999.

Lockwood, Annea. *A Sound Map of the Hudson River*. Lovely Music LCD 2081, 1989.

———. *Breaking the Surface*. Lovely Music LCD 2082, 1999.

Matthews, Kaffe. *cd Bea*. Annette Works AWcd0002, 1998.

Mileece. *Formations*. Lo Recordings LCD 30, 2002.

DJ Minx. *A Walk in the Park EP*. Minus 33mp3, 2004. MP3 download.

Miss Dinky. *Melodias Venenosas*. Traum 005 CD, 2001.

Misstress Barbara. *Relentless Beats, vol. 2*. Moonshine Music MM 80165–2, 2002.

Morabito, Susan. *Love to Dance*. Whirling Records 3006, 1999.

Morgenstern, Barbara. *Vermona ET 6–1*. Monika 05, 1999.

Mori, Ikue. *Garden*. Tzadik TZ 7020, 1996.

Mutamassik. *Masri Mokkassar: Definitive Works*. Sound-Ink SIK 015, 2005.

Neotropic. *Laundraphonic*. Ntone Records NTONE 18, 1996. 12".

———. "The Horse Trainer." *Prestatyn*. Council Folk Recordings CF CD 001, 2006. EP.

Neuberg, Amy X. *Residue*. Other Minds OM 1007–02, 2004.

Neutral. *Motion Of*. Hymen CD 718, 2002

Norton, Doris. *The Double Side of the Science*. Musik Research CD/MR 0148, 1990.

o.blaat. *Two Novels: Gaze/In the Cochlea*. Crónica CD 012, 2004.

Oliveros, Pauline. *Crone Music*. Lovely Music LCD 1903, 1990.

———. *Alien Bog/Beautiful Soop*. Pogus Productions P21012–2, 1997.

———. *Electronic Works*. Paradigm Discs PD 04, 1997.

Oram, Daphne. *Oramics*. Paradigm Discs PD 021, 2007. 2XCD.

Parenti, Susan. "No, Honey, I can do it." *Sonic Circuits IX*. Innova 118, 2002.

Parker, Andrea. *Kiss My Arp*. Mo Wax MWR 099 CD, 1999.

Parker, Donna. *Debutante*. Twisted Village TW-1064, 2006. LP.

Parkins, Zeena, and Ikue Mori, *Phantom Orchard*. Mego 071 CD, 2004.

Payne, Maggi. *Crystal*. Lovely Music LCD 2061, 1991.

Peaches. *The Teaches of Peaches*. XL Recordings XL CD 163, 2002.

Peebles, Sarah. *Insect Groove*. c74 007, 2002.

Radigue, Eliane. *Songs of Milarepa*. Lovely Music CD 2001, 1998. 2xCD.

Ratkje, Maja. *Voice*. Rune Grammophon RCD 2028, 2002.

DJ Rekha. *Basement Bhangra*. Koch Records, 2007.

Robindore, Brigitte. "L'Autel de la Perte et la Transformation." *CCMIX: New Electroacoustic Music from Paris*. Mode 98/99, 2001. 2xCD.

Rockmore, Clara. *The Art of the Theremin*. Delos DE 1014, 1987.

Rodgers, Tara. *Butterfly Effects*. Safety Valve, 2007.

Rosenfeld, Marina. *theforestthegardenthesea*. Charhizma CHA 003, 1999.

Rylan, Jessica. *Interior Designs*. Important Records IMP REC 134, 2007.

Saariaho, Kaija. "Jardin Secret 1." *Portrait of Kaija Saariaho*. BIS Records CD-307, 1994.

Sawako. *Hum*. 12k 1035, 2005.

Scaletti, Carla. "sunSurgeAutomata." *CDCM Computer Music Vol. 3*. Centaur CRC 2045, 1988.

Schimana, Elisabeth. *Touchless*. ORF Kunstradio, 1998.

Shortee. *The Dreamer*. Bomb Hip Hop BOMB 2042, 1999.

[sic] . . . *And Rabbits Named Friday*. Squirrelgirl SQRL 002, 2002.

Sonami, Laetitia. "What Happened." *Imaginary Landscapes: New Electronic Music*. Nonesuch 9 79235–2, 1989.

Spiegel, Laurie. *Unseen Worlds*. Infinity Series IS 88802–2, 1991.

———. *Obsolete Systems*. Electronic Music Foundation EMF CD 019, 2001.

Studer, Fredy, and DJ M. Singe. *Duos 14–20*. For Four Ears FOR 1242, 2001.

Tobin, Nancy. *Duo des Aigus*. MmeButterfly CD1, 2007.

Tracy + The Plastics. *Muscler's Guide to Videonics*. Chainsaw CHSW 23, 2001.

Val-Inc. *Craig Taborn: The Val-Inc Remixes*. Thirsty Ear THI 5147.1, 2004. 12".

Westerkamp, Hildegard. *Transformations*. Empreintes Digitales IMED 9631, 1996.

Z, Pamela. *A Delay Is Better*. Starkland ST213- CD, 2004.

Ten Compilations

4 Women No Cry, vol. 1 and 2 (Tusia Beridze [aka TBA], Rosario Blefari, Catarina Pratter and Eglantine Gouzy; Dorit Chrysler, Iris, Mico, and Monotekktoni). Monika 042 CD, 2005; 052 CD, 2006.

Bitstreams: Sound Works from the Exhibition at the Whitney Museum of American Art. JDK 06, 2001 (includes Ann Hamilton, Andrea Parkins, and others).

Digital Empire: DJ Girl. K-Tel, 2000.

Female of the Species. Law & Auder LA13 CD, 1999. 2xCD.

Flav-o-Pac: Memeograph I. Soundlab SL FLAV CD, 1999. Produced by Singe & Verb.

Girl Monster. Chicks on Speed Records COSR 33 CD, 2006. 3xCD.

New Music for Electronic and Recorded Media: Women in Electronic Music. CRI 728, 1997 (originally released by 1750 Arch Recordings in 1977).

Ohm: The Early Gurus of Electronic Music. Ellipsis Arts 3694, 2005, DVD (includes video footage of Bebe Barron, Pauline Oliveros, Laurie Spiegel, and others).

Pioneers of Electronic Music. New World Records 80644–2, 2006 (includes Pril Smiley and Alice Shields).

Women Take Back the Noise. Ubuibi 2006. 3xCD with circuit-bent packaging.

References

Achard, Ken. 2005. *The Peavey Revolution: Hartley Peavey: The Gear, the Company, and the All-American Success Story*. San Francisco: Backbeat Books.

Ahmed, Sara. 2004. *The Cultural Politics of Emotion*. New York: Routledge.

———. 2006. *Queer Phenomenology: Orientations, Objects, Others*. Durham, N.C.: Duke University Press.

Amacher, Maryanne. 1994. "Synaptic Island: A Psybertonal Topology." *Architecture as a Translation of Music*, edited by E. Martin, 32–35. New York: Princeton Architectural Press (Pamphlet Architecture 16).

———. 2004. Psychoacoustic Phenomena in Musical Composition: Some Features of a Perceptual Geography. *FO(A)RM* 3: 16–25.

"Around the World in News, Science." 1936. *Washington Post*, May 31, PY4.

Balsamo, Anne. 1996. *Technologies of the Gendered Body: Reading Cyborg Women*. Durham, N.C.: Duke University Press.

Bernstein, David W., ed. 2008. *The San Francisco Tape Music Center: 1960s Counterculture and the Avant-Garde*. Berkeley: University of California Press.

Bodle, Carrie. 2006. "Sonification/Listening Up." *Leonardo Music Journal* 16, special section: "Sound and the Social Organization of Space," guest edited by T. Rodgers: 51–52.

Born, Georgina. 1995. *Rationalizing Culture: IRCAM, Boulez, and the Institutionalization of the Musical Avant-Garde*. Berkeley: University of California Press.

Bosma, Hanna. 2003. "Bodies of Evidence, Singing Cyborgs and Other Gender Issues in Electrovocal Music." *Organised Sound* 8 (1): 5–17.

Bradby, Barbara. 1993. "Sampling Sexuality: Gender, Technology and the Body in Dance Music." *Popular Music* 12 (2): 155–76.

Brady, Erika. 1999. *A Spiral Way: How the Phonograph Changed Ethnography*. Jackson: University Press of Mississippi.

Bridges, Elizabeth. 2005. "Love Parade GmbH vs. Ladyfest: Electronic Music as a Mode of Feminist Expression in Contemporary German Culture." *Women in German Yearbook* 21: 215–40.

Brün, Herbert, with Arun Chandra, ed. 2004. *When Music Resists Meaning: The Major Writings of Herbert Brün.* Middletown, Conn.: Wesleyan University Press.

Bumiller, Elisabeth. 1996. "Can Clubland Live in Quality-of-Life Era?" *New York Times*, August 4, 33.

Cascone, Kim. 2000. "The Aesthetics of Failure: 'Post-Digital' Tendencies in Contemporary Computer Music." *Computer Music Journal* 24 (4): 12–18.

Cepeda, Raquel. 2001. "Ladies First." *Village Voice*, July 17.

Chadabe, Joel. 1997. *Electric Sound: The Past and Promise of Electronic Music.* Upper Saddle River, N.J.: Prentice Hall.

Chanan, Michael. 1995. *Repeated Takes: A Short History of Recording and Its Effects on Music.* New York: Verso.

Cixous, Hélène. 1976. "The Laugh of the Medusa." Translated by K. Cohen and P. Cohen. *Signs* 1 (4): 875–93.

Coleman, Beth, and Howard Goldkrand. 2006. "Anatomy of an Amalgamation." *Leonardo Music Journal* 16, special section: "Sound and the Social Organization of Space," guest edited by T. Rodgers: 53.

Collins, Nicolas. 2006. *Handmade Electronic Music: The Art of Hardware Hacking.* New York: Routledge.

Cooper, Carol. 1995. "Disco Knights: Hidden Heroes of the New York Dance Music Underground." *Social Text* 45 (Winter): 159–65.

Cotter, Holland. 2002. "The Mama of Dada." *New York Times Book Review*, May 19, 50.

Cox, Christoph, and Daniel Warner, eds. 2004. *Audio Culture: Readings in Modern Music.* New York: Continuum.

Crafts, Susan D., Daniel Cavicchi, and Charles Keil. 1993. *My Music: Explorations of Music in Daily Life.* Hanover, N.H.: Wesleyan University Press.

Cuddy-Keane, Melba. 2000. "Virginia Woolf, Sound Technologies, and the New Aurality." *Virginia Woolf in the Age of Mechanical Reproduction*, edited by P. L. Caughie, 69–113. New York: Garland.

Cusick, Suzanne G. 1994. "Feminist Theory, Music Theory, and the Mind/Body Problem." *Perspectives of New Music* 32 (1): 8–27.

Darter, Tom, and Greg Armbruster. 1984. *The Art of Electronic Music.* New York: William Morrow.

Davis, Erik. 2002. "Songs in the Key of F12." *Wired* 10 (5).

de Lauretis, Teresa. 1987. *Technologies of Gender: Essays on Theory, Film, and Fiction.* Bloomington: Indiana University Press.

Diamond, Beverley. 2000. "The Interpretation of Gender Issues in Musical Life Stories of Prince Edward Islanders." *Music and Gender: Negotiating Shifting Worlds*, edited by P. Moisala and B. Diamond, 99–139. Urbana: University of Illinois Press.

Doane, Mary Ann. 1999. "Technophilia: Technology, Representation, and the Feminine." *Cybersexualities: A Reader on Feminist Theory, Cyborgs and Cyberspace*, edited and with an introduction by J. Wolmark, 20–33. Edinburgh: Edinburgh University Press.

Dove. 2003. "Kuttin Kandi: More Than a Woman." http://www.daveyd.com/ (visited April 29, 2008).

Doyle, Peter. 2005. *Echo and Reverb: Fabricating Space in Popular Music Recording, 1900–1960.* Middletown, Conn.: Wesleyan University Press.

D'Souza, Aruna. 2002. "A World of Sound." *Art in America* (April): 110–15, 161.

Duckworth, William. 1995. *Talking Music: Conversations with John Cage, Philip Glass, Laurie Anderson, and Five Generations of American Experimental Composers.* New York: Schirmer Books.

Edwards, Paul N. 1996. *The Closed World: Computers and the Politics of Discourse in Cold War America.* Cambridge, Mass.: MIT Press.

Epstein, Helen. 1974. " 'The Cello Can't Play These Chords': An Electronic Music Maker." *New York Times*, July 21, 93.

Farrugia, Rebekah. 2004. "*Sisterdjs* in the House: Electronic/Dance Music and Women-Centered Spaces on the Net." *Women's Studies in Communication* 27 (2): 236–62.

Female Pressure website. 2008. http://www.femalepressure.net/ (visited April 30, 2008).

Fikentscher, Kai. 2000. *"You Better Work!" Underground Dance Music in New York City.* Hanover, N.H.: Wesleyan University Press.

Fuentes, Annette, and Barbara Ehrenreich. 1983. *Women in the Global Factory.* Boston: South End Press.

Fullman, Ellen. 1994. "Sonic Space of the Long-Stringed Instrument." *Architecture as a Translation of Music*, edited by E. Martin, 46–49. New York: Princeton Architectural Press (Pamphlet Architecture 16).

———. 2003. "The Long String Instrument." *Musicworks* 85 (Spring): 21–28.

Gagne, Cole. 1993. *Soundpieces 2: Interviews with American Composers.* Metuchen, N.J.: Scarecrow Press.

Gammel, Irene. 2003. *Baroness Elsa: Gender, Dada, and Everyday Modernity—A Cultural Biography.* Cambridge, Mass.: MIT Press.

Gamper, David, with Pauline Oliveros. 1998. "A Performer-Controlled Live Sound-Processing System: New Developments and Implementations of the Expanded Instrument System." *Leonardo Music Journal* 8: 33–38.

Garrison, Ednie Kaeh. 2005. "Are We On a Wavelength Yet? On Feminist Oceanography, Radios, and Third Wave Feminism." *Different Wavelengths: Studies of the Contemporary Women's Movement*, edited by J. Reger, 237–56. New York: Routledge.

Gercke, Hans. 2000. "The Garden of Dreams: About the Work of Christina Kubisch." *Klangraumlichtzeit*, edited by C. Kubisch, 42–49. Heidelberg: Kerher Verlag.

Ghazala, Reed. 2005. *Circuit-Bending: Build Your Own Alien Instruments.* Indianapolis: Wiley.

Gilbert, Jeremy, and Ewan Pearson. 1999. *Discographies: Dance Music, Culture and the Politics of Sound*. London: Routledge.

Gitelman, Lisa. 2006. *Always Already New: Media, History, and the Data of Culture*. Cambridge, Mass.: MIT Press.

Goldberg, Adele. 1984. *Smalltalk-80: The Interactive Programming Environment*. Reading, Mass.: Addison-Wesley.

Goldstein, Carolyn M. 1997. "From Service to Sales: Home Economics in Light and Power: 1920–1940." *Technology and Culture* 38 (1): 121–52.

Golianopoulos, Thomas. 2006. "Female MCs." *Scratch* 13 (September/October).

Grant, Annette. 2004. "Art: Let 7 Million Sheets of Paper Fall." *New York Times*, April 11, AR31.

Grossman, Rachel. 1980. "Women's Place in the Integrated Circuit." *Radical America* 14 (1): 29–49.

Grosz, Elizabeth. 1994. *Volatile Bodies: Toward a Corporeal Feminism*. Bloomington: Indiana University Press.

———. 1995. "Women, Chora, Dwelling." *Space, Time, and Perversion: Essays on the Politics of Bodies*. New York: Routledge.

———. 2005. *Time Travels: Feminism, Nature, Power*. Durham, N.C.: Duke University Press.

Guevara, Nancy. 1996. Women Writin' Rappin' Breakin.' *Dropping Science: Critical Essays on Rap Music and Hip Hop Culture*, edited by W. E. Perkins, 49–62. Philadelphia: Temple University Press.

Halberstam, Judith. 2005. *In a Queer Time and Place: Transgender Bodies, Subcultural Lives*. New York: New York University Press.

———. 2007. "Keeping Time with Lesbians on Ecstasy." *Women and Music* 11: 51–58.

Hammonds, Evelynn. 1997. "Toward a Genealogy of Black Female Sexuality: The Problematic of Silence." *Feminist Genealogies, Colonial Legacies, Democratic Futures*, edited by M. J. Alexander and C. T. Mohanty, 170–82. New York: Routledge.

Haraway, Donna. 1991. *Simians, Cyborgs, and Women: The Reinvention of Nature*. New York: Routledge.

Hayles, N. Katherine. 1999. *How We Became Posthuman: Virtual Bodies in Cybernetics, Literature, and Informatics*. Chicago: University of Chicago Press.

Hebert, James. 2008. "Deejaying Still Holds the Key to Her Heart." *San Diego Tribune*, March 16, E3.

Hedges, Elaine, and Shelley Fisher Fishkin, eds. 1994. *Listening to Silences: New Essays in Feminist Criticism*. New York: Oxford University Press.

Hinkle-Turner, Elizabeth. 2006. *Women Composers and Music Technology in the United States: Crossing the Line*. Aldershot, UK: Ashgate.

Hodgson, Brian. 2001. "Delia Derbyshire: Pioneer of Electronic Music Who Produced the Distinctive Sound of Dr. Who." *Guardian*, July 7, 22.

hooks, bell. 1984. *Feminist Theory: From Margin to Center*. Boston: South End Press.

Huber, David Miles, and Robert E. Runstein. 1997. *Modern Recording Techniques*. 5th ed. Oxford: Focal Press.

Hume, Christine. 2006. "Improvisational Insurrection: The Sound Poetry of Tracie Morris." *Contemporary Literature* 47 (3): 415–39.

Hutton, Jo. 2003. "Daphne Oram: Inventor, Writer and Composer." *Organised Sound* 8 (3): 49–56.

Irigaray, Luce. 1985. *This Sex Which Is Not One*. Translated by C. Porter with C. Burke. Ithaca, N.Y.: Cornell University Press.

———. 1993. *An Ethics of Sexual Difference*. Translated by C. Burke and G. C. Gill. Ithaca, N.Y.: Cornell University Press.

Kahn, Douglas. 1999. *Noise Water Meat: A History of Sound in the Arts*. Cambridge, Mass.: MIT Press.

Kantrowitz, Barbara, and Julie Scelfo. 2004. "American Masala." *Newsweek*, March 22, 50.

Katz, Lina. 2000. "Weekend Mambo March Aims to Bump and Grind Cabaret Law into the Ground: No Dancing Allowed." *Village Voice*, August 22.

Katz, Mark. 2004. *Capturing Sound: How Technology Has Changed Music*. Berkeley: University of California Press.

———. 2006. "Men, Women, and Turntables: Gender and the DJ Battle." *Musical Quarterly* 89 (4): 580–99.

Kearney, Mary Celeste. 1997. "The Missing Links: Riot Grrrl—Feminism—Lesbian Culture." *Sexing the Groove: Popular Music and Gender*, edited by S. Whiteley, 207–29. London: Routledge.

Keightley, Keir. 1996. "'Turn it down!' She Shrieked: Gender, Domestic Space, and High Fidelity, 1948–59." *Popular Music* 15 (2): 149–77.

Kubisch, Christina. 2006. "Works with Electromagnetic Induction." http://www.christinakubisch.de/ (visited March 9, 2007).

La Ferla, Ruth. 2007. "Setting the Beat, and the Style." *New York Times*, November 29, G1.

Landi, Ann. 2001. "Sonic Boom." *ARTnews* (December): 106–7.

Lee, Benjamin, and Edward LiPuma. 2002. "Cultures of Circulation: The Imaginations of Modernity." *Public Culture* 14 (1): 191–213.

Lee, Iara. 1998. *Modulations: Cinema for the Ear*. USA: Caipirinha Productions. DVD, 74 min.

Le Tigre. 1999. *Le Tigre*. Mr. Lady Records MRLR 07.

Levine, Robert, and Bill Werde. 2003. "Superproducers: They're Reinventing the Sound of Music. And the Music Industry." *Wired* 11 (10).

Lewis, George. 1996. "Improvised Music after 1950: Afrological and Eurological Perspectives." *Black Music Research* 16 (1): 91–121.

———. 2000. "Too Many Notes: Computers, Complexity and Culture in *Voyager*." *Leonardo Music Journal* 10: 33–39.

———. 2007. "The Virtual Discourses of Pamela Z." *Journal of the Society for American Music* 1: 57–77.

Licht, Alan. 1999. "Maryanne Amacher." *Wire* 181 (March).

Light, Jennifer. 1999. "When Computers Were Women." *Technology and Culture* 40 (3): 455–83.

"Lily Greenham: Lingual Music" (album notes and review). 2008. http://stalk.net/paradigm/pd22.html (visited April 30, 2008).

Lockheart, Paula. 2003. "A History of Early Microphone Singing, 1925–39: American Mainstream Popular Singing at the Advent of Electronic Microphone Amplification." *Popular Music and Society* 26 (3): 367–85.

Loli, Giulia. 2006. Letter to *Scratch* magazine. Rough Americana website. http://www.roughamericana.com/ (visited March 4, 2007).

MacDonald, Corina. 2007. "An Interview with Tara Rodgers." *Vague Terrain 08: Process* (November). http://www.vagueterrain.net/ (visited April 23, 2008).

Malloy, Judy, ed. 2003. *Women, Art, and Technology*. Cambridge, Mass.: MIT Press.

Maloney, Kathleen. 2000. "Recognition or Division?" *XLR8R* 39: 38.

"Maria Chavez: Those Eyes of Hers" (album review). 2005. *Vital Weekly*, no. 464. http://www.vitalweekly.net (visited February 23, 2007).

Martin, Steven M. 2001. *Theremin: An Electronic Odyssey*. USA: MGM. DVD, 82 min.

Massey, Doreen B. 2005. *For Space*. London: Sage.

Mathews, Max. 2008. http://www.csounds.com/mathews/ (visited April 23, 2008).

McCartney, Andra. 1995. "Inventing Images: Constructing and Contesting Gender in Thinking about Electroacoustic Music." *Leonardo Music Journal* 5: 57–66.

———. 2000. "Sounding Places with Hildegard Westerkamp." PhD diss., York University.

———. 2002. "New Games in the Digital Playground: Women Composers Learning and Teaching Electroacoustic Music." *Feminism and Psychology* 12 (2): 160–67.

———. 2003. "In and Out of the Sound Studio." *Organised Sound* 8 (1): 89–96.

———. 2006. "Gender, Genre and Elecroacoustic Soundmaking Practices." *Intersections: Canadian Journal of Music* 26 (2): 20–48.

McCartney, Andra, and Ellen Waterman. 2006. "Introduction: In and Out of the Sound Studio." *Intersections: Canadian Journal of Music* 26 (2): 3–19.

McClary, Susan. 1991. *Feminine Endings: Music, Gender, and Sexuality*. Minneapolis: University of Minnesota Press.

McDonnell, Evelyn. 1998. "Why Aren't More Geeks with the Gizmos Girls?" *New York Times*, April 12, AR34.

McDonnell, Evelyn, and Ann Powers, eds. 1995. *Rock She Wrote: Women Write about Rock, Pop, and Rap.* New York: Delta.

McRobbie, Angela. 1999. "'Come Alive London!' A Dialogue with Dance Music." *In the Culture Society: Art, Fashion, and Popular Music,* 144–56. New York: Routledge.

———. 2004. "Notes on Postfeminism and Popular Culture: Bridget Jones and the New Gender Regime." *All about the Girl: Culture, Power, and Identity,* edited by A. Harris, 3–14. New York: Routledge.

Milano, Dominic. 1979a. "Wendy Carlos." *Contemporary Keyboard* (December): 32–35+.

———. 1979b. "Rachel Elkind." *Contemporary Keyboard* (December): 36–37.

Mockus, Martha. 2008. *Sounding Out: Pauline Oliveros and Lesbian Musicality.* New York: Routledge.

Montague, Stephen. 1991. "Rediscovering Leon Theremin." *Tempo* 177 (June): 18–23.

Morris, Adelaide. 1997. "Sound Technologies and the Modernist Epic: H.D. on the Air. *Sound States: Innovative Poetics and Acoustical Technologies,* edited by A. Morris, 32–55. Chapel Hill: University of North Carolina Press.

Morris, Tracie. 2007. "Poetics Statement: Sound Making Notes." *American Poets in the Twenty-First Century: The New Poetics,* edited by C. Rankine and L. Sewell, 210–15. Middletown, Conn.: Wesleyan University Press.

Morton, David. 2000. *Off the Record: Technology and Culture of Sound Recording in America.* New Brunswick, N.J.: Rutgers University Press.

Moten, Fred. 2008. "Rough Americana" (recording review). *Journal of the Society for American Music* 2: 283–87.

Mumford, Lewis. 1966. *Technics and Human Development.* New York: Harcourt Brace Jovanovich.

Neset, Anne Hilde. 2001. "Go To: Pinknoises." *Wire* 204 (February): 83.

"Novelty Feature at the Stadium." 1947. *New York Times,* July 31, 17.

Oldenziel, Ruth. 1999. *Making Technology Masculine: Men, Women and Modern Machines in America, 1870–1945.* Amsterdam: Amsterdam University Press.

Oliveros, Pauline. 1984. *Software for People: Collected Writings 1963–80.* Baltimore, Md.: Smith Publications.

———. 1998. "Breaking the Silence." http://www.deeplistening.org (visited April 8, 2007).

———. 2005. *Deep Listening: A Composer's Sound Practice.* New York: iUniverse.

Oliveros, Pauline, and Fred Maus. 1994. "A Conversation about Feminism and Music." *Perspectives of New Music* 32 (2) (Summer): 174–93.

Oram, Daphne. 1972. *An Individual Note of Music, Sound and Electronics.* London: Galliard Paperbacks.

Owen, Frank, with Tricia Romano. 1997. "Spin Sisters: Women Step Up to the Decks." *Village Voice*, December 2, 30–32, 35.

Park, Jane C. H. 2004. "Cibo Matto's *Stereotype A*: Articulating Asian American Hip Hop." *East Main Street: Asian American Popular Culture*, edited by S. Davé, L. Nishime, and T. G. Owen, 292–312. New York: New York University Press.

Pease, Cynthia. 1978. "Women and the Man's World of Audio." *High Fidelity* 28 (7): 16.

Peebles, Sarah. 1996. "High-Tech versus My-Tech: Developing Systems for Electroacoustic Improvisation and Composition." *Musicworks* 66: 4–13.

Peril, Lynn. 2002. *Pink Think: Becoming a Woman in Many Uneasy Lessons.* New York: W. W. Norton.

Perlman, Marc. 2004. "Golden Ears and Meter Readers: The Contest for Epistemic Authority in Audiophilia." *Social Studies of Science* 34 (5): 783–807.

Peterson, George. 1987. "Women in Sound Reinforcement: Four Success Stories." *Mix: The Recording Industry Magazine* (June): 46–120.

Pilar, Praba. 2005. *Cyberlabia: Gendered Thoughts and Conversations on Cyberspace.* Oakland, Calif.: Tela Press.

Pinch, Trevor, and Frank Trocco. 2002. *Analog Days: The Invention and Impact of the Moog Synthesizer.* Cambridge, Mass.: Harvard University Press.

Pini, Maria. 2001. *Club Cultures and Female Subjectivity: The Move from Home to House.* New York: Palgrave.

Plant, Sadie. 1997. *Zeros + Ones: Digital Women + the New Technoculture.* New York: Doubleday.

Polli, Andrea. 2005. "*Atmospherics/Weather Works*: A Spatialized Meteorological Data Sonification Project." *Leonardo* 38 (1): 31–36.

———. 2006. "*Heat and the Heartbeat of the City*: Sonifying Data Describing Climate Change." *Leonardo Music Journal* 16: 44–45.

Potts, Sally Dorgan. 1994. "Women in Audio." *EQ* (May): 50–57.

Powers, Ann. 1994. "When Women Venture Forth." *New York Times*, October 9, H32.

Ptak, Carly. 2008. Here See website. http://www.heresee.com/cptak.htm (visited April 23, 2008).

Rabinovitch, Simona. 2000. "Female Forté: The Achievements of Women DJs in the 90s." *XLR8R* 39: 34–36.

Raimist, Rachel. 1999. *Nobody Knows My Name.* USA. VHS, 58 min.

Reynolds, Simon. 1998. *Generation Ecstasy: Into the World of Techno and Rave Culture.* Boston, Mass.: Little, Brown.

Rich, Adrienne. 2001. *Arts of the Possible: Essays and Conversations.* New York: W. W. Norton.

Riley, Denise. 1988. "*Am I That Name?*" *Feminism and the Category of "Women" in History.* Minneapolis: University of Minnesota Press.

Roads, Curtis. 1996. *The Computer Music Tutorial*. Cambridge, Mass.: MIT Press.

Rodgers, Tara. 2003. "On the Process and Aesthetics of Sampling in Electronic Music Production." *Organised Sound* 8 (3): 313–20.

———. 2006. "Butterfly Effects: Synthesis, Emergence, and Transduction." "Wild Nature and the Digital Life," special issue of *Leonardo Electronic Almanac* 14 (7–8). http://leoalmanac.org/ (visited November 30, 2006).

Romano, Tricia. 1998. "Call me Madame DJ." *Seattle Weekly*, May 20.

Rose, Tricia. 1994. *Black Noise: Rap Music and Black Culture in Contemporary America*. Hanover, N.H.: Wesleyan University Press.

Russolo, Luigi. 1913. "The Art of Noises: Futurist Manifesto." *The Art of Noises*, 23–30. Translated with an introduction by B. Brown. New York: Pendragon Press, 1986.

Ryzik, Melena. 2007. "Bhangra's Ambassador, Keeping the Party Spinning." *New York Times*, December 6, E1.

Sandstrom, Boden. 2000. "Women Mix Engineers and the Power of Sound." *Music and Gender: Negotiating Shifting Worlds*, edited by P. Moisala and B. Diamond, 289–305. Urbana: University of Illinois Press.

Sawchuk, Kim. 1994. "Pirate Writing: Radiophonic Strategies for Feminist Techno-Perverts." *Radio Rethink: Art, Sound and Transmission*, edited by D. Augitis and D. Lander, 201–22. Banff, Alberta: Walter Phillips Gallery.

Scaletti, Carla. 2002. "Computer Music Languages, Kyma, and the Future." *Computer Music Journal* 26 (4): 69–82.

Schaub, Mirjam. 2005. *Janet Cardiff: The Walk Book*. Cologne: Walther König.

Schloss, Joseph G. 2004. *Making Beats: The Art of Sample-Based Hip-Hop*. Middletown, Conn.: Wesleyan University Press.

Scott, Bonnie Kime. 2000. "The Subversive Mechanics of Woolf's Gramophone in *Between the Acts*." *Virginia Woolf in the Age of Mechanical Reproduction*, edited by P. L. Caughie, 97–114. New York: Garland.

Scott, Joan Wallach. 1988. *Gender and the Politics of History*. New York: Columbia University Press.

"Separate and Equal: Girls-Only Electronica Site." 2001. *Artbyte* 3 (6) (March–April): 16.

Sherburne, Philip. 2002. "If Electronic Music Is So Progressive, Why Is the Album Art So Sexist?" *Neumu*, April 19. http://www.neumu.net/ (visited January 18, 2007).

Sherman, Howard. 1982. "Riding the New Waves." *dB: The Sound Engineering Magazine* (July): 28–33.

Siegler, Dylan. 2000a. "Heather Heart." *XLR8R* 39: 35.

———. 2000b. "Kuttin Kandi." *XLR8R* 39: 36.

Smith, Richard R. 1995. *Fender: The Sound Heard 'Round the World*. Fullerton, Calif.: Garfish.

Snapper, Juliana. 2004. "Scratching the Surface: Time and Identity in Hip-Hop Turntablism." *European Journal of Cultural Studies* 7 (1): 9–25.

Sofia, Zoë. 2000. "Container Technologies." *Hypatia* 15 (2): 181–201.

Spiegel, Laurie. 1998. "Graphical Groove: Memorium for a Visual Music System." *Organised Sound* 3 (3): 187–91.

———. 2008. "Laurie Spiegel's Retiary Ramblings." http://www.retiary .org/ls/ (visited April 30, 2008).

Spivak, Gayatri Chakravorty. 1981. "French Feminism in an International Frame." *Yale French Studies* 62, Feminist Readings: French Texts/American Contexts: 154–84.

Stanley, Autumn. 1983. "Women Hold Up Two-Thirds of the Sky: Notes for a Revised History of Technology." *Machina Ex Dea: Feminist Perspectives on Technology*, edited by J. Rothschild, 5–22. New York: Pergamon Press.

Sterne, Jonathan. 2003. *The Audible Past: Cultural Origins of Sound Reproduction.* Durham, N.C.: Duke University Press.

Stosuy, Brandon. 2007. "Interview: Björk." Pitchfork, March 23. http:// www.pitchforkmedia.com/ (visited April 28, 2008).

Strange, Allen. 1972. *Electronic Music: Systems, Techniques, and Controls.* Dubuque, Ia.: William C. Brown.

Straw, Will. 1997. "Sizing Up Record Collections: Gender and Connoisseurship in Rock Music Culture." *Sexing the Groove: Popular Music and Gender*, edited by S. Whiteley, 3–16. London: Routledge.

Sweeney, Camille. 2002. "Downtown Girls." *New York Times Magazine*, March 17.

Taylor, Timothy D. 1993. "The Gendered Construction of the Musical Self: The Music of Pauline Oliveros." *Musical Quarterly* 77 (3): 385–96.

———. 2001. *Strange Sounds: Music, Technology and Culture.* New York: Routledge.

Théberge, Paul. 1997. *Any Sound You Can Imagine: Making Music/Consuming Technology.* Hanover, N.H.: Wesleyan University Press.

Tillmann-Healy, Lisa M. 2003. "Friendship as Method." *Qualitative Inquiry* 9 (5): 729–49.

Truax, Barry, ed. 1999. *Handbook for Acoustic Ecology.* 2nd ed. Vancouver, BC: World Soundscape Project, Simon Fraser University, and ARC Publications. http://www.sfu.ca/sonic-studio/handbook/ (visited March 26, 2007).

———. 2003. "Homoeroticism and Electroacoustic Music: Absence and Personal Voice." *Organised Sound* 8 (1): 117–24.

Turkle, Sherry. 1984. *The Second Self: Computers and the Human Spirit.* New York: Simon and Schuster.

Vaziri, Aidin. 1998. "Iara Lee: Eyes of Electronica." *Res* 1 (1). Available at the *Modulations* website, http://www.caipirinha.com/ (visited March 9, 2007).

310

Verini, James. 2003. "A New Spin on L.A. Art." *Los Angeles Times*, January 30, E16.

von Foerster, Heinz, and James W. Beauchamp, eds. 1969. *Music by Computers*. New York: John Wiley.

Wajcman, Judy. *Technofeminism*. 2004. Cambridge: Polity Press.

Walker, Jane, and Jackie Pelle. 2001. *Spinsters*. Canada. VHS, 48 min.

Warren, Tamara. 2003. "Girl in the Machine." *Nylon* (February).

Waterman, Ellen. 2007. "Radio Bodies: Discourse, Performance, Resonance." *Radio Territories*, edited by E. G. Jensen and B. Labelle, 118–34. Los Angeles: Errant Bodies Press.

Weheliye, Alexander G. 2002. "'Feenin': Posthuman Voices in Contemporary Black Popular Music." *Social Text* 71 (20, 2): 21–47.

Westerkamp, Hildegard. 2000. "The Local and Global 'Language' of Environmental Sound." Paper presented at Sound Escape, International Conference on Acoustic Ecology, Peterborough, Ontario, Canada, June 28–July 2. Hildegard Westerkamp website. http://www.sfu.ca/~westerka/ (visited April 24, 2008).

———. 2002. "Linking Soundscape Composition and Acoustic Ecology." *Organised Sound* 7 (1): 51–56.

Wierzbicki, James. 2005. *Louis and Bebe Barron's Forbidden Planet: A Film Score Guide*. Lanham, Md.: Scarecrow Press.

Wilson, Sarah. 2004. "Gertrude Stein and the Radio." *Modernism/Modernity* 11 (2): 261–78.

Woolf, Virginia. 2005. *A Room of One's Own*. Orlando, Fla.: Harvest Books.

Young, Gayle. 1982. "The How and Why of Instrument Design." *Musicworks* 21 (Fall).

Young, Iris Marion. 2005. *On Female Body Experience: "Throwing Like a Girl" and Other Essays*. New York: Oxford University Press.

Z, Pamela. 2003. "A Tool Is a Tool." *Women, Art, and Technology*, edited by J. Malloy, 348–61. Cambridge, Mass.: MIT Press.

Zvonar, Richard. 2004. "Bebe Barron: Strange Cues from the Id." *e | i* 3 (Spring): 18–23.

Index

Tara Rodgers is an independent writer and musician
and the founder of Pinknoises.com, a website devoted
to women DJs, electronic musicians, and sound artists.
She is currently a Ph.D. candidate in communication
studies at McGill University.

Library of Congress Cataloging-in-Publication Data
Rodgers, Tara, 1973–
Pink noises : women on electronic music and sound /
Tara Rodgers.
p. cm.
Includes bibliographical references and index.
ISBN 978-0-8223-4661-6 (cloth : alk. paper)
ISBN 978-0-8223-4673-9 (pbk. : alk. paper)
1. Women musicians—Interviews. 2. Disc jockeys—
Interviews. 3. Electronic music—History and criticism.
I. Title.
ML82.R65 2010
786.7092'2—dc22   2009039109